PHILOSOPHY, POLITICS AND SOCIETY

(Second Series)

Philosophy, Politics and Society

(Second Series)

A COLLECTION EDITED BY

PETER LASLETT
and
W. G. RUNCIMAN

OXFORD
BASIL BLACKWELL
1972

© BASIL BLACKWELL 1962

Reprinted 1964, 1967, 1969, 1972

ISBN 0 631 04880 4

PRINTED IN GREAT BRITAIN BY OFFSET LITHOGRAPHY BY
BILLING AND SONS LTD., GUILDFORD AND LONDON

CONTENTS

INTRODUCTION

THE first collection of essays under this title was published six years ago. This second is somewhat wider in its range, and we hope does rather more to justify the heading, especially the final term. The limitation to writers in this country has been abandoned, and two scholars have contributed from America, one from Germany. Five out of the ten essays have been written for the volume, as against three out of ten in its predecessor: only two have previously appeared in Britain.

The introduction of 1956 was written at the height of what one of us calls 'the heyday of Weldonism'. Heads were being gravely shaken at that time over the state of theorizing about politics, and doubts about its future expressed in many places other than at Oxford, where Mr. Weldon and the philosophical analysts of language had their most important seat. It so happened, however, that the forthright statement made in that Introduction—'For the moment, anyway, political philosophy is dead'—became the text most cited from the volume as a whole. It would be very satisfactory if we were able here to proclaim the resurrection, unreservedly and with enthusiasm. We cannot quite; but the mood is very different and very much more favourable than it was six years ago. The philosophical situation has changed markedly, even at Oxford. Books like Professor Hampshire's sensitive appeal to the philosophic imagination *Thought and Action* (1960) or Mr. Strawson's *Individuals* (1959) now command the attention previously accorded to those strictly analytical works, both ethical and epistemological, which then exercised such an influence. The emphasis on action in particular may be seen expressed at several points in the present collection.

We cannot point to a particular work on the relation of philosophy to politics which has made the late Mr. Weldon's *Vocabulary of Politics* entirely obsolete. But in *The Concept of Law* (1961) Professor Hart has in fact fulfilled the prophecy made in 1956 that the philosophers of law would be the first to turn linguistic analysis to positive use. We believe that this is the most important work for the general sociology of law and politics as well as for their philosophy to have appeared since political philosophy was proclaimed to be dead six years ago. In addition, Mr. Benn and Mr. Peters published in 1959 a work on *Social Principles and the Democratic State* which does proceed in the traditional way, and which sets out to argue from philosophical presuppositions to the recommendation of a cautious utilitarianism.

In Isaiah Berlin's contribution to this volume the reader will find some discussion of the reasons why it was never justifiable to pronounce that political philosophy had no future, though nowhere, we believe, will he find it stated that the reaction against the scepticism of the 1950s has gone so far as to restore the traditional *status quo*. We are confident, however, that there are signs throughout this book of a new interest in political theory. This interest comes from the much greater attention which philosophers and those in the humane studies generally have begun to show in the methods and results of social science.

'The central problem of sociology,' says Mr. Peter Winch in *The Idea of a Social Science* (1958), 'that of giving an account of the nature of social phenomena in general, itself belongs to philosophy.' The sort of reaction which this implies against the positivist outlook is significant both of contemporary philosophy and of sociology itself. Sociologists are perhaps less willing than they were to dismiss contemporary philosophizing, whatever its content, as of no use or importance to them. At the same time, the English philosopher of the 1960s concedes to the expert in the empirical facts about society and the state a recognition which he never enjoyed in the traditional order. An attempt to represent something both of the symmetry and the contrast between the work of the sociologist and the philosopher will be found in the juxtaposition of Mr. Williams's essay on Equality with that of Professor Dahrendorf.

It is, indeed, the political sociologists who have made some of the most significant contributions to particular problems of politics. In the works of such recent American authors as Lazarsfeld and Lipset, as well as in the earlier writings of Joseph Schumpeter, or in Max Weber himself (perhaps the most frequently cited authority in this volume) there is much of the greatest relevance to the traditional philosopher of politics. But these authors are concerned more to diagnose than to recommend; and it remains true that very few among our academic contemporaries are prepared to give positive advice, or even to talk prescriptively at all, about political matters. Of our contributors, perhaps Professor Rawls goes furthest towards a recommendation in his forceful advocacy of a modified contractarianism against the utilitarian principle which is so universally assumed to have displaced it: a measure of the change of outlook which this represents may be had by comparing his position with what Miss Macdonald had to say about the social contract in 1951.[1] But even this is still very different from the forthright recommendations of the traditional political theorists.

This, we feel, is the more extraordinary and the more perplexing because there has never been in recent generations a more obvious opening for prescriptive political theory, which tells us what we ought to do and why. When Lord Russell sits down on the pavement to protest against nuclear disarmament and finds himself arrested for it, he is proclaiming that he is at liberty to go back on that obligation to political authority which was and is still regarded as lying at the heart of all the problems of political philosophy. When he takes this action as the leader of a mass movement he is recommending to the community as a whole that in the most important of all respects the established governments of contemporary countries have forfeited the right to obedience on the part of conscientious and critical citizens.

Perhaps it is understandable that Lord Russell, though himself the best known of all living philosophers, found it impossible to respond to our request to contribute a theoretical essay on the Campaign for Nuclear Disarmament and its attitude to political obligation, although we understand he has made a contribution to a less academic collection to be published later this year. But it is more surprising that no other philosopher sharing some or all of his views should have come forward to examine the theoretical issues raised by this political protest. This is an almost literal vindication of the ironical suggestion made in the Introduction of 1956 that Hiroshima and Belsen have made the politics of our contemporary world so horrific that no one has the time or inclination to chisel out a new theory of political obligation.

We made a determined attempt to find examples of prescriptive discussion, in theoretical terms, of the other political dilem-

[1] See 'The Language of Political Theory' in *Logic and Language*, First Series, 1951 (edited by J. N. Flew).

mas of the time, but were unfortunate also in this. Lord Devlin's recent lectures on morality and the law could not be included here since we have learnt that they are to have a book to themselves. Only one essay of this sort became available to us, Miss Hannah Arendt's very interesting discussion in theoretical terms of Negro education in the southern United States, using the categories of public and private which are a general theme of her political philosophy.[1] We felt in the end unwilling to allow this piece to stand alone in a volume which had inevitably taken on a different character.

There is one further gap to record. The emphasis which is laid here on the social science of our day and its connexion with political philosophy required that we should try to represent the studies of the political anthropologists. Once again we have to report our inability to find a suitable essay, an essay which should, shall we say, present in a terse, generalized form the implications in this field of Professor Gluckman's important work on *The Judicial Process amongst the Barotse* (1955). We were referred by those who now practise this difficult discipline to the classic statements contained in *African Political Systems* (1940).[2] We are convinced that the political anthropologists have further developed their ideas since that time, but we are forced to record that it does not seem to be in directions which they are yet anxious to report to political theorists and philosophers.

The wish to cover additional topics does not mean, however, that we are either ungrateful to our present contributors, or pessimistic about the future. We feel that if and when a third series called *Philosophy, Politics and Society* appears in England it will record an attitude to political philosophy which has indeed been completely transformed, and that the transformation must be along the lines implied by the contents of the present volume.

Trinity College,   *January* 1962.
Cambridge.

---

[1] See the periodical *Dissent*, published in New York, issue of Fall, 1959.
[2] *African Political Systems*, edited by M. Fortes and E. E. Evans-Pritchard, with a preface by A. R. Radcliffe-Brown. See also I. Schapera, *Government and Politics in Tribal Society* (1956), and *Tribes Without Rulers* (1958), edited by John Middleton and David Tait.

PHILOSOPHY, POLITICS AND SOCIETY
(SECOND SERIES)

I

DOES POLITICAL THEORY STILL EXIST?[1]
by Isaiah Berlin

I

IS there still such a subject as Political Theory? This query, put with suspicious frequency in English speaking countries, questions the very credentials of the subject: it suggests that political philosophy, whatever it may have been in the past, is to-day dead or dying. The principal symptom which seems to support this belief is that no commanding work of political philosophy has appeared in the twentieth century. By a commanding work in the field of general ideas I mean at the very least one that has in a large area converted paradoxes into platitudes or vice versa. This seems to me no more (but also no less) than an adequate criterion of the characteristic in question.

But this is scarcely conclusive evidence. There exist only two good reasons for certifying the demise of a discipline: one is that its central presuppositions, empirical, or metaphysical, or logical, are no longer accepted because they have (with the world of which they were a part) withered away, or because they have been discredited or refuted. The other is that new disciplines have come to perform the work originally undertaken by the older study. These disciplines may have their own limitations, but they exist, they function, and have either inherited or usurped the functions of their predecessors: there is no room left for the ancestor from whom they spring. This is the fate

[1] The original version of this article appeared in French in the *Revue Francaise de Science Politique*, Vol. XI, no. 2, 1961. It has since been revised by the author whose thanks are due to Professor S. N. Hampshire, Professor H. L. A. Hart, Professor F. Rossi Landi, Mr. P. L. Gardiner, Mr. G. Warnock, and most of all to Mr. M. W. Dick, for reading and commenting on it in its earlier form.

that overtook astrology, alchemy, phrenology (positivists, both old and new, would include theology and metaphysics). The postulates on which these disciplines were based were either destroyed by argument or collapsed for other reasons; consequently they are to-day regarded merely as instances of systematic delusion.

This type of systematic parricide is, in effect, the history of the natural sciences in their relation to philosophy, and so has a direct bearing upon the question before us. The relevant consideration is this: there exist at least two classes of problems to which men have succeeded in obtaining clear answers. The first have been so formulated that they can (at least in principle, if not always in practice) be answered by observation and by inference from observed data. These determine the domains of natural science and of everyday common sense. Whether I ask simple questions about whether there is any food in the cupboard, or what kind of birds are to be found in Patagonia, or the intentions of an individual; or more complicated ones about the structure of matter, or the behaviour of social classes or international markets; I know that the answer, to have any genuine claim to truth, must rest on someone's observation of what exists or happens in the spatio-temporal world. Some would say 'organized observation'. I should be inclined to agree: observation is an activity, and part and parcel of the intention and the conceptual world of the observer. But differences on this issue, while they are crucial for the philosophy of science and the theory of knowledge, do not affect my argument. All the generalizations and hypotheses and models with which the most sophisticated sciences work, can be established and discredited ultimately only by the data of inspection or introspection.

The second type of question to which we can hope to obtain clear answers is formal. Given certain propositions called axioms, together with rules for deducing other propositions from them, I can proceed by mere calculation. The answers to my questions will be valid or invalid according to whether the rules that I accept without question as part of a given discipline, have been correctly used. Such disciplines contain no statements based on observation of fact, and therefore are not nowadays expected to provide information about the universe, whether or not they are used in providing it. Mathematics and formal logic are, of course, the best known examples of formal sciences of this type, but heraldry, chess, and theories of games in general, are similar applications of the formal methods which govern such disciplines.

These two methods of answering questions may be, very generally, denominated empirical and formal. Among the characteristics of both are at least these:

(a) That even if we do not know the answer to a given question, we know what kinds of methods are appropriate in looking for the answer; we know what kinds of answers are relevant to these questions, even if they are not true. If I am asked how the Soviet system of criminal law functions or why Mr. Kennedy was elected President of the United States, I may not be able to answer the question, but I know within what region the relevant evidence must lie, and how an expert would use such evidence to obtain the answer; I must be able to state this in very general terms, if only to show that I have understood the question. Similarly, if I am asked for the proof of Fermat's theorem, I may not be able to give it, indeed I may know that no one has yet been able to provide it, but I also know what kinds of demonstration would count as answers to this problem, even though they may be incorrect or inconclusive, and discriminate these from assertions which are irrelevant to the topic. In other words, in all these cases, even if I do not know the answer, I know where to look for it, or how to identify an authority or expert who knows how to set about looking for it.

(b) This means, in effect, that where the concepts are firm, clear and generally accepted, and the methods of reasoning, arriving at conclusions, etc., are agreed between men (at least the majority of those who have anything to do with these matters) there and only there is it possible to construct a science, formal or empirical. Wherever this is not the case—where the concepts are vague or too much in dispute, and methods of argument and the minimum qualifications that constitute an expert are not generally agreed, where we find frequent recriminations about what can or what cannot claim to be a law, an established hypothesis, an undisputed truth, and so on, we are at best in the realm of quasi-science. The principal candidates for inclusion into the charmed circle, who have not succeeded in passing the required tests, are the occupants of the large, rich and central, but unstable, volcanic and misty region of 'ideologies'.

One of the rough and ready tests for finding out which region we are in, is whether a set of rules, accepted by the great majority of experts in the subject, and capable of being incorporated in a text-book, can be applied in the field in question. To the degree to which such rules are applicable, a discipline approaches the coveted condition of an accepted science. Psychology, sociology, semantics, logic, perhaps certain branches of economics, are in a no-man's-land, some nearer, some further from the frontier which demarcates, less or more clearly, the frontiers of the established sciences.

(c) But besides these two major categories, there arise questions which fall outside either group. It is not only that we may not know the answers to certain questions, but that we are not clear how to set about trying to answer them—where to look—what would constitute evidence for an answer and what would not. When I am asked 'Where is the image in the mirror?' or 'Can time stand still?' I am not sure what kind of question it is that is being asked, or whether indeed it makes any sense at all. I am in not much better plight with some traditional questions which have probably been asked since the dawn of thought, such as: 'How did the world begin?', and, following that, 'What happened before the beginning?' Some say that these are not legitimate questions; but then what makes them illegitimate? There is something that I am trying to ask; for I am certainly puzzled by something. When I ask 'Why can I not be in two places at once?' 'Why can I not get back into the past?' or, to move to another region, 'What is justice?' or 'Is justice objective, absolute, etc.?' or again 'How can we ever be sure that an action is just?' —no obvious method of settling these questions lies to hand. One of the surest hallmarks of a philosophical question—for this is what all these questions are—is that we are puzzled from the very outset, that there is no automatic technique, no universally recognized expertise, for dealing with such questions. We discover that we do not feel sure how to set about clearing our minds, finding out the truth, accepting or rejecting earlier answers to these questions. Neither induction (in its widest sense of scientific reasoning) nor direct observation (appropriate to empirical enquiries), nor deduction (demanded by formal problems), seem to be of help. Once we do feel quite clear about how we should proceed, the questions no longer seem philosophical.

The history—and indeed the advance—of human thought (this is perhaps a truism) have, in fact, largely consisted in the gradual shuffling of all the basic questions that men ask into one or the other of two well-organized compartments—the empirical and the formal. Wherever concepts grow firm and clear and acquire universal acceptance, a new science, natural or formal, comes into being. To use a simile that I cannot claim to have invented, philosophy is like a radiant sun that, from time to time. throws off portions of itself; these masses, when they cool down, acquire a firm and recognizable structure of their own and acquire independent careers as tidy and regular planets; but the central sun continues on its path, and does not seem to diminish in mass or radiance. The 'status' and vitality of philosophy is another matter, and seems to be directly connected with the extent to which it deals with issues that are of concern to the common man. The relation of philosophy to opinion and conduct is a central question both of history and sociology, too large to be considered here. What concerns us is that philosophy in one state of development may turn into a science in the next.

It is no confusion of thought that caused astronomy, for example, to be regarded as a philosophical discipline in, say, the times of Scotus Erigena, when its concepts and methods were not what we should to-day regard as firm or clear, and the part played by observation in relation to *a priori* teleological notions (e.g. the yearning of each body to realize the full perfection of its nature) made it impossible to determine whether the amalgam that went under the name of the knowledge of celestial bodies was empirical or formal. As soon as clear concepts and specific techniques developed, the science of astronomy emerged. In other words, astronomy in its beginning could not be relegated to either compartment, even if such compartments as the empirical and the formal had been clearly distinguished; and it was, of course, part of the 'philosophical' status of early mediaeval astronomy that the civilization of that time (Marxists would say 'the superstructure') did not permit the distinction between the two compartments to be clearly demarcated.

What, therefore, is characteristic of specifically philosophical questions is that they do not (and some of them perhaps never will) satisfy conditions required by an independent science, the principal among which is that the path to their solution must be implicit in their very formulation. Nevertheless, there are some subjects which clearly are near the point of taking flight and divorcing themselves from the main body in which they were born, much as physics and mathematics and chemistry and biology have done in their day. One of these is semantics; another is psychology; with one foot, however reluctantly, they are still sunk in philosophical soil; but they show signs of a tendency to tear themselves loose and emancipate themselves, with only historical memories to tell them of their earlier, more confused, if in some respects richer, years.

II

Among the topics that remain obstinately philosophical, and have, despite repeated efforts, failed to transform themselves into sciences, are some that in their very essence involve value judgements. Ethics, æsthetics, criticism explicitly concerned with general ideas, all but the most technical types of history and scholarship, still live at various points of this limbo, unable or unwilling to emerge by either (the empirical or the formal) door. The mere fact that value judgements are relevant to an intellectual pursuit is clearly not sufficient to disqualify it from being a recognized science. The concept of normal health certainly embodies a valuation, and although there is sufficient universal consensus about what constitutes good health, a normal state, disease and so on, this concept, nevertheless, does not enter as an intrinsic element into the sciences of anatomy, physiology, pathology, etc. Pursuit of health may be the strongest sociological and psychological (and moral) factor in creating and promoting these sciences; it may determine which problems and aspects of the subject have been most ardently attended to; but it is not referred to in the science itself, any more than the uses of history or logic need be mentioned in historical or logical works. If so clear, universally accepted, 'objective', a value as that of desirable state of health is extruded from the structure of the natural sciences, this fact is even more conspicuous in more controversial fields. The attempts, from Plato to our own day (particularly persistent and numerous in the eighteenth century) to found objective sciences of ethics and æsthetics on the basis of universally accepted values, or of methods of discovering them, have met with little success; relativism, subjectivism, romanticism, scepticism with regard to values, keep breaking in. What, we may ask at this point, is the position of political theory? What are its most typical problems? Are they empirical, or formal, or neither? Do they necessarily entail questions of value? Are they on the way to independent status, or are they by their very nature compelled to remain only an element in some wider body of thought?

Among the problems which form the core of traditional political theory are those, for instance, of the nature of equality, of rights, law, authority, rules. We demand the analysis of these concepts, or ask how these expressions function in our language, or what forms of behaviour they prescribe or forbid and why, or into what system of value or outlook they fit, and in what way. When we ask, what is perhaps the most fundamental of all political questions—'Why should anyone obey anyone else?', we ask not 'Why do men obey'—something that empirical psychology, anthropology and sociology might be able to answer; nor yet 'Who obeys whom, when and where, and determined by what causes?' which could perhaps be answered on the basis of evidence drawn from these and similar fields. When we ask why a man should obey, we are asking for the explanation of what is normative in such notions as authority, sovereignty, liberty, and the justification of their validity in political arguments. These are words in the name of which orders are issued, men are coerced, wars are fought, new societies are created and old ones destroyed—expressions which play as great a part as any in our lives to-day. What makes such questions *prima facie* philosophical is the fact that no wide agreement exists on the meaning of some of the concepts involved. There are sharp differences on what constitute valid reasons for actions in these fields; on how the relevant propositions are to be established or even rendered plausible; on who or what constitutes recognized authority for deciding these questions; and there is consequently no consensus on the frontier between valid public criticism and subversion, or freedom and oppression and the like. So long as conflicting replies to such questions continue to be given by different schools and thinkers, the prospects of establishing a science in this field, whether empirical or formal, seem remote. Indeed, it seems clear that disagreements about the analysis of value concepts, as

2

often as not, spring from profounder differences, since the notions of, say, rights or justice or liberty will be radically dissimilar for theists and atheists, mechanistic determinists and Christians, Hegelians and empiricists, romantic irrationalists and Marxists, and so forth. It seems no less clear that these differences are not, at least *prima facie*, either logical or empirical, and have usually and rightly been classified as irreducibly philosophical.

This carries at least one important implication. If we ask the Kantian question, 'In what kind of world is political philosophy —the kind of discussion and argument in which it consists— in principle possible?' the answer must be 'Only in a world where ends collide'. In a society dominated by a single goal there could in principle only be arguments about the best means to attain this end—and arguments about means are technical, that is, scientific and empirical in character: they can be settled by experience and observation or whatever other methods are used to discover causes and correlations; they can, at least in principle, be reduced to positive sciences. In such a society no serious questions about political ends or values could arise, only empirical ones about the most effective paths to the goal. And indeed, something amounting to this was, in effect, asserted by Saint-Simon and Comte; and, on some interpretations of his thought, by Marx also, at any rate after 'prehistory', i.e. the class war, is over, and man's true 'history'—the united attack on nature to obtain goods upon whose desirability the whole of society is agreed—has begun. It follows that the only society in which political philosophy in its traditional sense, that is, an enquiry concerned not solely with elucidation of concepts, but with the critical examination of presuppositions and assumptions, and the questioning of the order of priorities and ultimate ends, is possible, is a society in which there is no total acceptance of any single end. There may be a variety of reasons for this: because no single end has been accepted by a sufficient number of persons; because no one end can be regarded as ultimate, since there can, in principle, exist no guarantee that other values may not at some time engage men's reason or their passions; because no unique, final end can be found—inasmuch as men can pursue many distinct ends, none of them means to, or parts of, one another; and so on. Some among these ends may be public or political; nor is there any reason to suppose that all of them must, even in principle, be compatible with one another. Unless political philosophy is confined to the analysis of concepts or expressions, it can be pursued consistently only in a pluralist, or potentially pluralist, society. But since all analysis, however abstract, itself involves a critical approach to the assumptions under analysis, this distinction remains purely academic. Rigid monism is compatible with philosophical analysis only in theory. The plight of philosophy under despotism in our own times provides conclusive concrete evidence for this thesis.

III

Let me try to make this clearer. If we could construct a society in which it was believed universally (or at least by as many people as believe that the purpose of medicine is to promote or maintain health and are agreed about what constitutes health) that there was only one overriding human purpose: for example, a technocratic society dedicated to the single end of the richest realization of all human faculties; or a utilitarian society dedicated to the greatest happiness of men; or a Thomist or communist or Platonic or anarchist, or any other society which is monistic in this sense—then plainly all that would matter would be to find the right roads to the attainment of the universally accepted end.

This statement needs to be qualified in at least two respects. The schema is in the first place artificially over-simplified. In practice, the kind of goal that can command the allegiance of a society—happiness, power, obedience to the divine will, national glory, individual self-realization, or some other ultimate pattern of life, is so general that it leaves open the question of what kind of lives or conduct incarnate it. No society can be so 'monolithic' that there is no gap between its culminating purpose and the means towards it—a gap filled with secondary ends, penultimate values, which are not means to the final end, but elements in it or expressions of it; and these in their turn incarnate themselves in still more specific purposes at still lower levels, and so on downwards to the particular problem of everyday conduct. 'What is to be done?' is a question which can occur at any level —from the highest to the lowest: doubts and disputes concerning the values involved at any of these levels, and the relationships of these values to one another can arise at any point.

These questions are not purely technical and empirical, not merely problems about the best means to a given end, nor are they mere questions of logical consistency, that is, formal and deductive: but properly philosophical. To take contemporary examples: what is claimed for integration of negroes and whites in the Southern states of the United States is not that it is a means towards achieving a goal external to itself—social justice or equality—but that it is itself a form of it, a value in the hierarchy of values. Or again 'one vote one man', or the rights of minorities or of colonial territories, are, likewise, not simply questions of machinery—a particular means of promoting equality which could, in theory, be equally well realized by other means, say by more ingenious voting devices—but, for those who believe in these principles, are intrinsic ingredients in the ideal of social equality, and consequently to be pursued as such, and not solely for the sake of their results. It follows that even in a society dominated by a single supreme purpose, questions of what is to be done, especially when the subordinate ends come into conflict, cannot be automatically answered by deductive reasoning from accepted premises, aided by adequate knowledge of facts, as certain thinkers, Aristotle at times, or Bertrand Russell in his middle phase, or a good many Catholic casuists, seem to have assumed.

Moreover, and this is our second qualification, it might well be the case that although the formulæ accepted by a society were sacred and immutable, they might carry different—and perhaps incompatible—meanings for different persons and in different situations; philosophical analysis of the relevant concepts might well bring out sharp disagreements. This has been the case conspicuously where the purpose or ideal of a society is expressed in such vague and general terms as the common good, or the fulfilment of the law of God, or rights to life, liberty and the pursuit of happiness and the like.

Nevertheless, and in spite of these qualifications, the stylized model of a society whose ends are given once and for all, and which is merely concerned with discovery of means, is a useful abstraction. It is useful because it demonstrates that to acknowledge the reality of political questions presupposes a pluralism of values—whether ultimate ones, or on the lower slopes of the hierarchy of values, recognition of which is incompatible with a technocratic or authoritarian everything-is-either-an-indisputable-end-or-a-means, monistic structure of values. Nor is the monistic situation entirely a figment of theory. In critical situations where deviation from the norm may involve disastrous consequences—in battles, surgical operating rooms, revolutions, the end is wholly concrete, varying interpretations of it are out of place and all action is conceived as a means towards it alone. It is one of the stratagems of totalitarian régimes to represent all situations as critical emergencies, demanding ruthless elimination of all goals, interpretations, forms of behaviour save for one absolutely specific, concrete, immediate end, binding on everyone, which calls for ends and means so narrow and clearly definable that it is easy to impose sanctions for failing to pursue them.

To find roads is the business of experts. It is therefore reasonable for such a society to put itself into the hands of specialists of tested experience, knowledge, gifts and probity, whose business it is, to use St.-Simon's simile, to conduct the human caravan to the oasis the reality and desirability of which are recognized by all. In such a society, whatever its other characteristics, we should expect to find intensive study of social causation, especially of what types of political organization yield the best results, that is, are best at advancing society towards the overriding goal. Political thought in such a society would be fed by all the evidence that can be supplied by the empirical sciences of history, psychology, anthropology, sociology, comparative law, penology, biology, physiology and so forth. The goal (and the best ways of avoiding obstacles to it) may become clearer as the result of careful studies of human thought and behaviour; and its general character must not at any stage be obscure or doubtful; otherwise differences of value judgement will creep into the political sciences as well, and inject what can only be called philosophical issues (or issues of principle) incapable of being resolved by either empirical or formal means. Differences of interpretation of fact—provided these are uncontaminated by disagreements about the ends of life—can be permitted; but if political theory is to be converted into an applied science, what is needed is a single dominant model—like the doctor's model of a healthy body—accepted by the whole, or the greater part, of the society in question. The model will be its 'ideological foundation'.

Although such a model is a necessary condition for such a science, it may not, even then, begin to be a sufficient one.

It is at this point that the deep division between the monists and pluralists becomes crucial and conspicuous. On one side stand Platonists and Aristotelians, Stoics and Thomists, positivists and Marxists, and all those who seek to translate political problems into scientific terms. For them human ends are objective: men are what they are, or change in accordance with discoverable laws; and their needs or interests or duties can be established by the correct (naturalistic, or transcendental, or theological) methods. Given that we can penetrate past error and confusion by true and reliable modes of investigation—metaphysical insight or the social sciences, or some other dependable instrument— and thereby establish what is good for men and how to effect this, the only unsolved problems will be more or less technical: how to obtain the means for securing these ends, and how to distribute what the technical means provide in a socially and psychologically best manner. This, in the most general terms, is the ideal both of the enlightened atheists of the eighteenth century and the positivists of the nineteenth; of some Marxists of the twentieth, and of those Churches which know the end for which man is made, and know that it is in principle attainable—or at least is such that the road towards it can be discerned—here, below.

On the other side are those who believe in some form of original sin or the impossibility of human perfection, and therefore tend to be sceptical of the empirical attainability of any final solution to the deepest human problems. With them are to be found the sceptics and relativists and also those who believe that the very efforts to solve the problem of one age or culture alter both the men who strive to do so and those for whose benefit the solutions are applied, and thereby create new men and new problems, the character of which cannot to-day be anticipated, let alone analysed or solved, by men bounded by their own historical horizons. Here, too, belong the many sects of subjectivists and irrationalists; and in particular those romantic thinkers who hold that ends of action are not discovered, but are created by individuals or cultures or nations as works of art are, so that the answer to the question 'What should we do?' is undiscoverable not because it is beyond our powers to find the answer, but because the question is not one of fact at all, the solution lies not in discovering something which is what it is, whether it is discovered or not—a proposition or formula, an objective good, a principle, a system of values objective or subjective, a relationship between a mind and something non-mental—but resides in action: something which cannot be found, only invented—an act of will or faith or creation obedient to no pre-existent rules or laws or facts. Here too stand those twentieth century heirs of romanticism, the existentialists, with their belief in the free self-commitment by individuals to actions or forms of life determined by the agent choosing freely; such choice does not take account of objective standards, since these are held to be a form of illusion or 'false consciousness', and the belief in such figments is psychologically traced to fear of freedom—of being abandoned, left to one's own resources—a terror which leads to uncritical acceptance of systems claiming objective authority, spurious theological or metaphysical cosmologies which undertake to guarantee the eternal validity of moral or intellectual rules and principles. Not far from here, too, are fatalists and mystics, as well as those who believe that accident dominates history, and other irrationalists; but also those indeterminists and those troubled rationalists who doubt the possibility of discovering a fixed human nature obedient to invariant laws; especially those for whom the proposition that the future needs of men and their satisfaction are predictable does not fit into an idea of human nature which entails such concepts as will, choice, effort, purpose, with their presupposition of the perpetual opening of new paths of action—a presupposition which enters into the very definition of what we mean by man. This last is the position adopted by those modern Marxists who, in the face of the cruder and more popular versions of the doctrine, have understood the implications of their own premises and principles.

IV

Men's beliefs in the sphere of conduct are part of their conception of themselves and others as human beings; and this conception in its turn, whether conscious or not, is intrinsic to their picture of the world. This picture may be complete and coherent, or shadowy or confused, but almost always, and especially in the case of those who have attempted to articulate what they conceive to be the structure of thought or reality, it can be shown to be dominated by one or more models or paradigms: mechanistic, organic, æsthetic, logical, mystical, shaped by the strongest influence of the day—religious, scientific, metaphysical or artistic. This model or paradigm determines the content as well as the form of beliefs and behaviour. A man who, like Aristotle, or Thomas Aquinas, believes that all things are definable in terms of their purpose, and that nature is a hierarchy or an ascending pyramid of such purposive entities, is committed to the view that the end of human life consists in self-fulfilment, the character of which must depend on the kind of nature that a man has, and on the place that he occupies in the harmonious activity of the entire universal, self-realizing enterprise. It follows that the political philosophy, and, more particularly, the diagnosis of political possibilities and purposes of an Aristotelian or a Thomist, will *ipso facto* be radically different from that of, let us say, someone who has learned from Hobbes or Spinoza or any modern positivist that there are no purposes in nature, that there are only causal (or functional or statistical) laws, only repetitive cycles of events, which may, however, within limits, be harnessed to fulfil the purposes of men; with the corollary that the pursuit of purposes is itself nothing but a product in the human consciousness of natural processes the laws of which men can neither significantly alter nor account for, if by accounting is meant giving an explanation in terms of the goals of a creator who does not exist, or of a nature of which it is meaningless to say that it pursues purposes —for what is that but to attempt to apply to it a subjective human category, to fall into the fallacy of animism or anthropomorphism?

The case is similar with regard to the issue of freedom and authority. The question, 'Why should I obey (rather than do as I like)?' will be (and has been) answered in one way by those who, like Luther, or Bodin, or the Russian Slavophils and many others whose thoughts have been deeply coloured by biblical imagery, conceive of life (although in very different fashions) in terms of the relations of children to their father, and of laws as his commands, where loyalty, obedience, love, and the presence of immediate authority, are all unquestioned, and surround life from birth to death as real and palpable relationships or agencies. This question will be answered very differently by the followers of, say, Plato, or Kant (divided by a whole heaven as these thinkers are) who believe in permanent, impersonal, universal, objective truths, conceived on the model of logical or mathematical or physical laws, by analogy with which their political concepts will be formed. Yet other, and wholly dissimilar, sets of answers will be determined by the great vitalistic conceptions, the model for which is drawn from the facts of growth as conceived in early biology, and for which reality is an organic, qualitative process, not analysable into quantitative units. Others again will originate in minds dominated by the image of some central force, thrusting forward in many guises, like some gnostic or Brahmin notion of perpetual self-creation; or be traceable to a concept drawn from artistic activity, in which the universe is seen not as an unconscious, quasi-biological process of the spirit or the flesh, but as the endless creation of a demiurge, in which freedom and self-fulfilment lie in the recognition by men of themselves as involved in the purposive process of cosmic creation—a vision fully revealed only to those beings to whom the nature of the world is disclosed, at least fragmentarily, through their own experience as creators (something of this kind emanated from the doctrines of Fichte, Schelling, Carlyle, Nietzsche and other romantic thinkers, as well as Bergson and in places Hegel, and, in his youth, Marx, who were obsessed by æsthetico-biological models); some among these, anarchists and irrationalists, conceive of reality as freedom from all rules and set ideals—fetters, even when they are self-imposed, upon the free creative spirit—a doctrine of which we have heard, if anything, too much. The model itself may be regarded as the product of historical factors: the social (and psychological) consequences of the development of productive forces, as Marx taught, or the effects in the minds of individuals of purely psychological processes which Freud and his disciples have investigated. The study of myths, rationalizations, ideologies and obsessive patterns of many kinds, has become a great and fertile preoccupation of our time. The fundamental assumption underlying this approach is that the 'ideological' model has not been arrived at by rational methods, but is the product of causal factors; it may disguise itself in rational dress, but, given the historical, or economic, or geographical, or psychological situation, must, in any case, have emerged in one form or another.

For political thinkers, however, the primary question is not that of genesis and conditions of growth, but that of validity and truth: does the model distort reality? Does it blind us to real differences and similarities and generate other, fictitious ones? Does it suppress, violate, invent, deceive? In the case of scientific (or common-sense) explanations or hypotheses, the tests of validity include increase in the power of accurate (or more refined) prediction or control of the behaviour of the subject matter. Is political thought practical and empirical in this sense? Machiavelli, and in differing degrees Hobbes, Spinoza, Helvétius, Marx, at times speak as if this were so. This is one of the interpretations of the famous doctrine of the unity of theory and practice. But is it an adequate account of the purpose or achievements of—to take only the moderns—Locke or Kant or Rousseau or Mill or the liberals, the existentialists, the logical positivists and linguistic analysts and Natural Law theorists of our own day? and if not, why not?

To return to the notion of models. It is by now a commonplace that the data of observation can be accommodated to almost any theoretical model. Those who are obsessed by one model can accept facts, general propositions, hypotheses and even methods of argument, adopted and perfected by those who were dominated by quite a different model. For this reason, political theory, if by theories we mean no more than causal or functional hypotheses and explanations designed to account only for what happens—in this case for what men have thought or done or will think or do—can perfectly well be a progressive empirical enquiry, capable of detaching itself from its original metaphysical or ethical foundations, and sufficiently adaptable to preserve through many changes of intellectual climate its own character and development as an independent science. After all, even mathematics, although bound up with—and obstructed by—metaphysics and theology, has nevertheless progressed from the days of the Greeks to our own; so too have the natural sciences, at any rate since the seventeenth century, despite vast upheavals in the general *Weltanschauungen* of the societies in which they were created.

But I should like to say once again that unless political theory is conceived in narrowly sociological terms, it differs from political science or any other empirical enquiry in being concerned with somewhat different fields; namely with such questions as what is specifically human and what is not, and why; whether specific categories, say those of purpose or of belonging to a group, or law are indispensable to understanding what men are; and so, inevitably, with the source, scope and validity of certain human goals. If this is its task, it cannot, from the very nature of its interests, avoid evaluation; it is thoroughly committed not only to the analysis of, but to conclusions about the validity of, ideas of the good and the bad, the permitted and the forbidden, the harmonious and the discordant problems which any discussion of liberty or justice or authority or political morality is sooner or later bound to encounter. These central conceptions, moral, political, æsthetic, have altered as the all-inclusive metaphysical models in which they are an essential element have themselves altered. Any change in the central model is a change in the ways in which the data of experience are perceived and interpreted. The degree to which such categories are shot through with evaluation will doubtless depend on their direct connexion with human desires and interests. Statements about physical nature can achieve neutrality in this respect; this is more difficult when the data are those of history, and nearly impossible in the case of moral and social life, where the words themselves are inescapably charged with ethical or æsthetic or political content.

To suppose, then, that there have been or could be ages without political philosophy, is like supposing that as there are ages of faith, so there are or could be ages of total disbelief. But this is an absurd notion: there is no human activity without some kind of general outlook: scepticism, cynicism, refusal to dabble in abstract issues or to question values, hard boiled opportunism, contempt for theorizing, all the varieties of nihilism, are, of course, themselves metaphysical and ethical positions, committal attitudes. Whatever else the existentialists have taught us, they have made this fact plain. The idea of a completely *Wertfrei* theory (or model) of human action (as contrasted, say, with animal behaviour) rests on a naïve misconception of what objectivity or neutrality in the social studies must be.

V

The notion that a simile or model, drawn from one sphere, is necessarily misleading when applied to another, and that it is possible to think without such analogies in some direct fashion—'face-to-face' with the facts—will not bear criticism. To think is to generalize, to generalize is to compare. To think of one phenomenon or cluster of phenomena is to think in terms of its resemblances and differences with others. This is by now a hoary platitude. It follows that without parallels and analogies between one sphere and another of thought and action, whether conscious or not, the unity of our experience—our experience itself— would not be possible. All language and thought is, in this sense, necessarily 'metaphorical'. The models, once they are made conscious and explicit, may turn out to be obsolete or misleading. Yet even the most discredited among these models in politics— the social contract, patriarchalism, the organic society and so forth, must have started with some initial validity to have had the influence on thought that they have had.

No analogy powerful enough to govern the concepts of generations of men can have been wholly specious. When Jean Bodin or Herder or the Russian Slavophils or the German sociologist Tönnies transfer the notion of family nexus to political life, they remind us of aspects of relationships between men united by traditional bonds or bound by common habits and loyalties, which had been misrepresented by the Stoics or Machiavelli or Bentham or Nietzsche or Herbert Spencer. So, too, assimilation of law to a command issued by some constituted authority in any one of the three types of social order distinguished by Max Weber, throws some light on the concept of law. Similarly, the social contract is a model which to this day helps to explain something of what it is that men feel to be wrong when a politician pronounces an entire class of the population (say, capitalists or negroes) to be outside the community—not entitled to the benefits conferred by the state and its laws. So too, Lenin's image of the factory which needs no supervision by coercive policemen after the state has withered away; Maistre's image of the executioner and his victims as the cornerstone of all authority, or of life as a perpetual battlefield in which only terror of supernatural power keeps men from

mutual extermination; the state's role as traffic policeman and
night watchman (Lassalle's contemptuous description of the
Liberal ideal); Locke's analogy of government with trusteeship;
the constant use by Burke and the entire Romantic movement of
metaphors drawn from organic growth and decay; the Soviet
model of an army on the march, with its accompanying attributes
and values, such as uncritical loyalty, faith in leadership, and
military goals such as the need to overtake, destroy, conquer
some specified enemy—all these illuminate some types of social
experience.

The great distortions, the errors and crimes that have sought
their inspiration and justification in such images, are evidence of
mechanical extrapolation, or over-enthusiastic application of
what, at most, explains a sector of life, to the whole. It is a form
of the ancient fallacy of the Ionian philosophers, who wanted a
single answer to the question: 'What are all things made of?'
Everything is not made of water, nor fire, nor is explained by the
irresistible march towards the world state or the classless society.
The history of thought and culture is, as Hegel showed with
great brilliance, a changing pattern of great liberating ideas which
inevitably turn into suffocating straitjackets, and so stimulate
their own destruction by new, emancipating, and at the same
time, enslaving conceptions. The first step to the understanding
of men is the bringing to consciousness of the model or models
that dominate and penetrate their thought and action. Like all
attempts to make men aware of the categories in which they think,
it is a difficult and sometimes painful activity, likely to produce
deeply disquieting results. The second task is to analyse the model
itself, and this commits the analyst to accepting or modifying or
rejecting it, and, in the last case, to providing a more adequate
one in its stead.

It is seldom, moreover, that there is only one model that
determines our thought; men (or cultures) obsessed by single
models are rare, and while they may be more coherent at their
strongest, they tend to collapse more violently when, in the
end, their concepts are blown up by reality—experienced events,
'inner' or 'outer', that get in the way. Most men wander hither
and thither, guided and, at times, hypnotized by more than one
model, which they seldom trouble to make consistent, or even
fragments of models which themselves form a part of some none

too coherent or firm pattern or patterns. To drag them into the light makes it possible to explain them and sometimes to explain them away. The purpose of such analysis is to clarify; but clarification may expose shortcomings and subvert what it describes. That has often and quite justly been charged against political thought, which, at its best, does not disclaim this dangerous power. The ultimate test of the adequacy of the basic patterns by which we think and act is the only test that common sense or the sciences afford, namely, whether it fits in with the general lines on which we think and communicate; and if some among these in turn are called into question, then the final measure is, as it always must be, direct confrontation with the concrete data of observation and introspection which these concepts and categories and habits order and render intelligible. In this sense, political theory, like any other form of thought that deals with the real world, rests on empirical experience, though in what sense of 'empirical' still remains to be discussed.

VI

When one protests (as we ourselves did above) that the application of such (social or political) models or combinations of overlapping models, which at most hold a part of our experience, causes distortion when applied beyond it; how do we set about to justify this charge? How do we know that the result is distortion? We usually think this because the universal application of a simile or a pattern—say that of the general will, or the organic society, or basic structure and superstructure, or the liberating myth—seems to those who reject it to ignore something that they know directly of human nature and thereby to do violence to what we are, or what we know, by forcing it into the Procrustean bed of some rigid dogma; that is to say, that we protest in the name of our own view of what men are, have been, could be.

How do we know these things? How do we know what is and what is not an adequate programme for human beings in given historical circumstances? Is this knowledge sociological, or psychological? Is it empirical at all, or metaphysical and even theological? How do we argue with those whose notions are different from ours? Hume, Helvétius, Condorcet, Comte, are clear that such knowledge must be based on empirical data and the methods of the natural sciences, all else is imaginary and worthless.

The temptation to accept this simple solution was (and is) very great. The conflict of the rival explanations (or models) of social and individual life had, by the late eighteenth century, grown to be a scandal. If one examines what answers were offered, let us say, between the death of Newton and the birth of Darwin, to a central political question—why anyone should obey anyone else—the babel of voices is appalling, perhaps the most confused in recorded history. Some said that I should obey those rules or institutions submission to which alone would fulfil my nature, with the rider that my needs and the correct path to their satisfaction were clear only to those privileged observers who grasped at least some part of the great hierarchy of being. Others said that I should obey this or that authority or law because only in that way could I (without aid of experts) fulfil my 'true' nature, or be able to fit into a harmonious whole. Some supposed this whole to be static; others taught that it was dynamic, but could not agree on whether it moved in recurrent cycles, or a straight, or spiral, or irregular evolutionary line, or by a series of oscillations leading to 'dialectical' explosions; or again, whether it was teleological or functional or causally determined.

Some conceived the ultimate universal pattern in mechanistic, others in organic, others still, in æsthetic terms. There were those who said that men must obey because they had promised to do so, or others had promised on their behalf; or that they were behaving as if they had promised and this was tantamount to having promised, whether they admitted this or no; or, if this seemed unconvincing, that it were best that they should behave as if they had so promised, since otherwise no one would know where he was and chaos would ensue. Some told men to obey because they would be happier if they did, or because the majority, or all men, would be happier; or because it was God's will that they should obey, or the will of the sovereign, or of the majority, or of the best or wisest, or of history, or of their state, or their race, or their culture, or their church.

They were told also that they must obey because the natural law laid down that they must do so, but there were differences about how the precepts of natural law were to be discovered,

whether by rational or by empirical means, or by intuition, and
again, by common men or only by the experts; the experts in their
turn were identified by some with natural scientists, by others
with specialists in metaphysics or theology, or perhaps in some
other discipline—mass psychology, mystical revelation, the laws
of history, of economics, of natural evolution, of a new synthesis
of all or some of these. Some people supposed that truth in these
matters could be discovered by a faculty which they called moral
sense, or common sense or the perception of the fitness of things,
or that it consisted in what they had been told by their parents
or nurses or was to be found in accepted views which it was mere
perversity to question, or came from one or other of many
sources of this sort which Bentham mocks at so gaily and effectively. Some (and perhaps these have always been the majority)
felt it to be in some degree subversive to raise such questions at all.

This situation caused justified indignation in a country dominated by free enquiry and its greatest triumph, Newtonian science.
Surely this monstrous muddle could be cleared away by the strong
new broom of scientific method—a similar chaos had, after all,
not so long ago prevailed in the natural sciences too. Galileo and
Newton—and the light of reason and experiment—had silenced
for ever the idle chatter of the ignoramus, the dark muttering of
the metaphysician, the thunder of the preacher, the hysterical
shrieks of the obscurantist. All genuine questions were questions
of discoverable fact—*calculemus*, Condorcet declared, was to be
the motto of the new method; all problems must be so refor-
mulated that inspection of the facts—aided by mathematical
techniques—would answer them decisively, with a clear,
universally valid, empirical statement of verifiable fact.

VII

Nevertheless, attempts by the *philosophes* of the eighteenth
century to turn philosophy, and particularly moral and political
philosophy, into an empirical science, into individual and social
psychology, did not succeed. They failed over politics because
our political notions are part of our conception of what it is to
be human, and this is not solely a question of fact, as facts are
conceived by the natural sciences; nor the product of conscious
reflection upon the specific discoveries of anthropology or

sociology or psychology, although all these are relevant and indeed indispensable to an adequate notion of the nature of man in general, or of particular groups of men in particular circumstances. Our conscious idea of man—of how men differ from other entities, of what is human and what is not human or inhuman—involves the use of some among the basic categories in terms of which we perceive and order and interpret data. To analyse the concept of man is to recognize these categories for what they are. To do this is to realize that they are categories, that is, that they are not themselves subjects for scientific hypotheses about the data which they order.

The analogy with the sciences which dominates the pre-Kantian thinkers of the eighteenth century—Locke, Hume and Condillac, for example, is a typical misapplication of a model that works in one sphere to a region where it will obscure at least as much as it illuminates.

Let me try to make this more specific. When the theological and metaphysical models of the Middle Ages were swept away by the sciences of the seventeenth and eighteenth centuries, they disappeared largely because they could not compete in describing, predicting, controlling the contents of the external world with new disciplines. To the extent to which man was regarded as an object in material nature the sciences of man—psychology, anthropology, economics, sociology and so on—began to supplant their theologico-metaphysical predecessors. The questions of the philosophers were affected by this; some were answered or rendered obsolete: but some remained unanswered. The new human sciences studied men's actual habits; they promised, and in some cases, provided, analyses of what men said, wanted, admired, abhorred; they were prepared to supply empirical evidence for this, or experimental demonstration; but their efforts to solve normative problems were less successful. They tried to reduce questions of value to questions of fact—of what caused what kind of men to feel or behave as they did in various circumstances. But when Kant or Herder or Dostoevsky or Marx duly rejected the encyclopædists' answers, the charge against them was not solely that of faulty observation or invalid inference; it was that of a failure to recognize what it is to be a man, that is, failure to take into account the nature of the framework— the basic categories—in terms of which we think and act and

3

assume others to think and act, if communication between us is to work.

In other words, the problem the solutions of which were found insufficient is not in the usual sense empirical, and certainly not formal, but something that is not adequately described by either term. When Rousseau (whether he understood him correctly or not) rejected Hobbes's account of political obligation on the ground that Hobbes seemed to him to explain it by mere fear of superior force, Rousseau claimed not that Hobbes had not seen certain relevant empirical, psychologically discoverable, facts, nor that he had argued incorrectly from what he had seen—but that his account was in conflict with what, in thinking of human beings as human, and distinguishing them, even the most degraded among them, not only in explicit thought, but in our feelings and in our action, from beings that we regard as inhuman or non-human, we all know men to be. His argument is not that the facts used to construct Hobbes's model had gaps in them, but that the model was inadequate in principle; it was inadequate not because this or that psychological or sociological correlation had been missed out, but because it was based on a failure to understand what we mean by motive, purpose, value, personality and the like.

When Kant breaks with the naturalistic tradition, or Marx rejects the political morality of Bentham, or Tolstoy expresses a low opinion of the doctrines of Karl Marx, they are not complaining merely of empirical ignorance or poor logic or insufficient experimental evidence, or internal incoherence. They denounce their adversaries mainly for not understanding what men are and what relationships between them—or between them and outside forces—make them men; they complain of blindness not to the transient aspects of such relations, but to those constant characteristics (such as discrimination of right from good for Kant, or, for Marx, systematic self-transmutation by their own labour) that they regard as fundamental to the notion of man as such. Their criticisms relate to the adequacy of the categories in terms of which we discuss men's ends or duties or interests, the permanent framework in terms of which, not about which, ordinary empirical disagreements can arise.

What are these categories? How do we discover them? If not empirically, then by what means? How universal and unchanging are they? How do they enter into and shape the models and paradigms in terms of which we think and respond? Do we discover what they are by attention to thought, or action, or unconscious processes, and how do we reconcile these various sources of knowledge? These are characteristically philosophical questions, since they are questions about the all but permanent ways in which we think, decide, perceive, judge, and not about the data of experience—the items themselves. The test of the adequate working of the methods, analogies, models which operate in discovering and classifying the behaviour of these empirical data (as natural science and common sense do) is ultimately empirical: it is the degree of their success in forming a coherent and enduring conceptual system.

To apply these models and methods to the framework itself by means of which we perceive and think about them, is a major fallacy by the analysis of which Kant transformed philosophy. In politics it was committed (by Hume and Russell, for example) when enquiry into the empirical characteristics of men was confounded with the analysis of the notion of man (or 'self' or 'observer' or 'moral agent' or 'individual' or 'soul', etc.) in terms of which the empirical characteristics were themselves collected and described. Kant supposed these categories to be discoverable *a priori*. We need not accept this; this was an unwarranted conclusion from the valid perception that there exist central features of our experience that are invariant and omnipresent, or at least much less variable than the vast variety of its empirical characteristics, and for that reason deserve to be distinguished by the name of categories. This is evident enough in the case of the external world: the three-dimensionality of (psychological, common sense) space, for example, or the solidity of things in it, or 'the irreversibility' of the time order, are among the most familiar and inalienable kinds of characteristics in terms of which we think and act. Empirical sciences of these properties do not exist, not because they exhibit no regularities—on the contrary they are the very paradigm of the concept of regularity itself— but because they are presupposed in the very language in which we formulate empirical experience. That is why it seems absurd to ask for evidence for their existence, and imaginary examples are enough to exhibit their structure; for they are presupposed in our commonest acts of thought or decision; and where imaginary examples are, for the purpose of an enquiry, as good as, or even better than, empirical data drawn from actual experience, we may be sure that the enquiry is not, in the normal sense, an empirical one. Such permanent features are to be found in the moral and political and social worlds too: less stable and universal, perhaps, than in the physical one, but just as indispensable for any kind of intersubjective communication, and therefore for thought and action. An enquiry that proceeds by examples, and is therefore not scientific, but not formal, that is deductive, either, is most likely to be philosophical.

There is an ultimate sense, of course, in which such facts as that space has three dimensions, or that men are beings who demand reasons or make choices, are simply given: brute facts and not *a priori* truths; it is not absurd to suppose that things could have been otherwise. But if they had been (or will one day be) other than they are now, our entire conceptual apparatus —thought, volition, feeling, language, and therefore our very nature, would have been (or will be) different in ways that it is impossible or difficult to describe with the concepts and words available to us as we are to-day. Political categories (and values) are a part of this all but inescapable web of ways of living, acting and thinking, a network liable to change only as a result of radical changes in reality, or through dissociation from reality on the part of individuals, that is to say, madness.

VIII

The basic categories (with their corresponding concepts) in terms of which we define men—such notions as society, freedom, sense of time and change, suffering, happiness, productivity, good and bad, right and wrong, choice, effort, truth, illusion (to take them wholly at random)—are not matters of induction and hypothesis. To think of someone as a human being is *ipso facto* to bring all these notions into play: so that to say of someone that he is a man, but that choice, or the notion of truth, mean nothing to him, would be eccentric: it would clash with what we mean by 'man' not as a matter of verbal definition (which is alterable at will), but as intrinsic to the way in which we think, and (as a matter of 'brute' fact) evidently cannot but think.

This will hold of values too (among them political ones) in terms of which men are defined. Thus, if I say of someone that he is kind or cruel, loves truth or is indifferent to it, he remains human in either case. But if I find a man to whom it literally makes no difference whether he kicks a pebble or kills his family, since either would be an antidote to *ennui* or inactivity, I shall not be disposed, like consistent relativists, to attribute to him merely a different code of morality from my own or that of most men, or declare that we disagree on essentials, but shall begin to speak of insanity and inhumanity; I shall be inclined to consider him mad, as a man who thinks he is Napoleon is mad; which is a way of saying that I do not regard such a being as being fully a man at all. It is cases of this kind, which seem to make it clear that ability to recognize universal—or almost universal—values, enters into our analysis of such fundamental concepts as 'man', 'rational', 'sane', 'natural', etc.—which are usually thought of as descriptive and not evaluative—that lie at the basis of modern translations into empirical terms of the kernel of truth in the old *a priori* Natural Law doctrines. It is considerations such as these, urged by neo-Aristotelians and the followers of the later doctrines of Wittgenstein, that have shaken the faith of some devoted empiricists in the complete logical gulf between descriptive statements and statements of value, and have cast doubt on the celebrated distinction derived from Hume.

Extreme cases of this sort are of philosophical importance because they make it clear that such questions are not answered by either empirical observation or formal deduction. Hence those who confine themselves to observation of human behaviour and empirical hypotheses about it, psychologists, sociologists, historians, however profound and original they may be, are not, as such, political theorists, even though they may have much to say that is crucial in the field of political philosophy. That is why we do not consider such dedicated empiricists as the students, say, of the formation and behaviour of parties or élites or classes, or of the methods and consequences of various types of democratic procedure, to be political philosophers or social theorists in the larger sense.

Such men are in the first place students of facts, and aspire to formulate hypotheses and laws like the natural scientists. Yet as a rule these thinkers cannot go any further: they tend to analyse men's social and political ideas in the light of some overriding belief of their own—for example, that the purpose of all life is or should be the service of God, however interpreted; or on the contrary that it is the pursuit of experimentally discoverable individual or collective satisfaction; or that it lies in the self-realization of a historical (or psychological or æsthetic) pattern, grasp of which alone can explain men to themselves and give meaning to their thoughts and action; or, on the contrary, that there exists no human purpose; or that men cannot but seek conflicting ends; or cannot (without ceasing to be human) avoid activities that must end in self-frustration, so that the very notion of a final solution is an absurdity. In so far as it is such fundamental conceptions of man that determine political doctrines (and who will deny that political problems, e.g. about what men and groups can or should be or do, depend logically and directly on what man's nature is taken to be?), it is clear that those who are governed by these great integrating syntheses bring to their study something other than empirical data.

If we examine the models, paradigms, conceptual structures that govern various outlooks whether consciously or not, and compare the various concepts and categories involved with respect, for example, to their internal consistency or their ex-planatory force, then what we are engaged upon is not psychology or sociology or logic or epistemology, but moral or social or political theory, or all these at once, depending on whether we confine ourselves to individuals, or to groups, or to the particular types of human arrangements that are classified as political, or deal with them all in one. No amount of careful empirical observation and bold and fruitful hypothesis will explain to us what those men see who see the state as a divine institution, or what their words mean and how they relate to reality; nor what those believe who tell us that the state was sent upon us only for our sins; or those who say that it is a school through which we must go before we are adult and free and can dispense with it; or that it is a work of art; or a utilitarian device; or the incarnation of natural law; or a committee of the ruling class; or the highest stage of the self-developing human spirit; or a piece of criminal folly. But unless we understand (by an effort of imaginative insight such as novelists usually possess in a higher degree than logicians) what notions of man's nature (or absence of them) are incorporated in these political outlooks, what in each case is the dominant model, we shall not understand our own or any human society: neither the conceptions of reason and nature which governed Stoics or Thomists or govern the European Christian Democrats to-day; nor the very different image which is at the heart of the holy war in which the national-Marxist movements in Africa or in Asia, are or may soon be marching; nor the very different notions that animate the liberal and democratic compromises of the West.

It is by now a platitude to say that understanding human thought and action is in large measure understanding what problems and perplexities they strive with. When these problems, whether empirical and formal, have been conceived in terms of models of reality so ancient, widely accepted and stable, that we use them to this day, we understand the problems and difficulties and the attempted solutions without explicit reference to the governing categories; for these, being common to us and to cultures remote from us, do not obtrude themselves on us; stay, as it were, out of sight. In other cases (and this is conspicuously true of politics) the models have not stood still: some of the notions of which they were compounded are no longer familiar. Yet unless we have the knowledge and imagination to transpose ourselves into states of mind dominated by the now discarded or obsolescent model, the thoughts and actions that had them at their centre will remain opaque to us. It is failure to perform this difficult operation that marks much of the history of ideas, and turns it into either a superficial literary exercise, or a dead catalogue of strange, at times almost incomprehensible, errors and confusions.

This may not matter too much in the empirical and formal disciplines, where the test of a belief is, or should be, verification or logical coherence: and where one can accept the latest solutions, and reject the falsified or incoherent solutions of the past without bothering (if one is incurious) to understand why they were ever held. But philosophical doctrines are not established or discredited in this final fashion: for they are concerned with —indeed they owe their existence to—problems that cannot be settled in these ways. They are not concerned with specific facts, but with ways of looking at them; they do not consist of first order propositions concerning the world. They are second or higher order statements about whole classes of descriptions of, or responses to, the world and man's activities in it; and these are in turn determined by models, networks of categories, descriptive, evaluative, and hybrids compounded of the two, in which the two functions cannot be disentangled even in thought—categories which if not eternal and universal, are far more stable and widespread than those of the sciences; sufficiently continuous, indeed, to constitute a common world which we share with mediæval and classical thinkers.

Ionian cosmology, the biology of Aristotle, Stoic logic, Arab algebra, Cartesian physics, may be of interest to historical specialists, but need not occupy the minds of physicists or biologists or mathematicians who are solely interested in the discovery of new truth. In these studies there is genuine progress: what is past is largely obsolete. But the political philosophy of Plato or Aristotle or Machiavelli, the moral views of the Hebrew prophets or of the Gospels or of the Roman jurists or of the mediæval Church—these, whether in the original or in the works of their modern expositors, are incomparably more intelligible and more relevant to our own preoccupations than the sciences of antiquity. The subject matter of these disciplines—the most general characteristics of men as such, that is, as beings engaged in moral or social or spiritual activities—seems to present problems which preserve a considerable degree of continuity and similarity from one age and culture to another. Methods of dealing with them vary greatly; but none have as yet achieved so decisive a victory as to sweep all their rivals into oblivion. The inadequate models of political thought evidently have, by and large, perished and been forgotten; the great illuminating models are still controversial to-day, stir us still to adherence or criticism or violent indignation.

We might take as examples Professor Karl Popper's denunciation of Plato's political theory or Irving Babbitt's philippics against Rousseau, Simone Weil's violent distaste for the morality of the Old Testament, or the frequent attacks made to-day on eighteenth-century positivism or 'scientism' in political ethics.[1] Some of the classical constructions are in conflict with one another, but, inasmuch as each rests on a vivid vision of permanent human attributes and is capable of satisfying some enquiring minds in each generation, no matter how different the circumstances of time and place, the models of Plato, or of Aristotle, or of Judaism, Christianity, Kantian liberalism, romanticism,

---

[1] What thinker to-day entertains violent emotions towards the errors of Cartesian physicists or mediæval mapmakers?

historicism, all survive and contend with each other to-day in a variety of guises. If men or circumstances alter radically, or new empirical knowledge is gained which will revolutionize our conception of man, then certainly, some of these edifices will cease to be relevant and will be forgotten like the ethics and metaphysics of the Egyptians or the Incas. But so long as men are as they are, the debate will continue in terms set by these visions and others like them: each will gain or lose in influence as events force this or that aspect of men into prominence. One thing alone is certain, that save to those who understand and even feel what a philosophical question is, how it differs from empirical or formal question (although this difference need not be explicitly present to the mind, and overlapping or borderline questions are frequent enough) the answers—in this case the main political doctrines of the West—may well seem intellectual fancies, detached philosophical speculations and constructions without much relation to acts or events.

Only those who can to some degree re-enact within themselves the states of mind of men tormented by questions to which these theories claim to be solutions, or at any rate the states of mind of those who may accept the solutions uncritically but would, without them, fall into a state of insecurity and anxiety—only these are capable of grasping what part philosophical views, and especially political doctrines, have played in history, at any rate in the West. The work of the logicians or physicists of the past has receded because it has been superseded. But there is something absurd in the suggestion that we reject Plato's political doctrines or Kant's æsthetics or ethics because they have been 'superseded'. This consideration alone should prevent facile assimilation of the two cases. It may be objected to this line of argument that we look upon old ethical or political doctrines as still worth discussion because they are part of our cultural tradition—that if Greek philosophy, biblical ethics, etc., had not been an intrinsic element in Western education, they would by now have been as remote from us as early Chinese speculation. But this merely takes the argument a step backwards: it is true that if the general characteristics of our normal experience had altered radically enough—through a revolution in our knowledge or some natural upheaval which altered our reactions—these ancient categories would probably by now have been felt to be as obsolete as those

of Hammurabi or the epic of Gilgamesh. That this is not so is
doubtless due partly to the fact that our experience is itself
organized and 'coloured' by ethical or political categories that
we have inherited from our ancestors, ancient spectacles through
which we are still looking. But the spectacles would long ago
have caused us to blunder and stumble and would have given
way to others, or been modified out of recognition as our physical
and biological and mathematical spectacles have been, if they
had not still performed their task more or less adequately: which
argues a certain degree of continuity in at least two millennia of
moral and political consciousness.

                                 IX

We may be told that whatever we may maintain about the
sources motives or justification of our beliefs, the content of what
adherents of divers philosophies believe tends to be similar if
they belong to the same social or economic or cultural milieu or
have other—psychological or physiological—characteristics in
common. The English philosophers, T. H. Green and J. S. Mill,
preached philosophically contradictory doctrines: Green was a
quasi-Hegelian metaphysician, Mill a Humean empiricist, yet
their political conclusions were close to one another's; both were
humane Victorian liberals with a good deal of sympathy for
socialism. This, we shall further be told, was because men are
conditioned to believe what they believe by objective historical
factors—their social position, or the class structure of their
society and their position in it, although their own (erroneous)
rationalizations of their beliefs may be as widely different as
those of Mill and Green.

So, too, it has been said, the outlook—the 'operational ideas'—
of Fascists and Communists display a surprising degree of similarity, given the extreme opposition and incompatibility of the
official axioms from which these movements logically start. Hence
the plausibility of some of the methods of the 'sociology of knowledge', whether Marxist or Paretian or psycho-analytic, and of
the various eclectic forms which, in the hands of Weber, Mann-
heim and others, this instrument has acquired. Certainly such
theorists have cast light on the obscure roots of our beliefs. We
may be conditioned to believe what we believe irrationally, by

circumstances mainly beyond our control, and perhaps beyond our knowledge too. But whatever may in fact causally determine our beliefs, it would be a gratuitous abdication of our powers of reasoning—based on a confusion of natural science with philosophical enquiry—not to want to know what we believe, and for what reason, what the metaphysical implications of such beliefs are, what their relation is to other types of belief, what criteria of value and truth they involve, and so what reason we have to think them true or valid. Rationality rests on the belief that one can think and act for reasons that one can understand, and not merely as the product of occult causal factors which breed 'ideologies', and cannot, in any case, be altered by their victims. So long as rational curiosity exists—a desire for justification and explanation in terms of motives and reasons, and not only of causes or functional correlations or statistical probabilities—political theory will not wholly perish from the earth, however many of its rivals, such as sociology, philosophical analysis, social psychology, political science, economics, jurisprudence, semantics, may claim to have dispelled its imaginary realm.

It is a strange paradox that political theory should seem to lead so shadowy an existence at a time when, for the first time in history, literally the whole of mankind is violently divided by issues the reality of which is, and has always been, the sole *raison d'être* of this branch of study. But this, we may be sure, is not the end of the story. Neo-Marxism, neo-Thomism, nationalism, historicism, existentialism, anti-essentialist liberalism and socialism, transpositions of doctrines of natural rights and natural law into empirical terms, discoveries made by skilful application of models derived from economic and related techniques to political behaviour, and the collisions, combinations and consequences in action of these ideas, indicate not the death of a great tradition, but, if anything, new and unpredictable developments.

SOCIOLOGICAL EVIDENCE AND POLITICAL THEORY

by W. G. Runciman

WHEN the suggestion was voiced in the first volume of *Philosophy, Politics and Society* that political philosophy might be dead, it was received in some quarters with alarm and indignation but more often with a very proper scepticism. For we all know, after all, that political philosophizing can go on no matter how rigorously we may want to press the distinction of facts and values. It may be hard enough in practice to win a political argument, but we reveal our belief that it is in principle winnable by embarking on it at all; moreover, we know very well that some political theories that have been discredited have been rightly discredited but that others still need to be taken account of; and so on. This is not to say that there has been quite so lively a revival of political theory as the scepticism about its death might have led one to expect. But in the years since the heyday of Weldonism it has ceased to be necessary to argue the case that political philosophy is possible at all. On the other hand, it remains as good a question as ever to ask of the proponent of any given political theory what evidence (if any) would persuade him to abandon it. In this paper, I want to consider some of the issues which this question raises, and in particular to discuss three cases where the work of social scientists has a specific bearing on political theory. In so doing, I want also to draw attention to the contribution made on this topic by Max Weber.

I

I make at the outset two assumptions: first, as already indicated, that political philosophy is in principle possible given that we are prepared to engage in political argument at all; and second, that the propositions which political philosophers are concerned to establish or defend are some sorts of moral propositions.

The case for these two assumptions has recently been argued with some force by Benn and Peters,[1] but I must make clear that in sharing their view up to this point I do not share their further contention that all political arguments may be subsumed under a single moral heading, for which the criterion is impartiality. This further argument, which has been effectively criticized elsewhere,[2] must involve an improper assimilation of two different notions of social justice; and as Weber at one point argues, there is a conflict irreconcilable by any single ethical norm between the notion of justice represented by (in his example) Schmoller and that represented by Babeuf. I shall return to this point later; but for the moment, I only want to make clear that by likening political arguments to ethical arguments I am not suggesting that there is only one relevant political morality.

One further preliminary consideration should perhaps be dealt with at this point, namely the alleged 'subjectivism' or 'relativism' of all political (or moral or æsthetic) beliefs. The sceptic, to whom any political belief is as unarguable as a taste for ice cream, is likely to lend weight to his attack by pointing to the indisputable variety of political beliefs and the lack of any universally accepted criterion for appraising them. This, however, is not really the point. No matter how many people or communities sociologists might discover who believed for various reasons that the earth is flat, we should not be disposed (or not, at any rate, simply for that reason) to abandon our conviction that it is round. The point is rather whether any evidence is adduced which might shake our conviction; and this applies in the case of a political belief just as much as a scientific one.

Let us consider, for example, the political proposal that the state should torture and execute all widows and orphans. It is surely difficult to maintain that this sort of suggestion should be taken any more seriously than the claim that the earth is flat; and it is not, therefore, the simple diversity of beliefs which makes different political attitudes seem immune to arbitration—indeed, some such attitudes may be dismissed as confidently as a refusal to accept the discoveries of natural science. The difficulty in fact comes only when dealing with beliefs which cannot be so

---

[1] S. I. Benn and R. S. Peters, *Social Principles and the Democratic State.*
[2] Brian M. Barry, 'Justice and the Common Good', *Analysis*, XXI (1961), pp. 86–90.

cavalierly rejected but which are nevertheless impervious to evidence.

Examples of such beliefs (leaving aside the psychological factors which may be involved in clinging to them) might be the Roman Catholic conception of Natural Law or certain of the more rigid tenets of so-called 'vulgar' Marxism. These are impervious to evidence not because their proponents do not adduce any in support of their position, but because the conclusions argued from the evidence rest upon an interpretation which, if consistently maintained, can be guaranteed in advance to cover any fact which the observer might bring back from the sociological study of the contingent world. We may, of course, succeed in controverting such people on grounds of consistency; or we may, precisely by forcing them to be consistent, put them into a position which we believe must cause them some discomfiture, whether or not they are willing to admit to it. But there may be nothing more to be done. Indeed, it may be that if we were to ask, for instance, a believing Catholic what evidence of any kind could convince him to abandon the doctrine of natural law, the answer would be none. This is not to say that he will never change his mind. But if he does, we shall be more likely to use words like 'conversion' or 'loss of belief' to describe the occurrence than to treat it as equivalent, say, to the process whereby someone comes to accept the truth of a historical fact.

It is obvious, however, that political beliefs are in general not of this kind. This is particularly clear in such cases as a utilitarian position, which necessarily involves a susceptibility to empirical psychological or sociological evidence: any utilitarian assertion about political or moral duty may be disputed by questioning its implications in terms of the pain or pleasure caused. But in any instance where there is an answer to 'what makes you think so?' a political belief is in principle susceptible to argument just as much as an assertion of the most respectably empirical kind. It may not prove possible to settle such an argument conclusively, or even to settle precisely what evidence would be accepted by both parties as decisive. But it certainly does not follow from this that political beliefs are necessarily and in principle immune to the adducing of logical or empirical evidence.

By way of illustration, let me give one example of a bad argument and another of a good one; or more precisely, one bad argument against a tenable position and one good argument against an untenable one. The bad argument is taken from Hegel,[1] and reads as follows: 'To hold that every single person should share in deliberating and deciding on political matters of general concern on the ground that all individuals are members of the state, that its concerns are their concerns, and that it is their right that what is done should be done with their knowledge and volition, is tantamount to a proposal to put the democratic element without any rational form into the organism of the state although it is only in virtue of the possession of such a form that the state is an organism at all.' The good argument is taken from T. H. Huxley's critique of the Social Darwinists:[2] 'It strikes me that men who are accustomed to contemplate the active or passive extirpation of the weak, the unfortunate, and the super-fluous; who justify that conduct on the ground that it has the sanction of the cosmic process, and is the only way of ensuring the progress of the race, who, if they are consistent, must rank medicine among the black arts and count the physician a mis-chievous preserver of the unfit; on whose matrimonial under-takings the principles of the stud have the chief influence; whose whole lives, therefore, are an education in the noble art of sup-pressing natural affection and sympathy, are not likely to have any large stock of these commodities left.'

I do not mean that the good argument is good because it settles the question definitively; but to achieve its purpose it does not need to. To show that an ethical doctrine entails that ministering to the sick is wicked is quite enough to stultify it as it stands (though of course counter-moves could be made, if only by modifying the categorical assertion that any interference in cosmic selection is wrong). Similarly, Hegel may be right in asserting that it is foolish to advocate a certain sort of universal democracy. But it is not difficult to show that this conclusion is not entailed by the question-begging use of 'rational form' and the irrelevant assertion that the state must be an organism—the only arguments adduced in the passage concerned. These two examples are, of course, a long way short of demonstrating what a good full-scale political theory would look like or of providing a map of the logical bridges between prescriptive statements and

---

[1] *Philosophy of Right* (ed. Knox), Section 308.
[2] Quoted by R. Hofstadter, *Social Darwinism in American Thought*, p. 95.

those non-prescriptive assertions (whether logical or empirical) which would controvert or modify them. But they serve as reassurance (if needed) that political arguments are not merely an exchange of boos and hurrahs and they suggest that it may be worth while to classify the ways in which argument about political positions can be relevant to the positions held.

The best such classification that I know of is given by Max Weber, although I shall later dissent in one major respect from his views. According to Weber, there are three and only three purposes which can be served by arguments about questions of value (*Wertungsdiskussionen*). First of all, the meaning of a value-judgement may be analysed and it may be discovered what other evaluative axioms it can logically be derived from or can logically be derived from it. Secondly, it is possible to argue about the actions implied by a set of value-judgements when an existing factual situation is assessed in terms of these value-judgements only. Thirdly, the factual consequences of such actions may be debated in the light of either the means necessary to carry them out or the further consequences (which may be incompatible with the original value-judgement) which must result from such actions. This third type of argument, says Weber, may lead to four sorts of conclusions by which the initial value-judgement will be directly modified. In the first place, the initial prescriptive statement may be shown to be impossible to fulfil. Secondly, it may be possible to realize but only at the cost of further consequences which would themselves violate it. Thirdly, it may be possible only by means not taken into account in the formulation of the original value-judgement. Finally, there may be other value-judgements which were not originally considered but which, though incompatible with the recommended policy, are also accepted by its proponents.

It needs little reflection to see that these three types of argument cover a very great deal; indeed, they cover precisely what political arguments are in practice about. This still leaves our previous cases where the holder of a political belief—Weber himself uses the example of a convinced syndicalist—will not accept any argument at all, not because (like the widow and orphan killer) he is mad, but because certain objectives have for him an absolute value to which no considerations of feasibility or consequence are relevant. But it would be a mistake to suppose that the syndicalist (whom I shall return to later) need be quite so un-shakeable as Weber himself would have us believe. It is some-times (and rightly) maintained that political viewpoints can never be proved, but only well or badly defended.[1] But such defences are just what political arguments consist of; and there are few even of convinced syndicalists who if asked why they hold the view they do will not give answers debatable by some rules of logic and evidence that they would themselves accept.

This is not to say that political persuasion is effected only by the adducing of further evidence. An interesting case is where persuasion is effected in such a way as may often happen with æsthetic judgements, where we may say, for example, 'Try looking at these Picassos a little longer and you'll find you come to like them'. I do not want to argue that there is not an important distinction between cases of this kind and such 'manipulative' techniques of persuasion as mob oratory or subliminal advertising; but they are also different from those cases where some further evidence is in fact adduced (e.g. by suggesting that Picasso is in some demonstrable respect similar to a painter whom the person concerned is known to like). An analogous case in political argu-ment is perhaps where someone conjures up the picture of the ideal society implied by his political beliefs and tries thereby (but without adducing further argument) to secure his inter-locutor's assent to them. The difficulty here is that æsthetic assent may be given to two incompatible ideals such, for instance, as honesty and kindness, or on a more political level, the two different conceptions of social justice cited, as we saw earlier, by Weber. But such conflicts need not, of course, be always irrecon-cilable, or at least not as often as Weber tends to imply; and the first move out of them, if there is to be one at all, is to conduct precisely the sort of argument or discussion which Weber classifies.

II

One of the things which Weber's analysis makes clear is how often it is feasibility which constitutes the crucial criterion by which a political argument may be settled; and it is such argu-ments which, if established, very often require the abandonment

---

[1] E.g. by Margaret Macdonald in her Essay on 'Natural Rights' in *Philosophy, Politics and Society* (1956), p. 52.

of a prescriptive political position. To illustrate this, I want to consider briefly three books which are importantly relevant to the classical theory of democracy. None of them sets out to advance a new *Weltanschauung*, and all three were written not by political philosophers but by social scientists. But they each contain general propositions of an 'if . . . then' form which have a clear and direct relevance (though in each case in a very different way) to the central tenets of democratic theory. The three books are: Schumpeter's *Capitalism, Socialism and Democracy*, Lazarsfeld's *The People's Choice* (together with the subsequent study *Voting*) and Arrow's *Social Choice and Individual Values*.

The idea of Schumpeter's which is of interest here (and which should be initially credited to Mosca) is that free competition between élites is the best guarantee of political freedom; and this assertion rests to a large extent upon the factual claim that, as Schumpeter firmly puts it, 'voters do not decide issues'. Schumpeter, in fact, asks us to stand on its head the accepted causal postulate of democratic theory. The results and processes of elections are, in his view, the dependent and not the independent variable in the political process; and in any case, 'even if the opinions and desires of individual citizens were perfectly definite and independent data for the democratic process to work with, and even if everyone acted on them with rationality and promptitude, it would not necessarily follow that the political decisions produced by that process from the raw material of those individual volitions would represent anything that could in any convincing sense be called the will of the people'. I think it is probably true to say that this second assertion is generally accepted as correct (Arrow, as we shall see, is also relevant), but that the first represents a considerable underestimate of the importance of the electorate. However, even if Schumpeter is only partially right, his view is hardly less important to the theorist of democracy; indeed it illustrates in part the basic difference between the philosopher and the sociologist of politics. The traditional philosophers of politics (who could, after all, have no idea how universal suffrage might work in practice) were largely concerned to justify by *a priori* argument the sort of system which they would like to see realized; the political sociologist, on the other hand, asks what sort of system is possible under what sort of conditions and with what sort of probable consequences. Whether or not he starts with a prescriptive view-point, his evidence both about feasibilities and consequences is likely to influence directly such a viewpoint; and this is precisely what Schumpeter sets out to do.

To the holder of what we can loosely call a Rousseauist position, Schumpeter's argument may be relevant in one or more of the ways classified by Weber. Probably it will imply either that the Rousseauist prescriptions are impossible to fulfil or that they are possible only at the cost of undesired consequences. But for the present argument, the interest of the Mosca–Schumpeter doctrine is that its force depends not on its prescriptive content so much as its sociological validity.

The same is, of course, particularly true of Marx. We may share all of Marx's horror and indignation at the effects which he witnessed of the capitalist system; but to accept also his political theory (whereby to work for the violent abolition of the bour-geois state is the real duty of the citizen body) we must agree with the social laws to which he attributed the validity of natural science. If political freedom can *only* be realized by the withering away of the state, then it is wrong to perpetuate it by means of piecemeal social reform; similarly, if political freedom can *only* be realized by free competition of élites, then it is wrong to advocate plebiscitary one-party democracy. Of course, it is not as simple as that; for we must settle just what we mean by 'political freedom', 'withering away of the state', 'competition of élites' and so on; and we may find that we either cannot or need not go further than the first of Weber's categories of *Wertungs-diskussionen*. But this does not alter my central point; the value of Schumpeter's political theory rests very largely on the validity of his sociological evidence. Do voters decide issues or not? And if not, does it not follow that a competition of élites is the only way to try to fulfil the aspirations of classical democratic theory?

If we turn now to Lazarsfeld, the implications of his work for political theory are less immediately apparent. The importance of Lazarsfeld's work has been justly recognized irrespective of its relevance to the political theorist, for it has effected a revision of our picture of voting behaviour whose acceptance should not blind us to its originality. By developing techniques peculiarly appropriate to voting behaviour (voting being not only a meaningful but a quantifiable action), Lazarsfeld and his associates have shown just how differently actual voters behave from the model citizens of classical democratic theory. Of course a number of observers (most notably Ostrogorski and Graham Wallas) had seen that this was so before Lazarsfeld; but it is Lazarsfeld who has shown how it is possible to answer the questions how far, in what way and under what conditions the conclusion holds, and who has arrived at answers which have been largely confirmed by his successors. These answers have very definite implications for political theory, some of which are briefly considered in the final chapter of *Voting*. We now have a vivid picture of to what extent voting is dictated by habit, how relatively few voters change their political allegiance[1] and how unlike the process of voting is to a rational choice between considered alternatives.

But is this falling short by the electorate from the classical ideal a bad thing or a good one? Is it possible, as the authors of *Voting* suggest, that apathy is in fact a political good? And if the electorate did make a fresh rational choice every election and did attach a real importance to that choice, would democracy (as understood in the Western two-party sense) be possible at all?

There is, obviously, no short or simple answer to these questions; but there can equally be no doubt that any useful theory of democracy must take our knowledge of voting behaviour into account. The case argued (or suggested) by the authors of *Voting* needs considerable elaboration, for they do not consider the different implications of apathy in the sense of non-extremism (extremism being a willingness to see the whole system changed even if indifferent as between existing parties) and non-partisanship (partisanship being an identification with one or other party but with in addition a commitment to the rules of the game). It could, for instance, be argued that non-extremism is a good thing but non-partisanship a bad one; and it might be that a low poll is sometimes a bad thing (showing that the electorate doesn't care at all) but sometimes also a good one (showing that the electorate doesn't care too intensely). My point, however, is once again only that Lazarsfeld's work has placed an important limit on the scope of *a priori* theorizing about democracy; and it has done so by producing sociological evidence directly relevant to the tenets

---

[1] Under, of course, more or less 'normal' circumstances; for scepticism of the Anglo-American voting studies, see H. Daudt, *Floating Voters and the Floating Vote* (1961).

of political theory. It is not evidence which necessarily supports either a left-wing or a right-wing view; but it is important precisely because any theory of democracy, whether left or right, must take account of it.

The third work, Arrow's, although principally concerned with the economists' problem of constructing a social welfare function, has in a sense the most clear-cut relevance to the problems of democratic theory. Arrow's General Possibility Theorem is a formal demonstration that 'If we exclude the possibility of inter-personal comparisons of utility, then the only methods of passing from individual tastes to social preferences which will be satis-factory and which will be defined for a wide range of sets of individual orderings are either imposed or dictatorial'. In other words, for the conditions of a genuine social ordering of pre-ferences to be satisfied, certain criteria of unanimity must initially have been fulfilled. (Some modifications of Arrow's theorem have been proposed, but I take it as it stands.) The implications of this conclusion for political theory, and particularly for idealist political theory, are briefly considered by Arrow in his final chapter, but (as with the final chapter of *Voting*) the implications are not worked out in any great detail. This does not, however, make the cogency of such implications any less clear. What sort of a theory of the General Will or of the Common Good it is worth trying to construct in the face of Arrow's conclusions cannot be settled on the basis of Arrow's conclusions alone; but no such theory (again, whether of the Left or Right) is worth attempting at all which does not carefully take account of them.

It is readily apparent that Arrow's argument is different in kind from the other two since unlike them it is purely deductive, whereas both Schumpeter and Lazarsfeld have drawn our attention to contingent facts about the political world. Although this does not affect its relevance to an argument about the feasi-bility of certain kinds of political recommendation, the difference is obviously an important one.

Purely deductive arguments, of which the propositions of game theory are perhaps in this context the most notable example, can be of direct relevance to the political theorist on a number of problems. For instance, the 'prisoner's dilemma' of game theory may be used to elucidate a formal difference between the will of all (uninformed rational choice) and the general will (informed rational choice with an effective promise to abide by it). Or it may be shown how under certain conditions a war of all against all gives the weakest the best chance of survival, and other examples of this kind. The application of such deductions, however, is always debatable and must rest on the contingent assumption that the appropriate conditions are fulfilled; and it therefore seems plausible to suggest that although purely deductive arguments may be relevant to a debate between the holders of rival political theories, such theories are likely more often or in addition to need to be defended by reference to sociological evidence.

III

This does not mean, however, that even the most solid and pervasive generalizations of political sociology will, if established, constitute evidence which necessarily favours one or other of several political theories (in the prescriptive sense) which may be mutually incompatible. This may be illustrated by reference to one of the most familiar problems in the study of political consensus and social stratification. Ever since Durkheim observed that stable poverty is the best guarantee of conservatism, sociologists have remarked on the apparent correlation between lack of opportunity and lack of discontent. To cite one of the best-known examples: Stouffer and associates, studying the American army during the Second World War, found that in the Air Force (where chances of promotion were highest) discontent with promotion was greatest, and in the Military Police (where chances of promotion were lowest) discontent with promotion was least. Now let us suppose (whether or not it is so) that there is a general validity in some proposition of this kind. The Right, of course, will eagerly embrace it as evidence for the assertion that equality of opportunity (or of status) is, as they have always maintained, a bad thing; by promoting envy, they argue, it merely leaves everyone unhappier than they were before. But the Left may feel no less well furnished with an argument for their own position: is it not, they may ask, precisely this situation which calls for remedy? Where superstition and ignorance can prolong an acceptance of deprivation and injustice, does this not make the situation more unacceptable rather than less so?

In an argument of this kind, it may be that there is a confrontation of two incompatible *Weltanschauungen* to which any evidence will be made subservient, and we are back once again with Weber's syndicalists on whom we shall have to try some other argument of a 'why do you think so?' kind. But my point is that if such arguments are capable of being settled to any extent or in any respect (and they demonstrably are, or people would not cite evidence in political argument at all), then this will be by reference to an argument such as classified by Weber and very often to an argument depending on 'what would happen if . . .'; or, in other words, to an argument based partly or wholly upon a sociological generalization. If a political position is open to argument at all (leaving aside the instances, which I briefly touched on, where people's views may be changed either by 'conversion' or by what one would want to call 'manipulative' techniques) it will be in the ways discussed by Weber; and though this may be purely formal argument (Weber's first type) it will also very often be argument to which contingent socio-logical evidence is relevant.

Objections will, of course, be raised at this point by those con-cerned to deny the possibility of any sociological generalization which can be sufficiently validated to entail the modification of a political theory. Once again, however, an adequate answer is suggested by Weber. Weber allows that every historical sequence is unique (in an additional sense to the Heraclitean truism that every event is unique); but he also emphasizes that every his-torical explanation must rest on nomothetic sociological assump-tions—if it did not, historians would be deprived of the use of even such words as 'dangerous'. What the sociologist does, having first understood the meaning of the actions he describes (Weber's famous *verstehen*), is then to test his explanatory generalizations against empirical evidence. This can be done, in principle, with such propositions as 'competition between élites is the best guarantee of political freedom' and 'too great involve-ment by the electorate is bad for two-party democracy' just as well as with such more 'scientific' looking assertions as 'Catholics are more likely than Protestants to vote Democrat even when socio-economic status is held constant'. And to the extent that such propositions can be validated, they may involve the modifi-cation of any political theory which is not irretrievably immune to argument.

I must end, however, by emphasizing the one important qualification which needs to be made to Weber's views. Weber, though allowing—as in the syndicalist example—that some political beliefs are less amenable to discussion than others, tends in general to imply (much as Weldon was to do) that any choice of attitude or *Weltanschauung* or political vocabulary is not only likely to be irreconcilable with any other but is also essentially arbitrary in nature. Weber, of course, took up this position in the context of an argument against the positivists of social science who wished to claim the possibility of a total objectivity for their assertions, and he was at pains to point out (rightly) that even the choice of formulation of a sociological question will involve a value-judgement. However, his implication that all choice of political attitude is equally arbitrary is, I think, demonstrably false (although it has also been held by people arguing purely as philosophers, in a way that Weber was not). Let us take Weber's own example of an argument with a syndicalist. Suppose that he takes a sort of anarchic Sorelian position whereby the first maxim of political conduct is that of organized resistance to any established government; for convenience, let us put it into the form of the proposition 'all government must be forcibly resisted'. If we ask him why, he may reply only (and this seems to be what Weber has in mind) 'because they are governments'; and if he goes no further than this, we may indeed wish to label his political beliefs as irrational or arbitrary, and attribute to his argument no higher status than to a claim that all red-headed men should be shot simply because their hair is red. If, however, he sets out to justify his position—let us say, by replying that 'all government is necessarily and by nature evil'—then we shall ask him for empirical evidence, and we shall thereby embark on an explicit sociological discussion. Two conclusions seem self-evident in this context: first, that we do wish to distinguish between purely arbitrary and non-arbitrary political beliefs; and second, that any recognition of amenability to evidence is a tacit recognition that the gulf between fact and value is not so unbridgeable as Weber himself elsewhere (and for a different purpose) claims.

Thus two conclusions follow from Weber's treatment of *Wertungsdiskussionen*, one of which he makes clear and one of which he in other contexts denies. As he makes clear, sociological evidence is likely to be crucially relevant to even the most abstract arguments about political theory. But in addition (and contrary to Weber's own dichotomy between fact and value), the fact of degrees of amenability to such evidence implies the possibility of a meaningful distinction between *Weltanschauungen*, whether or not these are as irreconcilable as Weber seems to think they will ultimately prove. Not only is it true that some political theories are more amenable than others to the citing of relevant evidence. It is also true that to recognize that this is so is to acknowledge that the separation of political theory from political sociology is not so radical as has sometimes been supposed and as Weber himself is apt to argue.

3

A MISTAKE ABOUT CAUSALITY IN SOCIAL SCIENCE

by Alasdair MacIntyre

'GENERALLY speaking,' wrote Hume, 'the errors in religion are dangerous; those in philosophy only ridiculous.' The aim of this paper is to show that philosophical errors can be dangerous too.

I

How are beliefs related to actions? Does what men believe alter their actions so as to make a difference to their social life? Or does their social life continue at least relatively independently of what they believe? Answers to these questions which appear at first sight very much opposed often have a great deal in common. What they usually have in common is the slide from the striking and controversial falsehood to the non-controversial apparent platitude. Pareto, the early Weber, Marx, all lay themselves open to charges of saying either (in the case of Pareto and Marx) that beliefs are essentially secondary, a by-product of a social life which drives forward independently, or (in the case of the early Weber) that ideas have an autonomous and effective role in social life.

All take up a bold and partisan position. All presently begin to qualify. Pareto at times proclaims the irrelevance of beliefs to conduct without qualification: 'A Chinese, a Moslem, a Calvinist, a Catholic, a Kantian, a Hegelian, a Materialist, all refrain from stealing: but each gives a different explanation for his conduct.' But the same Pareto in other passages is less truculent; he ascribes a socially subversive character to discussions in moral philosophy, for example. The early Weber enters the lists against those who would reduce Protestantism to a mere ideological reflection of the nascent capitalist economic order with a view to showing it as decisively formative of that order; the later Weber insists that he was merely investigating one direction of the causal chain. The other direction is equally open to investigation. And the most striking example of all is the transition from Marx's 'The mode of production in material life determines the social, political and intellectual life processes in general' to Engels's letter to Bloch: 'According to the materialist conception of history, the *ultimately* determining element in history is the production and reproduction of real life. More than this neither Marx nor I have ever asserted. Hence if somebody twists this into saying that the economic element is the *only* determining one, he transforms that proposition into an abstract, senseless phrase.'

The pattern in each case is the same. Beginning from a simple proclamation of either the influence of beliefs upon or the irrelevance of beliefs to actions, the initial view is then modified by the admission of counter-examples until all the protagonists come together in adherence to a facile interactionism. Beliefs and ideas influence social life; and social life influences beliefs and ideas. There is two-way causation.

About the empirical observations on which sociologists would base such a conclusion no one would wish to quarrel. But what about the concepts which provide the scheme into which the facts have been fitted? What indeed is the conceptual scheme which such diverse thinkers share? It contains two elements at least worth noticing and challenging.

The first is the view that beliefs and actions are distinct and separately identifiable social phenomena. The second is the view that causal connexion consists in constant conjunction. Social scientists are often extremely anxious to rid their study of what they conceive of as alien philosophical elements. It is therefore surprising how often their views on causation are a union of Hume's analysis with Mill's methods. This comes out very clearly in the Pareto quotation I have already cited—since refraining from stealing may be conjoined with any belief, no belief is constantly conjoined with refraining from stealing. Hence no belief is causally connected with refraining from stealing. Likewise Weber, to establish a causal link between Protestantism and capitalism, uses Mill's Method of Difference. He shows that in China and in India all the preconditions of capitalism evident in Europe were present, except for Protestantism. But capitalism did not arise. Hence we have good reason to suppose that Protestantism is the cause of capitalism.

It is worth pointing out that, if you hold the Humean view of causality, and you wish to investigate the relation of belief to action, you will probably involve yourself in treating belief and action as separate phenomena, since it is only between such that causality in the Humean sense can hold. This link between the two pieces of conceptual apparatus explains why to attack the separation of belief and action will also be to attack the applicability of the Humean conception of causality in this region.

On Hume's view (or rather, the most notorious of Hume's several slightly different views), for something to be the cause of something else, the two must be observed to be uniformly conjoined. If A constantly precedes B, and B uniformly follows A, then A is the cause of B. It follows that there is no necessity in causal relations. A is the cause of B, but equally B might have been the cause of A, or C the cause of either or both of them. All causal connexion is contingent and we can only discover what causal connexions do in fact hold by looking. We ought never to be surprised, on Hume's view, by what we discover, for we have no right to any prior expectations which might be overthrown. Anything may turn out to be causally connected with anything else. From this the following paradoxical conclusion follows for the social theorist, at least if he holds, as classical sociology has done, that beliefs and actions are distinct phenomena.

If beliefs and actions stand in a causal relationship (as that is understood by Hume) then it is purely contingent which beliefs are related to which actions. If we are looking for the cause of some action in the realm of beliefs, we can have no *a priori* expectations about where to look. Any belief might be the cause of any action. Suppose that we see a man spraying his roses with insecticide and interpret the statement 'He does it because he believes that green-fly are harmful to roses' as an ascription of Humean causality. Our justification for making the statement can now only be that we have observed a uniform correlation between the belief that green-fly are harmful and the action of spraying roses; but we might in establishing this uniformity have found any other to hold. The action of spraying roses might equally well be correlated with the belief that sunspots cause slumps or with the belief that the Pope is anti-Christ. It just *happens* to be correlated with the belief that green-fly are harmful to roses. We can bring out the nonsensical character of this conclusion and also why it is nonsensical by considering two further cases.

The first is the case of a man who is quite as concerned about the welfare of his roses as was the man in the earlier example. Moreover, his roses are covered with green-fly, but he just does not spray them with insecticide or take any similar measure. If the Humean view were applicable, we should still have to ask, 'But does he or does he not believe that green-fly are harmful to roses?' For the belief might turn out in this case to be correlated with the action of *not* spraying the roses. Moreover, if it did, this would show that there was no uniform correlation between the belief and the action, and hence it would follow that the belief was not to be counted as causally efficacious even in the cases where it did precede the action.

This is perhaps a final *reductio ad absurdum* of the view that belief and action are correlated in this way. If we came across this second type of case we should, having described it in the terms in which I have described it, have left no room for the question, 'But does he or does he not believe that green-fly are harmful to roses?' If a man is concerned about his roses, knows that they are covered with green-fly and does not spray them, *it follows* that he does not believe that green-fly are harmful to roses. To say that it follows is to say that his action in not spraying his roses already implies his beliefs about green-fly, and it does not point to them as an external sign of something else, his belief. His belief consists in acting in this way. To believe what he does is to act in a particular way.

This is enough to show that actions and beliefs are not separate phenomena, any more than (to cite an apt, if not precise, parallel) words and meanings are. If we do not extend the parallel further, it is perhaps not too misleading to say that just as we can talk intelligently about words and about meanings, and yet these are not two separate 'things', so actions and beliefs are not separate. And just as words may be said to express meanings, so actions may be said to express beliefs (and, as I shall argue, get their whole intelligibility from so doing). Note, incidentally, that beliefs can sometimes be considered apart from actions, but actions never apart from beliefs. Against this the following counter-example might be brought, based on my own two examples.

What are we to say, it might be asked by a determined

Humean, about a man who is and professes to be actively concerned about the welfare of his roses, knows that they are covered with green-fly, does not spray the roses with insecticide, but insists that he does believe that green-fly are harmful? Surely such a case is conceivable, and the very fact that it is conceivable shows that actions and beliefs are sharply distinguishable. But about this kind of case it is quite clear what one must say. This is not an agent whose beliefs and actions are at variance, so much as someone who if he has all these characteristics cannot be intelligible as a rational agent at all; he counts himself out of the class of beings recognizable as ordinary human agents, and hence cannot be cited as evidence. To this it will be objected that my argument is much too strong, and so it is. For all rational agents are inconsistent some of the time; and what I have hitherto considered is only the case where inconsistency is so extreme that we write off the subject as insane or at least disturbed. And what shall we say of the case where we cannot possibly write off the subject as insane but none the less his beliefs are inconsistent with his actions?

This depends upon the extent of the inconsistency. Where insanity or other mental disorder is ruled out, if a man says that he believes such and such, but his actions are totally discrepant with his answers, we are strongly inclined to call the avowals insincere or at least self-deceiving, to say that the man does not *really* believe what he says he believes. If on the other hand the discrepancy is a good deal less than total we simply characterize the agent as 'inconsistent'. And in doing so we bring out further the fact that the relation between belief and action is not contingent, but logical. For when Humeans ask rhetorically how an action could possibly be logically related to a belief, since only one belief can be logically related to another, they are in a way right. It is because actions express beliefs, because actions are a vehicle for our beliefs that they can be described as consistent or inconsistent with beliefs expressed in avowals. Actions, as much as utterances, belong to the realm of statements, concepts and beliefs; and the relation of belief to action is not external and contingent, but internal and conceptual.

We can understand in the light of this Aristotle's view that the conclusion of a practical syllogism is an action. In Aristotle's doctrine of the practical syllogism the major premise is an assertion that something is good for, suits, or pleases, somebody (e.g. 'Dry food suits any man'—the only merit of the example is that it is Aristotle's own); the minor premise is an assertion warranted by perception (e.g. 'Here's some dry food'); and the conclusion an action (e.g. the speaker eats it). The action thus follows from the premises in just the way in which a proposition follows from the premises in a theoretical syllogism. We can bring out the force of the 'follows from' in the last sentence by considering a close parallel with the theoretical syllogism. This is the case where a speaker appears to accept the premises of a valid syllogism and yet to resist the conclusion. He allows that a warm front brings rain and also that a warm front is approaching, but he refuses to say 'So it's going to rain'. There are only two possibilities open in such a case. *Either* the speaker thinks that an additional premise needs to be added to the argument, *or* he does not realize to what he has committed himself. If the latter is ruled out, then we can infer what kind of additional beliefs the speaker has, e.g. that he thinks the warm front may well be intercepted in its course by some other meteorologically relevant factor. In precisely the same way, where a speaker affirms premises and fails to act on them, we can make inferences as to his additional beliefs. Having said that dry food is good for man and that here is some dry food the speaker fails to eat. 'So you want to starve or you think that someone has poisoned this food, or you've just had a meal.' Either we can make an inference such as this or once again we have to charge the speaker with not realizing to what he has committed himself. In both cases, if the subject insists on simply affirming the premises and denying the conclusion, he becomes unintelligible: we literally do not know in the one case what he is saying and in the other case what he is doing.

It is important to notice that I have not committed myself by any of my earlier arguments to any identification of beliefs with actions. There is no necessary kinship therefore between my position and for instance a behaviourist analysis of belief into hypothetical and categorical statements about action. I would certainly argue that for it to be true that 'x believes that p', it is necessary that it be true that x either does or would behave in certain ways. But this is quite different from arguing that 'x believes that p' *means* that x does or would behave in such ways. Indeed it is absolutely necessary to maintain that beliefs and actions are not identical and that the former cannot be reduced to the latter. For all sorts of predicates can be appropriately applied to actions which cannot be applied to beliefs, and vice versa. Beliefs can be true or false, probable or improbable and so on. Actions cannot. Actions can be effective or ineffective, prompt or dilatory, and so on. Beliefs cannot. There remain a range of predicates which can without logical impropriety be applied to both. These include 'reasonable' and 'unreasonable', 'confused' and 'clear-headed' and so on. And we can now see one aspect of Hume's mistake in supposing that an action can only be called reasonable or unreasonable as being well designed or ill designed for its chosen end; it can also and more importantly be unreasonable in the context of the agent's beliefs. But now what is the relevance of all this to sociology?

My argument has run so far that sociologists as various as Engels, Pareto and Weber necessarily erred in presenting the role of ideas in social life and their relation to actions. For no matter how assiduous they were in presenting facts, they misconceived the logical character of what they collected. If we re-examine in this light, as one significant example, what Weber says of the relation of Protestantism to capitalism, we shall understand better the effect of this logical misunderstanding. Weber himself, in describing this relationship, has one or two additional logical unclarities. (I ought to say now since I am criticizing Weber that I only chose his work as an example because of its classical and permanent qualities of brilliance.) For example, what he specifically relates causally to Protestantism is what he calls 'the spirit of capitalism', a concept by means of which capitalist attitudes appear to be contrasted with capitalist activities. In fact, of course, an attitude can never be identified except in terms of the activities in which it is manifested. An attitude is precisely a propensity to do certain things, perhaps in a certain style. So that to talk about 'the spirit of capitalism' and its causes is to talk about the causes of a set of activities, viewed in a certain way, and not about something else. Moreover, Weber's contrast between the 'logical' influence of certain doctrines and the 'psychological' influence of certain doctrines is not always a clear one. The example he gives in the case of the doctrine of 'good works' in Protestantism will bring this out.

For the earliest Calvinists man's eternal fate is predestined by

God and nothing he can do can alter it. Moreover, there are no external signs to show who is predestined for heaven, who for hell. But the psychological pressure to know something as all-important as this was too much for Calvinists and from Beza they held that 'good works' were signs of election. So in time the performance of good works and election to salvation became identified for a doctrine which had originally kept them severely apart. Weber describes this as if the psychological pressure of the need to know if one were saved had distorted the logical consequences of Calvinism. But in fact Calvinism and Calvin himself had always had to accommodate the commandments to good works in the Bible. Calvin was committed to the following propositions: 1. God commands good works; 2. It is of the highest importance possible to do what God commands; 3. Good works are irrelevant to what is of most importance to you, your salvation or damnation. It is a requirement of logic, not of psychological pressures, that one of these propositions be modified; the alternative is contradiction. Moreover, unless it is the third proposition which is modified, preaching and legislation on morals, two central Calvinist activities, which are also rationally backed up by doctrine, lose their point. The development from Calvin to Beza is therefore a development in reasoning as much as say the development from Descartes to Spinoza, and talk about psychological pressures can be misleading. What is especially misleading about it is that it leads to underrating just what Weber at this stage wanted to stress, the power of ideas, that is of rationality.

The relationship which he in fact manages to pinpoint between Protestantism and capitalism is indeed a rational one. Weber in fact presents us with capitalist actions as the conclusion of a practical syllogism which has Protestant premises. To discern this logical relationship between belief and action was an enormous achievement. And because the achievement was this, the use of Mill's methods is entirely out of place; we do not need to juggle with causal alternatives. India and China did not strengthen and could not have weakened his case about Europe. For it is not a question of whether there is a purely contingent relationship between isolable phenomena. And so constant conjunction is neither here nor there. This explains perhaps why although we may want to modify this or that detail in the light of later work, the conviction which *The Protestant Ethic and the Spirit of Capitalism* carries is so immediate. One last concluding point: the statistical work done before and after on the correlation between Protestant beliefs and capitalist practice in Europe is not made in the least irrelevant by this interpretation. If I explain your actions as a conclusion from your premises, I must be able to identify both action and premises as yours. What the statistical material shows is that enough of the same people were Protestants and engaged in the relevant kinds of activity. Thus statistical enquiry has as great a role in sociology on this view as it ever had. But its correlations are put to uses which are not quite what classical sociology conceived them to be. Equally the task of comparison between the European and the Asian developments remains relevant. But its relevance is not that of the Humean causal connexion.

II

If the role of ideas in relation to actions is not that of Humean causes or Humean effects, what is it? Some light is perhaps cast on this by considering the familiar distinction between a physical movement and a human action. This distinction is obvious if we consider the criteria of identity in each case. The same physical movements may constitute in different contexts quite different actions. So a man may go through the same physical movements involved in signing his name and be concluding a treaty or paying a bill, which are quite different actions. But is not the man performing the same action in each case, namely signing his name? To this the answer is that writing one's name is never merely by itself an action; one is either signing a document or giving information or perhaps just doodling. All these are actions, but writing one's name is not. Equally, the same action may be constituted by quite different physical movements. Writing on paper, passing coin, even saying words may all constitute the same action of paying a bill.

When we talk about 'explaining human behaviour', we sometimes blur this distinction. Because there is no human action which does not involve physical movement we may suppose that to explain the movement is to explain the action. And this leads easily back to the view that to explain actions is to assign to them

Humean causes. For we do look for Humean causes for physical movement. What this view overlooks is that if we, on being asked for an explanation of what we have done, refer it to an antecedent condition of a Humean kind we precisely remove it from the class of actions and assign it to some other class, most probably the class of physical movements. My head nods and I am asked, 'Why did you nod your head?' If I answer by referring to a nervous tick, I point in the direction of a story about necessary and sufficient antecedent conditions, a story about nerves and muscles and possibly about conditioning in early childhood. Here the explanation will certainly be one of the Humean type, with reference to general laws, that is to constantly conjoined factors. But to explain the nod as a nervous tick is precisely to explain it not as something that I do, but as something that just happens. If on the other hand I explain the nod by saying that I had been asked a question and was answering it by a 'Yes', then I certainly explain the nod as an action. I do so by pointing to the purpose which it serves. This reference to the agent's purpose always carries with it implicitly and often explicitly a reference to some antecedent event or condition. But the relation between the action and its antecedents is certainly not one of constant conjunction. If I explain my nod of the head as an answer to an antecedent question, I certainly do not refer to a generalization stating some constant conjunction which holds between questions and answers. From the fact that a question has been asked it never follows that it will be given some particular answer or indeed any answer. What makes a reference to antecedent questions part of an explanation of what one was doing is that one is explaining the role of one's nod in carrying through a socially established and recognized practice, that of asking and answering questions. That is, the background to my explanation is formed by the customarily recognized rules of a particular social order.

I have now advanced a stronger thesis than that contained in the first part of the paper. There I argued that the Humean view of causality was inapplicable to the relation between beliefs and actions. Now I have argued that it is also inapplicable to the relation between an agent's earlier and later actions. What further follows from this about the relation of actions to beliefs? Consider the case where I am puzzled about myself. Why did I nod my head or move my hand? If it is the physical movement about which I am puzzled, my puzzlement can be removed by reading a book on neurology or something of the sort. Knowledge of general laws is what is needed and the agent can explain his movements in exactly the same way that anyone else can, by informing himself of their physiology. But if I am puzzled not about the physical movement, but about an action, it is quite otherwise. Nobody can remove my puzzlement by a reference to general laws. And in one sense nobody can remove my puzzlement except myself. But it is important to be clear in what sense this is true.

The privileged position which the agent enjoys in respect of the explanation of his actions is not such that the agent can explain his action better than anyone else. We may often be able to see what someone is after better than they can and so explain their actions. Some people are notoriously bad at recognizing their own loves, jealousies or ambitions. None the less if what the agent does is to count as an example of an action at all, his action is identified fundamentally as what it is by the description under which he deems it to fall. What is the point about the agent's description of his action? Let us establish three points in turn, each with a wider scope.

The first is that for an action to be such it must fall under some description which is socially recognizable as the description of an action. This is a truism. The point of including the phrase 'socially recognizable' in its formulation is that I cannot decide for myself what is or is not an action or a purpose. I can invent a new action, but if I do, what I am doing must be communicable to other people. The reason for this is quite simply that only if I can fulfil the conditions for making what I am doing intelligible to others, can I fulfil the condition of making what I am doing intelligible to me. For the intelligibility of the action consists precisely in it falling under a description which assigns (almost always implicitly) some purpose to the action. And descriptions are public property, just as and because language is public property. From this it also follows that if an action is to be *my* action the description under which it falls must be available to me. For anything I can do, I must be able to intend to do, and I can only intend to do what I can describe to myself in advance of action. (I do not of course mean that intentions are in fact always formulated in advance of action.)   Action which follows from a previously formed intention consists in making the world answer to my description of it.

An action then must fall under a description and *my* actions under a description available to me.   To these two points must be added a third.   I have already conceded that others may recognize what I am doing, fit an apter description to it, than I can.   It remains true that the agent's honest avowals have final authority. What he cannot avow as his purpose under any conditions could not be his purpose.   This is just a truistic extension of the phrase 'his purpose'.   (What psycho-analysis has done incidentally is immensely to widen our conception of the conditions under which such avowals can take place.)

The thesis then is that an agent can do only what he can describe. I can bring out the force of the thesis by an example of its application.   Clearly the application of the thesis is most obvious in cases of what we might call 'conscious' action and less so in cases of 'unconscious action'.   So consider the latter type of case.   An overworked programmer starts sleepwalking in the computing laboratory.   In his sleep he punches tape, working out the next stages of the programme on which he is currently engaged. When we describe this we shall say without hesitation that he worked out the programme in his sleep.   But a tramp who has climbed into the laboratory, falls asleep, sleep walks and punches tape.   He does not even know what a computer is.   Even if by chance the patterns on his tape formed a regular and orthodox sequence we should never say that he worked out a programme in his sleep, but only that in his sleep he punched tape and it happens that the pattern corresponds to a part of a programme. The difference between what we should say in the two cases is accounted for by the fact that the descriptions 'working out a programme' and 'working out some particular programme' were available to the computing assistant, but not to the tramp. So it does appear that our concept of action is delimited at this point, in just the way I have argued.   But now consider the following counter-example.

An agent can only do what he can describe.   But children can often do what they cannot yet describe.   A child in particular who learns to speak late may carry through many complex activities without being able to offer descriptions of them.   This example certainly necessitates a modification of the argument. The point is that the child can only learn such actions as are available to, or at least recognizable to, the adults who surround him. The child's actions count as actions because we can identify them as such in terms of *our* descriptions. The same is true of the actions of a deaf-mute. And this example thus helps to bring out a crucial point. The limits of what I can do are set by the limits of the descriptions *available* to me, not those I possess at any given moment. And the descriptions available to me are those current in the social group to which I belong.

This conceptual analysis is obviously of the highest importance for sociology. If the limits of action are the limits of description, then to analyse the ideas current in a society is also to discern the limits within which action necessarily moves in that society. The theory of ideology appears not as one more compartmentalized concept of the sociologist, but as part of his central concern with society as such. To identify the limits of social action in a given period is to identify the stock of descriptions current in that age. 'Reading history', says Stuart Hampshire, 'I learn that to ascribe certain intentions, now familiar, to men living in earlier centuries would be to put words into their mouths and minds which could not possibly have occurred there.'

The role of descriptions in action and the consequent place of understanding descriptions in the explanation of action are of course much more complex than the argument so far allows for. I have written as though a given stock of descriptions just was or was not available at a given time to a given social group. In fact, however, such descriptions occur as constituents of beliefs, speculations, and projects and as these are continually criticized, modified, rejected or improved, the stock of descriptions changes. The changes in human action are thus intimately linked to the thread of rational criticism in human history. To go any further we must notice another aspect of human action altogether.

Any action might have been other than it is; an agent always has alternatives. When a man has overwhelming reasons for doing one thing rather than another (at the point of a gun, say) we often describe him as having had no alternative. But if every alternative is excluded, so that no choice at all remains, what happens is no longer an action. It is because this is the case that

Humean-style explanations are so misleading. For the essence of explanation in terms of constant conjunction is that, given the antecedent conditions, subsequent events could not have fallen out other than they did. There are no alternatives. Since human actions always have alternatives, the whole concept of an action is falsified in the Humean pattern. (I am well aware that I am side-stepping a whole cluster of problems around the traditional free-will *versus* determinism argument. The side-stepping is intentional.)

From a number of different lines of argument it has therefore emerged that to look for the antecedents of an action is not to search for an invariant causal connexion, but to look for the available alternatives and to ask why the agent actualized one rather than another. Sometimes the explanation will refer to the agent's dispositions, sometimes to his choices. But since in human beings the exercise of choice has the key place in the formation of dispositions it is to choice that I shall attend. The explanation of a choice between alternatives is a matter of making clear what the agent's criterion was and why he made use of this criterion rather than another and to explain why the use of this criterion appears rational to those who invoke it. In other words, the internal relation of beliefs to action is such that in explaining the rules and conventions to which action in a given social order conform we cannot omit reference to the rationality or otherwise of those rules and conventions.

Explaining actions is explaining choices; and explaining choices is exhibiting why certain criteria define rational behaviour for a given society. To this we must now add that the beginning of an explanation of why certain criteria are taken to be rational in some societies is that they *are* rational. And since this has to enter into our explanation we cannot explain social behaviour independently of our own norms of rationality. But let us approach this from another point of view.

Suppose that a team of Martian social scientists is observing human behaviour. What they are watching we should describe as chess-playing, but unhappily they lack the concept of a game. Mars is gameless. They therefore do not discern the rule-governed character of the players' behaviour, although they arrive at many statistical generalizations about the movement of small pieces of wood by human beings. What is it that they do not understand when they fail to understand these movements as a game of chess?

They fail of course first of all to grasp the players' actions as distinct from their physical movements. It is not that they wrongly *explain* what is done; rather they fail to *identify* the actions which are to be explained. Secondly it is not just that they cannot explain the rule-governed actions of the players; they fail also to notice cases of rule-breaking or cases of miscalculation based on misapprehension of the rules. Suppose a group of chess-players who, when the end-game is between a king on one side and a king and a pawn on the other, continue to play indefinitely in the belief that mate cannot be indefinitely evaded. To explain this behaviour we should have to explain why they believed this and such an explanation would have to start from identifying this belief as both false and susceptible of exposure in the light of their knowledge of the rules of chess. If the belief were not false, there would be nothing to explain in this particular case; but we should still have something to explain, namely how they had learnt (rather than mislearnt) the rules of chess.

The analogy with a social system is clear. To explain actions within it we have to identify the rules and their connexion with reasonable or unreasonable, true or false beliefs. Thus we cannot explain actions by means of beliefs and not raise questions of truth or falsity, reason or unreason. For the explanation of why someone did something will be quite different if the agent's beliefs are true from what it will be if they are false, since there will be something quite different to explain. Thus in any society we shall only be able to identify what is going on if we have identified and assessed the established methods of reasoning and criticism in that society. And this will bring us into the sharpest conflict with any school of sociological thought which holds that questions of the truth or reasonableness of beliefs either ought not to be or cannot be raised by sociologists.

What is it that such an approach in social theory misses out which I want to include? Not just the nationality of social life, but the tension between it and other factors.

Earlier in the argument I defended the thesis that the limits of action are the limits of description, that the delineation of a society's concepts is therefore a, if not perhaps the, crucial step in the delineation of its life. I have also argued that the stock of descriptions and beliefs in a society changes and develops. We can in the light of these arguments suggest a classification of societies reminiscent of, but different from, those of Bergson and Popper. Bergson and Popper in slightly different ways contrast 'open' and 'closed' societies. I want a threefold classification into closed, open, and societies which were open but which are being turned back into closed societies. All primitive societies, especially isolated ones, tend to be closed. They have their concepts and their beliefs; they move in a closed conceptual circle. (The witchcraft of the Azande is an example of this.) Most later societies are open; there are established modes of criticism. But in many societies there is a concerted attempt to delimit the available stock of concepts and beliefs and at a certain point to return to a closed circle. There is always something slightly self-contradictory about this attempt; for to know that the circle has to be closed is to be aware that it is in fact open. This conscious falling back involves therefore an attempt to meet rational criticism by non-rational methods.

It follows that the analysis of an ideology must always fall into three parts; we have to identify what the ideas and beliefs are which compose it, we have to identify the kind of limits which they place upon action, and we have to examine what are the consequent means by which it either keeps open the way to rational criticism or attempts to prevent any criticism which does not fall inside the established conceptual framework. We shall only be able to do this if we examine what happens at the points where the ideology needs criticism most, that is, where it is false or unreasonable. And here once again we need to bring into our sociological explanation our own norms of rationality. What this means I shall now try to illustrate by the discussion of a particular and notorious example.

III

In the years 1935-8 four things happened in Russia. The second five-year plan was completed and the third started. The Stalin Constitution, 'the most democratic in the world', was enacted: it had largely been written by Bukharin and Radek. All the members of Lenin's Politbureau, except for Trotsky who

was in exile and Stalin himself, but including Radek and Bukharin, were found guilty of planning to assassinate Stalin and
restore capitalism and of a number of other crimes, including
causing the death of Maxim Gorky. And Stalin personally
wrote a philosophical work, *Dialectical and Historical Materialism*,
which appeared as part i chapter IV of the *History of the
C.P.S.U.* (B). What I want to try and explain in the light of the
previous argument is the relation of this last fact to the first three.
It is worth beginning by asking why Stalin should write a book
upon philosophy at all.

Deutscher's answer is that it was part of the creation of a
public image. 'As the prompter of the trials he remained invisible
to the public—he appeared before it in the role of philosopher,
historian and constitution maker.' But we must ask why this
public image was needed. Stalin had never shone as a theorist.
The answer is that Stalin needed both to assert the normative
character of certain ideas as an orthodoxy; and that he needed
to explain why alternative views could be discounted. In this
Stalin shared a characteristic of all contemporary ideologues.
Any theory about the role of theory in society is bound, if it is
to be convincing, to contain an account both of its rivals and of
itself. Moreover, social theories have another characteristic, as
yet unnoticed in the present argument, which must now be
brought out. It is a characteristic which sharply differentiates
the role of theory in the human sciences from that of theory in
the natural sciences.

The way people think about things (that is, natural science—
'things' includes human bodies) is appropriate or not depending
upon the nature of the things in question; the way people think
about people, themselves, is part of the reality about which they
are trying to think in appropriate ways. The concepts which we
employ to grasp what we are become part of what we are; or
rather that we use them in this way becomes part of what we are.
Thus in social theory we are using concepts to understand beings
who define themselves by means of their use of concepts, in some
cases the concepts that we are using in trying to understand them.
So to construct a theory and to propagate it is to afford people a
new means of self-comprehension; to give the theory currency
may well change the very behaviour which the theory attempts
to describe. Hence the much noted fact that social theories, unlike

theories in physics, can play a role in their own verification and falsification. How is this relevant to Stalinism?

It is highly relevant if the role of the theory is to reinforce and express a mode of behaviour; for then the occurrence of this type of behaviour appears to reinforce the hold of the theory. The system becomes self-enclosed. My argument will be that Stalinist thought in Russia aspired to become a closed system through the dominance of certain modes of behaviour which are delineated by the concepts in Stalin's book. What are these concepts? In order to understand what is specific to Stalinism we must set the book against the background which it had both for its author and its readers, the Marxist classics. What is in *Dialectical and Historical Materialism* which is not mere repetition?

First of all, that from among the formulas of classical Marxism, which are by no means all mutually consistent with one another, Stalin consistently selects those which allow him to fall back into a simple mechanistic materialism, such as Marx always avoided and even Engels sometimes denounced. So Stalin tells us 'that the world develops in accordance with the laws of the movement of matter'; 'that matter is primary since it is the source of sensations, ideas, mind, and that mind is secondary, derivative'; and hence also 'that the material life of society is an objective reality existing independently of the will of men . . .' This gives us an overall picture of social life as a series of causal chains originated outside human life in the physical universe. To these chains the Humean pattern of analysis applies perfectly and indeed it applies not only to the relation between one action and another but to the relation between ideas and actions. Ideas are effects and they are also causes. As causes they are subsidiary. They cannot initiate or obstruct change; they can only accelerate or decelerate a process already under way. 'There are old ideas and those which have outlived their day and which serve the interests of the moribund forces of society. Their significance lies in the fact that they hamper the development, the progress of society. Then there are new and advanced ideas and those which serve the interests of the advanced forces of society. Their significance lies in the fact that they facilitate the development, the progress of society. . . .'

Thus Stalin's first main contribution is a crude statement of the view which I have attempted in the earlier sections of this paper to refute. And it is extremely relevant to remark that these views of Stalin's are already known to be false within the Marxist tradition. One can refer not only to Hegel or to Marx's *Theses on Feuerbach* but to the battle against mechanistic materialism waged in the twenties in the Soviet Union by the partisans of Deborin. This philosophical debate did not follow any of the lines of political cleavage. Philosophers of both views were found in both Left and Right oppositions. When Stalin came to power he banned the philosophical debate in a manner reminiscent of that in which the papacy put an end to the discussions between Dominicans and Jesuits over free-will. His later enunciation of his own views was accompanied by a canonization of a book which was rarely, if ever, evoked in the earlier discussions, Lenin's *Materialism and Empirico-Criticism*. In this book Lenin expounds a mechanistic theory of knowledge which he seems to have abandoned in the later *Philosophical Notebooks* after reading Hegel.

The second feature of Stalin's philosophy, specific to it, is the silent abandonment in his statement of the so-called laws of dialectics of a principle dear to both Hegel and Engels, that of the negation of the negation. The function of this principle is extremely important to any Hegelianism. For it expresses the lack of finality in any conceptual scheme or state of affairs. Thus there is a tension in Hegel's writings between the concept of the negation of the negation and the concept of the Absolute. For it is the former which prevents any state of affairs or conceptual scheme being identified as the realization in concrete terms of Absolute Spirit. Hence when Hegel comes with greater or lesser degree of explicitness to identify the Prussian Monarchy socially and his own philosophy conceptually with the Absolute in its earthly realization, he necessarily has to let the principle of the negation of the negation fall into the background. That is to say, the principle functions as a safeguard against finality and against absolutizing any state of affairs or conceptual scheme as final. To remove it therefore as silently and as completely as Stalin does is to open the way for the Absolute.

The thesis which I want to argue is that Stalinism is a conceptual scheme which claims final and absolute truth for itself and does so in the interests of realizing one part of the Bolshevik programme at the expense of another. Marx himself had taken bourgeois democracy to be a sham because he believed that you could not distribute political power unless economic power were also distributed. A bourgeois society could not distribute economic power because it is an industrializing society; and an industrializing society is one in which a few men dispose by their decisions both of capital and of labour. It follows that an industrializing society cannot be democratic. Since Marx never envisaged socialism as other than the most radical form of democracy, he could only envisage it as coming into being in an already fully industrialized economy. When the Bolsheviks took power they inherited Marx's beliefs about democracy (*State and Revolution* is the text in point). But they also faced the task of industrialization. On this contradiction their theory broke. *Either* they could accept the objective impossibility of socialism (as Lenin did for the short run in NEP); *or* they could try to elaborate a new way round these difficulties, attempting to safeguard democracy for the future by inner-party democracy (which is roughly Trotsky's proposed way out in the later twenties); or they could accept industrialization and call it democracy (which is what Stalin did).

It was the use of mechanistic concepts which enabled Stalin to distort consciousness in this way. Mechanistic concepts are extremely tempting in an industrial society. The industrial manager knows that anything a man can do a machine can do. That is to say, all specifiable tasks for human beings can be reduced to routine movements which a machine can perform. The catch is in the word 'specifiable', but it is easy to ignore this and for the imagination to be impressed by the number of activities which appear to have been reduced to routine sequences of physical movement. Moreover, the image of mechanism also expresses admirably the necessary hierarchy of the industrializing process. Marx himself saw clearly that mechanistic materialism implies a distinction between those who are the causally manipulated and those who are somehow able to perform the manipulation. Writing of Robert Owen in the third of the *Theses on Feuerbach*, Marx said that 'The materialist doctrine that men are products of circumstance and upbringing, and that therefore changed men are products of other circumstances and changed upbringing, forgets that it is men who change circumstances and that the educator must himself be educated. Hence, the doctrine necessarily arrives at dividing society into two parts, of which one is superior to society. . . .' What Marx sees is that mechanistic concepts are tied to elucidating all change as someone acting upon someone else, leading them into a desired position. That the person is a reformer in his own eyes is irrelevant. I can change your views by arguing with you or by giving you injections. In the first place I appeal to impersonal canons of rationality and the relationship between us can only be elucidated by an account of established procedures of rule-following. The whole concept of democracy is bound up with this concept of rational argument, and the democratic concept of equality is partly to be elucidated with reference to the fact that rational argument appeals to criteria which entail a verdict that is irrespective of persons. If, however, I change your views by giving you injections, or by causal manipulation of any other kind, then I destroy this equality, for I see you as manipulated, myself as a manipulator.

In the tension between democracy and industrialization which faced the Bolsheviks, therefore, mechanistic concepts could play an important role in establishing a picture of human relations in which democratic equality was no longer a possibility. The name 'democracy' then became free-floating, available as an approval term for whatever purposes it might be required for. But the difficulty in redefining it was the existence of the Old Bolsheviks who in their own theories and practice, were the bearers of an alternative wider conceptual scheme (it is in the light of our canons of rationality that we can see it as wider), which prevented consciousness being closed to non-Stalinist alternatives. Hence terror. Terror is the closing of the circle against rationality. Rational argument can never insure you against alternatives, for by its very nature it leaves open the possibility of a better argument turning up. So if Stalin is to make into an Absolute the mechanistic consciousness he has to remove physically all traces of alternative.

The attempt is bound to fail. *1984* is impossible. But seeing why it is impossible will help us to understand the necessity not just of terrors but of trials, and not just of trials but of confessions. *1984* is impossible because in modern industrial society rational discourse is ineliminable. In order to control the apparatus which limits consciousness, you have to have agents. In order that they shall know what they are doing they must have a wider consciousness than they allow to others. So the fatal inroads of rationality begin. But, if *1984* is impossible, the gap can be closed in two ways. Your mechanistic conceptual scheme insists that all ideas are the effects of something else, in particular that they are the mirror-images cast by alien class-interest. So the assertion of this kind of causal relationship of beliefs and actions forges a vital link in the Stalinist argument. If actions cause ideas, and Stalinist ideas reflect proletarian class-interests, and non-Stalinist ideas reflect hostile class-interests, the conclusion follows that to have had non-Stalinist ideas means that you must have been performing non-Stalinist actions. It is this background which allows the inference from opposition to Stalin's views on collectivization to participation in a plot to assassinate Stalin. In Stalinist terms the whole thing is rational; it can only be challenged by leaving this closed circle. But to prevent this there is only one device: let those who have the alternative concepts themselves testify that the circle is closed by confessing that the inferences of Stalinism are correct and the conclusions true. Hence confessions. The relevance of *1984* to this is clear. To make a *1984* you need agents; and these agents at least are unimpressed by the confessions, for they extorted them. So they are the next danger. On this view it is no accident that Bukharin and Rakovsky were accompanied in the dock by the police-chief Yagoda and followed by the police-chief Yezhov.

The core of the argument is then that Stalinism can only be understood as a set of ideas which express the social dilemma of the Bolsheviks between democracy and industrialization and the way in which Stalin resolved this dilemma. About this argument two things must be said. First, it stresses the rationality of Stalinist actions; and this follows from the methodological argument of the earlier sections of the paper. It takes as a central problem for Stalinism how to exhibit as rational the manifestly irrational; how to turn an open society into a closed one. And secondly, this is only a starting point. I do not want to deny the role of other motivations in Stalinism; what I have been concerned to do is indeed to *identify* rather than to *explain*. But if one accepts this identification then we will have to take out a widely accepted class of explanations of Stalinism. This class includes all explanations of Stalinism which make questions of theory secondary, which sees Stalinism as the expression of the need for a God figure, say, or of the romantic cult of violence among intellectuals, or of the cult of personality. If the methodological part of this essay is correct, then actions are uninterpretable and unidentifiable apart from beliefs. And beliefs function not as an antecedent cause of, but as an expression of Stalinist social order and disorder. About the close of the English revolution, Marx wrote that 'Cromwell and the English people had borrowed the phraseology, the emotions and the illusions of the Old Testament as trappings for their own bourgeois revolution. As soon as they had reached the goal, as soon as the bourgeois transformation of English society had been effected, Locke supplanted Habakkuk.' This does not entail that either Locke or Habakkuk were mere superstructure; if this were the rational garb of a social order, we can only discern its shape as that which can be clothed in this way. We have to understand English society *through* Habakkuk and *through* Locke. Having said this we can safely parody Marx and say that 'Lenin and the Russian people had borrowed the phraseology, the emotions and the illusions of Marxist-Leninism as trappings for their own revolution. As soon as they had reached the goal, as soon as the industrializing transformation of Russian society had been undertaken, Stalin supplanted Marx.'

4

A PARADOX IN THE THEORY OF DEMOCRACY

by Richard Wollheim

THE invention of Democracy is traditionally attributed to Cleisthenes. Many will object to this attribution, not so much on factual grounds, as because it savours too much of a heroic or Promethean view of history. But in this case at least such a view might seem justified. We know little enough of the motives or sentiments of the great reformer, but of the enduring significance of what he achieved there can be no reasonable doubt. The institutions that he devised survived with only minor modifications as the political structure of Athens: around them there developed a creed or theory of popular government, of which only fragments have come down to us: and, finally, it was to those institutions that the word Δημόκρατία was initially applied. By the middle of the fifth century B.C. Democracy existed as a set of institutions, as a theory of government, and as a word. Since the institutions come first and prompted the rest, he who devised them may with good reason be celebrated as the inventor of Democracy.

From the days of Cleisthenes onwards Democracy has enjoyed a continuous, if often exiguous, history in Western culture. The political experience of Athens has never been forgotten and never totally dismissed, if only because it is recorded in texts that for quite extraneous reasons have made a sustained claim upon the attention or reverence of the educated.

However, although there has been continuity, there has also been change. In several important respects the Democracy of Antiquity differs, and should be distinguished, from the Democracy of the modern world: and this not just in practice, but also in theory. To take an obvious case: to the classical mind Democracy was linked *in an essential way* with certain specific political institutions. These links no longer exist. For the institutions with which the Ancients so intimately connected

71

Democracy either are no longer held to be connected, or even consistent, with Democracy, as in the case of public scrutiny or the lot, or else *are* still held to be connected with Democracy but not in a way which can be directly derived from the nature of Democracy, as, for instance, with the Rule of Law.

But the most important respect in which modern Democracy differs from classical Democracy is that whereas classical Democracy was a form of sectional government, to the modern mind Democracy is opposed to all forms of sectional government. The etymology of the word Democracy gives a clue to what the Ancients meant by it. For Democracy was regarded as a form of government parallel to, though different from, other forms of government designated by names having a parallel structure: Aristocracy, Oligarchy, Plutocracy, Ochlocracy. In each case power lay with a certain section of the population: the forms differed from one another according to the section with which power lay: and in each case the section was indicated by the prefix. In Aristocracy, it was the *aristoi* or the best: in Oligarchy, it was the *oligoi* or the few: in Plutocracy it was the *plutoi* or the rich: in Ochlocracy it was the *ochlos* or mob: in Democracy it was the *demos*. And the *demos* in the Greek city-state was a specific or determinate section of the population: the populace or the poor.

By contrast the modern conception of Democracy is of a form of government in which no restriction is placed upon the governing body: the governing body is identical with the citizen body. We might put the difference between the ancient and modern conceptions of Democracy like this: in both cases Democracy is the rule of the people; but in the classical theory the people is identified with a section or part of the population, whereas in modern theory the people is identified with the population as a whole.

Immediately a problem arises: if Democracy means the rule of the people *as a whole*, how can it be realized? For in any modern state the people is bound to be both *numerous* and *diverse*, and either of these characteristics by itself—let alone the conjunction of the two—surely must make a group of individuals incapable of effective rule. In antiquity, or at any rate in the political theory of antiquity, the problem does not arise. For the *demos* of the Greek city-state was, in the first place, relatively small: and, secondly, it was, or was supposed to be, united in interest, and therefore uniform in desire or want.

One solution to this problem is to suggest a return to the Greek conditions: or the suggestion is, rather, that the conditions which hold for the Greek *demos* should be made to hold for the population of a modern democracy. This population should, in the first place, be considerably reduced in size. And when it is no longer numerous, it will automatically cease to be diverse. Or if any diversity remains, this diversity will be purely phenomenal or apparent. This solution—which can roughly be equated with Rousseau's ideal of 'legitimate rule'—is obviously unacceptable. The restriction upon population is Utopian: and the 'true' or 'real' uniformity that it advocates, which is consistent with any degree of conscious diversity, is worthless.

Another solution consists in weakening the criteria attached to the notion of effective rule. For if we mean by 'ruling' 'devising and composing laws'—as the Greeks did—then it is clearly impossible for a numerous and diverse population to exercise collective rule. One answer, as we have seen, is that we should bring it about that the population in a Democracy is neither numerous nor diverse. Another answer is that we should mean something different by 'ruling': or that in elucidating Democracy we should employ a different concept of 'rule'. And it is this second answer that is, explicitly or implicitly, incorporated in most modern democratic theories. If modern theory insists that in a democracy the people in the sense of the whole population, not just a section of the population, should rule, it also insists that the people should rule in the sense not of devising or initiating legislation but of choosing or controlling it. And the significance of this is that it permits a people to rule despite its size and its diversity.

That size is no obstacle to the people ruling in what might be called this weakened sense should be evident. Since the control or choice of legislation does not require that the people should meet in general assembly, numbers do not impair its effectiveness. That diversity is equally no obstacle may be less apparent. That it is not derived directly from the fact that whereas to say that the people rule in the strong sense entails that everyone assents to the legislation enacted, to say that the people rule in the weak sense has no such entailment: popular rule, where rule means control, can be said to hold, even if a sizeable proportion of the population dissents from what is enacted.

However, even if popular rule is consistent with some degree of dissent, there must also be a degree of dissent with which it is inconsistent. Or to put it another way: for legislation to be said to be by the people, it must stand in some positive relation to what the individual citizens would like legislation to be like. How is this relation to be characterized?

In practice, of course, we say that legislation is democratic if (1) it concurs with what the majority of the population would like and (2) it is enacted because of this concurrence. It has however been argued that though the majority principle may be all right in practice, it certainly is inadequate to any ideal construction of Democracy: and since any justification of Democracy is most likely to relate to an ideal construction, this is important.

Before the inadequacies of the majority-principle can be brought out, an ambiguity in its formulation needs to be resolved. For the principle may be insisting on a concurrence of the legislation with an absolute majority, or merely with a plurality, of citizens' choices. If an absolute majority is intended, then the majority principle is acceptable in that it never selects legislation that is intuitively unacceptable, given the choices of the individual citizens: the trouble is, however, that over too large a range not just of possible but of likely cases the majority principle selects no absolute majority legislation at all. Accordingly if government is to be continuous, the absolute-majority principle needs to be supplemented by another principle, and for this role the obvious candidate is the plurality principle. This principle in all likely cases at any rate *does* select specific legislation, but the trouble is that the legislation it selects is in some cases counter intuitive—given, that is, the choice of the citizens.[1] An example will illustrate this.

Let us suppose that there are three policies from which the population must choose: A, B, C. Forty per cent. choose A, 35 per cent. choose B, and 25 per cent. choose C. On the simple majority principle A is selected. However, those who choose B prefer C to A, and those who choose C prefer B to A. In the light of this information, it is far from clear that A is the right

[1] Duncan Black, *Theory of Committees and Elections* (London, 1958), pp. 67-8.

selection if democratic rule is to be observed. For 60 per cent. prefer both B and C to A.

What this example brings out is that it is not always clear which policy or legislation should be enacted in a democracy, given the choices of the individual citizens—if all we take into account are the first choices of the citizens. We need to go below this and consider the whole preference-schedule of the individual citizens.

Following up this kind of criticism of the majority-principle, political scientists have envisaged the problem of Democracy as that of devising a function which would allow us to derive what might be called the 'democratic choice' from the ordered choices or preference-schedules of the individual citizens. It is only if we can construct such a function—the argument runs—that we can claim to have explicated the weak sense of 'rule' in which, according to *modern* theory, the people rule in a Democracy.

Recently, however, this approach has met with a reverse. For in his *Social Choice and Individual Values*, Arrow[1] has proved that it is impossible to construct a function that satisfies certain intuitive criteria. Arrow's specific concern was with what he called a 'social welfare function' whose task was to determine a complete 'social' preference schedule given the individual preference-schedules. However, it has more recently been shown[2] that Arrow's Impossibility Theorem also applies to the less ambitious project, which is more directly relevant to democracy, of constructing a function which would merely give us a 'social' first-choice on the basis of the individual preference-schedules.

I mention this problem, however, solely *en passant*: not because I intend to tackle it, but because I intend to ignore it. For the purpose of this paper, I intend to assume that the so-called problem of aggregation has been solved: that there exists a method or rule[3] for going from individual choices to some specific legislation such that we can justifiably call the enactment of that legislation an instance of democratic rule.

Having made this assumption, I now want to go on and

---

[1] Kenneth J. Arrow, *Social Choice and Individual Values* (New York, 1951), Ch. V.

[2] R. D. Luce and H. Raiffa, *Games and Decisions* (New York, 1957), Ch. 14.

[3] 'Rule' or 'method' here are to be understood in some very general sense that will satisfy even those who hold that 'the essence of democracy is something which must escape definition in terms of any functional relation between decisions and individual preferences'. I. M. D. Little, 'Social Choice and Individual Values', *Journal of Political Economy*, Vol. LX, no. 5, October 1952, p. 432.

envisage Democracy in terms of a certain machine which operates according to this method or rule. The machine—which we may for convenience call the democratic machine—operates in a discontinuous fashion. Into it are fed at fixed intervals the choices of the individual citizens. The machine then aggregates them according to the pre-established rule or method, and so comes up with what may be called a 'choice' of its own. Democratic rule is said to be achieved if throughout the period when the machine is not working, the most recent choice of the machine is acted upon. The question now arises: What is the authority of the choice expressed by the machine? More specifically, why should someone who has fed his choice into the machine and then is confronted by the machine with a choice non-identical with his own, feel any obligation to accept it?

In order however to advance the inquiry we must now note a distinction. For the choices that the individual citizen feeds into the democratic machine and on the basis of which the democratic 'choice' is made, are susceptible of two very different interpretations.

On the one hand, we may regard the choices as expressions of *want*. To say that a certain citizen chooses policy A or that he prefers policy A to policy B, is to say that he wants policy A more than any other policy or that he wants it more than policy B. The wants which the citizens' choices express need not, of course, be selfish or egotistical wants. When a man decides that he wants policy A more than policy B, he may well be moved not just by his own narrow interests but by a concern for the welfare of others. But all the same, in choosing A he is not asserting that the others want A, nor that A is in their interests, nor that A would be an ideal solution, nor that A ought to be realized; he would be asserting *tout court* that he wants A.

If we conceive the democratic machine as operating on choices in the sense of expressed wants, then our question resolves into something approximating to the old Utilitarian problem: Why should a man who wants A think that B ought to be the case, when B is not consistent with A but is arrived at by considering the wants of all the other citizens of the society? And I think that in this connexion it is only necessary to make two quite brief observations.

In the first place, there is no inconsistency whatsoever in

wanting A and thinking that B ought to be the case, even when A and B are themselves inconsistent. We may well have a desire and a moral belief that runs counter to that desire. Indeed there are moral philosophers who have held that morality would be inconceivable unless *some* of our moral beliefs ran counter to our desires.

However, though there is no inconsistency between wanting A and thinking that B ought to be the case, it should be equally obvious that the former could not serve as a reason for the latter nor the latter be derived from the former. Yet there seems a presumption in the question that just this is what is to be shown. Paradoxically though, Utilitarians (and I use the expression in a rather general way) seem to have held both that there was a *prima facie* inconsistency between wanting A and thinking that B ought to be the case, and also that this inconsistency was to be removed by showing that the belief that B ought to be the case was grounded in the want for A. But of course this last demand is an absurdity. It springs either from an absurdly exaggerated conception of what it is to prove consistency, i.e. that to prove two propositions are consistent one must show that one can be derived from the other, or else from a fundamentally egotistic conception of the basis of morality, i.e. that all one's moral beliefs are grounded in wants.

In fact the citizen who expresses a want for A and then, in deference to the operation of the democratic machine, thinks that B ought to be the case, thinks that B ought to be the case as the result of applying some higher-order principle to the effect that what the democratic machine chooses ought to be the case. He consults, in other words, his principles, he does not go back and consult again his wants. All he needs to be certain of is that his principles and his wants, though they may lead in different directions, are not actually inconsistent: and it seems very difficult to attach any sense even to the *possibility* that they could be.

However, it is now time to turn to another interpretation that can be put on the material which is characteristically fed into the democratic machine. On this view when the citizen chooses a certain policy or prefers one policy to another, he is expressing not a want but an *evaluation*. He chooses A or prefers A to B, because he thinks that A is the best policy, is the policy that ought to be enacted, or, alternatively, that A is a better policy than B or ought to be enacted in preference to B—not because he wants A more or needs it more than B. If it is objected at this stage that evaluations are based upon wants and therefore not to be contrasted with them, I can only reply that this may well be true if what is meant is that a man will often enough take his wants into account in arriving at his evaluations. But it does not follow from this that his evaluations are not different from his wants, nor that they cannot be placed in contrast to them. Indeed, the fact that evaluations may be based on wants is no more germane to our present discussion than it was to our earlier discussion that wants can be affected by evaluations.

Let us then regard the democratic machine as being fed with choices in the sense of evaluations. The evaluations are then aggregated by the machine in accordance with its established rule, and the machine comes up with a choice of its own. Anyone who accepts democracy is then obliged to think that the policy that the machine selects is the policy that ought to be enacted.

But immediately a difficulty arises. Let us imagine a citizen who feeds his choice for, say, A, or for A over B into the democratic machine. On the present interpretation, he is to be regarded as thereby expressing his opinion that A ought to be enacted. And now let us further suppose that the machine into which this and other choices have been fed comes up with its own choice, and its choice is for B. How can the citizen accept the machine's choice, which involves his thinking that B ought to be enacted when, as we already know, he is of the opinion, of the declared opinion, that A ought to be enacted?

Observe that we are confronted with a far more serious problem now when we interpret choices as evaluations than we were when we interpreted them as expressions of wants. For on the original interpretation the problem was (it will be remembered) that the acceptance of the machine's choice did not follow from one's own choice, which one had fed into the machine: the problem on this new interpretation is that the acceptance of the machine's choice seems to be incompatible with—not just not to follow from, but to be incompatible with—one's own original choice. For if a man expresses a choice for A and the machine expresses a choice for B, then the man, if he is to be a sound democratic, seems to be committed to the belief that A ought to be the case *and* to the belief that B ought to be the case.

Now, this is a serious matter. For I think it is fairly self-evident that, even if the dichotomy of 'expressed want' 'evaluation' is somewhat harsh, the choices that the citizens of a democracy make when they are called upon to make a choice are far closer to evaluations than to expressions of want. And I hold this not because of any particularly elevated view I have of political behaviour but because I think that the ordinary citizen, confronted by a political choice, is far more likely to know which of the two policies he thinks *ought to be* enacted than which of them he *wants* enacted. Accordingly he is more likely to vote in a way that reflects his evaluations than in a way that reflects his wants. If this is so, then the difficulty that I have described would seem to constitute a paradox in the very heart of democratic theory.

There are two obvious ways in which the paradox might be broken. One is by denying that in the circumstances the man is committed to the belief that A (i.e. the policy of his choice) ought to be enacted: the other is by denying that the man is committed to the belief that B (i.e. the policy of the machine's choice) ought to be enacted. Either of these two ways would be effective in resolving the paradox: both have considerable plausibility: but neither, I submit, is ultimately acceptable. Let me review the arguments:

1. It might be claimed that the man who feeds his choice for A into the democratic machine is not in fact committed to believing that A ought to be the case in the face of the machine's verdict, since, though the choice that he feeds into the machine is certainly an evaluation, it is an *interim*, not a final or definitive, evaluation. When he expresses his preference for A or for A over B, his preference (properly understood) is hypothetical. Written out it would be formulated in some such way as 'I think that A ought to be enacted, provided that other people, or enough other people, are of the same opinion'. The preference, the argument runs, is necessarily hypothetical, because when it is expressed, the man cannot know the preferences that will be expressed by his fellow-citizens. It is only when all these preferences have been fed into the machine, and the machine has operated on them and has come up with a preference of its own, that he has the requisite information on which to base a final as opposed to a provisional

or interim choice. And then when he is in this position what he does is to reiterate the preference of the machine: he chooses as it has chosen—that is to say, in the present case he chooses B.

Once we understand this—the argument runs—the paradox disappears. No longer is there any temptation to think of the unfortunate citizen as committed both to the belief that A ought to be enacted and to the belief that B ought to be enacted—for it should now be clear that he continues to hold that A ought to be enacted only up to the moment when he has reason to think that B ought to be enacted: as soon as he has reason to commit himself to B, i.e. as soon as the machine has expressed *its* choices on the basis of all the choices in the community, his commitment to A dissolves. The man, in other words, withdraws his support from A and gives it to B.

The argument has some plausibility; but not, I think, enough. For, to begin with, it cannot be correct to interpret the choices fed into the democratic machine as interim or hypothetical, i.e. as of the form 'I think that A ought to be enacted if other people or enough other people are of the same opinion'. And this for two reasons. First, a hypothetical choice, or a choice hypothetically expressed, generally implies some doubt whether the condition upon which the choice is dependent is or is not fulfilled. It would be inappropriate to express a choice hypothetically if one knew that the protasis was fulfilled: and it would be pointless to express it so if one knew that the protasis was unfulfilled. And yet in politics people sometimes vote knowing how the vote as a whole will go: sometimes, indeed, knowing full well that it will go in the opposite direction to that in which they cast their own vote. And we don't think that the behaviour of such people is irrational. Suppose that a man votes Liberal, knowing full well that only a rather small minority of the population is of his opinion. We may disagree with his behaviour, but surely we don't think it irrational. Yet surely we ought to do so, if in casting his vote for the Liberals he was in effect saying 'I want a Liberal policy to be enacted if other people or enough other people are of my opinion', though he was quite certain that there was no chance whatsoever of there being enough people who were of his opinion.

Secondly, to interpret the citizens' choices as hypothetical is to imply that there is a dependence between what policy the citizen

prefers and some other condition—in this case, how he thinks
that others will vote: so that the citizen allows this consideration
effectively to enter into his calculations when he decides which
policy he supports. But this implication is surely, in many cases
at least, unfounded. The citizen who votes for A cannot, without
further qualification, be understood as expressing a view that A
ought to be enacted if enough other people think so: because
he may well be of the opinion that whether A ought to be enacted
or not is *in some sense or other* independent of what other people
think. Or even if he thinks that there is some dependence between
what ought to be enacted and what others think, he may not
think that there is a *total* dependence: so that if a policy is outvoted, then it automatically follows that it ought not to be
enacted. Indeed, it would seem that democracy not merely
allows but positively demands that our political preferences have
a certain constancy to them and that they do not fluctuate with
the preferences of others. In other words, when the machine's
choice has been declared and we have given our adherence to it,
there is a sense in which we still do and should stand by our
original choice. What this sense is is still unclear, but that such a
sense exists is surely indubitable.

However, suppose we allow that the citizen's choices are really
hypothetical. Once we make this admission it is far from clear
why a choice which is reached by aggregating them on the
assumption that they are categorical or unconditional should
have any particular appeal or authority. It is not very difficult
to see why a choice which is based upon what are genuinely the
unconditional choices of individual citizens should have authority:
for such a choice would have been arrived at by considering what
the citizens of the society actually think ought to be done. But
if the democratic choice is the result of aggregating hypothetical
choices, then it is arrived at merely by considering what the
citizens of the society think ought to be done *under a certain set
of conditions*, i.e. when other people agree with them. But why
is this of such paramount significance? For is it not possible—
indeed, is it not suggested by the form of words employed—
that under a different set of conditions the citizens might well
want something different done? Why then should we attach
special prestige to what they think ought to be done if other
people agree with them? Why is this a privileged condition?

And, as far as I can see, the only reason for regarding any condition as privileged—in the sense that we are justified in detaching the remaining part of the preference and aggregating it—is that we are of the opinion that the condition is actually fulfilled. But it is quite clear that not in all cases of hypothetical choices will the condition be fulfilled. In some cases it will be, in others it will not be.

Moreover, if we take this suggestion for resolving the paradox of democracy *as a whole* we shall find a far stronger reason for thinking that a choice reached by aggregating hypothetical choices, where these hypothetical choices are choices conditional upon general agreement with the voter, has no natural authority. For it will be remembered that the voter who votes 'A if enough others agree with this', switches to B when the democratic machine comes up with B. Now if this is so, surely he might equally well have in the first place have voted B—for in voting B he would on this view merely have been expressing the view (which *is* surely his) that B ought to be enacted if enough people are of that opinion. Indeed it now seems as if the voter could quite legitimately have voted for *any* of the policies placed before him—provided only, of course, that he neither knows that enough other people would prefer that policy nor knows that not enough other people will prefer that policy, i.e. if the uncertainty proviso, which, as we have seen, is necessary for the making of a hypothetical choice, is fulfilled. In other words, if the vote for A is interpreted as 'A ought to be enacted if enough people are of the same opinion', and the voter is prepared to switch to support B if enough people are of that o pnion, it is obvious that 'A' as it appeared in his original vote was a variable, not a constant: a variable ranging over all the policies that are not obviously either winners or losers, not a constant designating one particular policy. If this is so, then it would be quite improper to take his vote literally, as meaning what it says—as one surely would do if one accepted a choice arrived at by aggregating it and similar votes. Accordingly the first attempt to solve our paradox must be rejected.

2. The other obvious way of breaking the paradox of Democracy would be by denying the other limb of the offending conjunction. Democracy—the argument would run—is government by compromise, and the role of the democratic machine is

to function as a kind of impersonal arbitrator. In so far as the
machine chooses a policy, it chooses a policy that it would be wise
or prudent to follow, not a policy that the citizen ought to follow.
And in so far as to believe in Democracy is to be prepared or
disposed to accept the machine's choice, it is to accept it as the
most sensible thing to do. The functioning of the democratic
machine influences one's behaviour, actual and potential: what it
does not do is increase one's obligations. On this view what one
feeds into the machine are one's evaluations to the effect that
this or that policy ought to be enacted: and these evaluations one
continues to adhere to even after the machine has operated upon
them. What the machine comes up with is the choice of a policy
that it would be prudential for all to support, and there is no
reason to postulate any incompatibility between the acceptance
of such a policy, on the one hand, and, on the other, the continued
adherence to one's own political beliefs. So once again the
paradox disappears.

Once again the argument is plausible, but I do not think that
ultimately it carries conviction. For, in the first place, it seems
to me unrealistic to say that our commitment to the machine's
choice, when the machine's choice does not concur with ours, is
purely tactical or prudential. For if it were, then some argument
analogous to that of Gyges's ring would apply. Suppose, once
again, that our choice is for A and that of the machine is for B.
Then if our support for B were purely tactical or prudential, we
should surely be content if the B government were somehow
outwitted and they found themselves, contrary to their own
inclinations but with the continued support of their electors,
putting through policy A. Yet I think it is fairly clear that if this
happened in reality, we should be displeased and would think
that something undesirable had occurred. If the machine chooses
B, there is a sense in which we think that B ought to be enacted
whether or not A could be. And this is more than tactical or
prudential support.

Secondly it does not seem correct to equate—as the present
argument does—belief in Democracy with a disposition to
accept the successive choices of the democratic machine. For
surely a man could be so disposed without believing in Democracy. He might, for instance, be prepared to go along with
Democracy, because he thought that he could achieve power by

no other means: although once he had achieved power he would probably try to end the democratic process. The problem, then, arises how we are to distinguish such a man from the genuine believer in Democracy. Surely the disposition to accept democratic results is common, and what must distinguish one from the other is the reason that each has for his acceptance. The genuine believer in Democracy is disposed to accept the successive choices of the democratic machine *because he believes that what the democratic machine chooses ought to be enacted.*

But once we make this concession the present solution to the paradox stands condemned. For if the believer in Democracy believes that what the democratic machine chooses ought to be enacted, then, whenever the machine actually chooses a policy, he must believe that that policy ought to be enacted: not just that it would be wise or tactical to support its enactment, but that it ought to be enacted. In other words, the believer in Democracy is in our example committed to the belief that B ought to be enacted.

So we must abandon this solution to the paradox: which, it might be said, requires the same sort of systematic reinterpretation of our ordinary behaviour that Hobbes (on the traditional interpretation, at any rate) found himself committed to when he asserted an analogous theory about the obligation or commitment we have not just simply to Democracy but to government as such.

The paradox of Democracy cannot, it seems, be resolved by denying either of the limbs of the offending conjunction that gives rise to it. The only remaining way of resolving it is to show that the two limbs are, contrary to appearances, not inconsistent, and therefore their conjunction is not offensive. In other words, what is now required is to show that in our example it is perfectly in order for one and the same citizen to assert that A ought to be enacted, where A is the policy of his choice, and B ought to be enacted, where B is the policy chosen by the democratic machine, even when A and B are not identical.

Now, if my arguments have been sound so far, it is evident that either the two assertions *are* compatible, or else Democracy is inconsistent. I doubt that any of us are prepared to regard Democracy as inconsistent: in consequence we are committed to the view that, in the circumstances of my example, A ought to be enacted and B ought to be enacted are compatible. What we need to see, though, is *how* they are compatible, and the rest of this paper I shall devote to expounding, I fear rather sketchily, one explanation.

The explanation I proffer presupposes a distinction between direct and oblique moral principles. Direct principles refer to the morality of actions, policies, motives, etc., where these are picked out or designated by means of some general descriptive expressions, e.g. *murder, envy, benevolence, birth-control, telling lies,* etc. Oblique principles, by contrast, refer to the morality of actions, policies, motives, etc., where these actions, policies, motives, etc., are not picked out by reference to some common quality or characteristic that they possess, but are identified by means of an artificial property bestowed upon them either as the result of an act of will of some individual or in consequence of the corporate action of some institution. This is a far from satisfactory formulation of the distinction, neither very clear nor very precise, but I think that it will do for my present purposes. Examples of direct principles would be *Murder is wrong, Birth-control is permissible.* Examples of oblique principles would be *What is commanded by the sovereign ought to be done,* or *What is willed by the people is right.*

Now, my suggestion is that two judgements of the form 'A ought to be the case' and 'B ought to be the case' are not incompatible even though A and B cannot be simultaneously realized *if* one of these judgements is asserted as a direct principle whereas the other is asserted as a derivation from an oblique principle— provided that the direct and the oblique principle are not themselves incompatible. Now, I am aware that the proviso might give rise to some difficulty, for it might be natural to think that A ought to be enacted was incompatible with any oblique principle from which B ought to be enacted could be derived, *ipso facto.* For my principle to have any area of operation, it is of course important to exclude incompatibility of this kind and to permit as relevant only incompatibility of a more immediate kind. And I hope that this restriction will be seen to be less artificial when it is realized that a judgement of the kind B ought to be enacted is derived from an oblique principle only by the introduction of certain further factual premises, e.g. B has been commanded by the Sovereign, B is the will of the people, etc.

Now I think it should be clear that my suggestion, if accepted, would resolve our paradox by the only mēans still available to us, i.e. by showing that the two limbs of the conjunction are not inconsistent. For—to return to the example—'A ought to be enacted' is asserted by the citizen who has been outvoted as a direct principle, whereas 'B ought to be enacted' is asserted by him as a derivation from an oblique principle, i.e. the principle of Democracy.

But the question now arises, What reason have I for putting forward my suggestion? How is its truth to be established? And the only answer I can give is, I am afraid, disappointing. The most I can do is to try to dispose of two reasons, two reasons which I am sure are misguided, for rejecting it.

1. Someone might maintain that 'A ought to be the case' and 'B ought to be the case' are clearly incompatible, and being incompatible they are incompatible in all circumstances: *a fortiori*, they are incompatible no matter what reasons may be adduced in favour of either of them. Against this forthright position I would like to urge a more sceptical attitude. It seems to me fairly evident that any judgement of the form 'X ought to be the case' acquires a different meaning when it is asserted as a derivation from an oblique principle from that which it has when it is asserted directly, cf., e.g. Jews ought to be given privileged treatment asserted in the 1930s as a derivation from some principle to the effect that victims of persecution should be given exceptional treatment, and the same proposition asserted simply as an expression of Jewish chauvinism. Now if this is so, if the meaning of a principle can vary with the reasons for which it is asserted, and if—as is usually admitted—incompatibility is intimately associated with meaning, there seems, at the very least, good reason not to be dogmatic that of the two principles it is true that, once incompatible, always incompatible.

2. Again, it might be argued against my suggestion, that 'A ought to be the case' and 'B ought to be the case' can never be consistently conjoined by anyone because the assertion of the first commits one to the implementation of A and the assertion of the second commits one to the implementation of B, and *ex hypothesi* this is impossible: for one cannot simultaneously commit oneself to the implementation of two policies that cannot be simultaneously realized.

Now this objection rests upon the identification of asserting (honestly asserting) that A ought to be the case with committing oneself to the implementation of A. And the identification is by no means self-evident. *Perhaps* honestly asserting 'I ought to do A' does commit one to the implementation of A—but it is surely megalomania further to identify 'A ought to be the case' with 'I ought to do A' or to think that belief in the one commits one to belief in the other.

However, even if we do allow that there *is* an element of commitment in any evaluation to the effect that, e.g. A ought to be the case, it is by no means clear in the present case that the degree of commitment is such as to preclude any commitment to the other. For it is surely evident that the commitment cannot be total. The democrat who believes in his political heart that A ought to be enacted cannot be totally committed to A. And if the commitment is short of totality, then there is in principle room for some commitment to B, even when B diverges from A. Indeed, when we think of the actual situation, it seems that our degree of commitment to the political policy we directly support never goes beyond arguing on its behalf, persuading others of its truth, etc.—whereas the degree of commitment we can plausibly be said to have to the choice of the democratic machine extends only to not resisting its implementation or perhaps to resisting any attempt to resist its implementation—and it seems perfectly possible to be simultaneously committed in these two different directions. Hence I conclude that the second objection to my suggestion fails.

5

ON THE ORIGIN OF SOCIAL INEQUALITY[1]
by Ralf Dahrendorf

EVEN in the affluent society, it remains a stubborn and re-
markable fact that men are unequally placed. There are
children who are ashamed of their parents because they think
that a university degree has made them into 'something better'.
There are people who decorate their houses with aerials without
having the television sets which belong to them, in order to
convince their neighbours that they could afford it. There are
firms which furnish their offices with movable walls because the
status of their employees is measured in square feet and every
room has to be enlarged on the promotion of its tenant. There
are clerical workers whose ambition it is to achieve a position
in which they can not only afford but are socially permitted to
own a two-tone car. Of course, such differences are no longer
directly sustained by the force of legal sanction which upholds
the system of privilege in a caste or estate society. Nevertheless,
our society is—quite apart from the cruder gradations of property
and income, prestige and power—characterized by a multitude
of differences of rank so subtle and yet so penetrating that one
cannot but be sceptical of the claim which is sometimes made
that a process of levelling has brought about the disappearance
of all inequalities. It is no longer usual to investigate the anxiety,
suffering and hardship which inequalities cause among men—
yet there are suicides because of poor examination results, divorces
based on 'social' incompatibility, crimes due to a feeling of social
inequality. Throughout our society social inequality is still
turning men against men.

These remarks are not meant to be a plea for equality. On the
contrary, I shall later agree with Kant, who calls 'inequality
among men' a 'rich source of much that is evil, but also of
everything that is good'. Yet the extreme effects of inequality
may serve to give the outline of the problem with which I am

---

[1] This essay was initially given as an inaugural lecture in the University of Tübingen
and has been translated for the present volume by the author.

concerned. Diderot has our sympathy when he states in his article 'Société' in the *Encyclopédie*: 'There is no more inequality between the different stations in life than there is among the different characters in a comedy: the end of the play finds all the players once again in a common position, and the brief period for which their play lasted did not and could not convince any two of them that one was really above or below the other.' But the life of men in society is not merely a comedy, and the hope that all will be equal in death is a feeble consolation for most. The question remains: why is there inequality among men? Where do its causes lie? Can it be reduced or even abolished altogether? Or do we have to accept it as a necessary element in the structure of human society?

In my remarks, I shall try to show that this was historically the first question asked by sociology. By surveying the various attempts to answer it a whole history of sociological thought might be written, and I shall at least give some indication of how this may be so. So far, however, as the problem of inequality is concerned, this history has achieved little more than to give it a different name: what was called in the eighteenth century the origin of inequality and in the nineteenth the formation of classes, we describe today as the theory of social stratification—without either the problem having changed or a satisfactory solution having been found for it. My reflections lead therefore to an attempt to sketch an explanation of the old problem which will, in my belief, take us a few steps beyond the positions reached so far.

The younger a branch of scholarship is, the more concerned are its historians to pursue its origins back into history at least as far as Greek antiquity. Historians of sociology are no exception to this rule. But if one regards the problem of inequality as a key to the history of sociology, it can be clearly shown both that Plato and Aristotle were definitely not sociologists, and also why they were not. It is always awkward to ascribe to an academic subject a precise date of birth, but this discussion may help us with reasonable plausibility to date the beginnings of sociology.

In 1792, a gentleman by the name of Meiners, 'Royal British Councillor and *rite* teacher of worldly wisdom in Göttingen', wrote some reflections on 'the causes of the inequality of estates among the most prominent European peoples'. His results were not unduly original: 'Inequality of natures produced unfailingly at all times inequality of rights. . . . If the negligent, the lazy, the untrained and the ignorant were to enjoy equal rights with those who display the contrary virtues, this would be as unnatural and unjust as if the child had equal rights to those of the adult, the weak and cowardly woman equal rights to those of the strong and courageous man, the villain equal security and respect with the meritorious citizen.'[1]

In view of the time when he wrote (three years after the beginning of the French Revolution), Mr. Meiners gives a highly characteristic version of an ideology which up to the present day and with only minor refinements is used by all societies which are worried about their survival to reassure themselves of the justice of their injustices. By repeating in a simplified form the errors of Aristotle, they assert a pre-established harmony of things natural and social, and above all a congruence of natural differences between men and social differences between their positions. It was, after all, Aristotle who had said: 'It is thus clear that there are *by nature* free men and slaves, and that servitude is agreeable and just for the latter. . . . Equally, the relation of the male and the female is *by nature* such that one is better and the other inferior, one dominates and the other is dominated. . . . With the barbarians, of course, the male and the dominated have the same rank. This is due to the fact that they do not possess a naturally dominating element. . . . This is why the poets say, "It is just that Greeks rule over barbarians", because the barbarian and the slave are *by nature* the same.'[2] Now this is just the attitude which makes impossible a sociological treatment of the problem, that is to say an explanation of inequality in terms of specifically social factors expressed in propositions capable of being empirically tested.

So far, I have talked about social inequality as if it was clear what is meant by this notion. Obviously, this is a somewhat optimistic assumption. The turner and the fitter, the general and the sergeant, the artistically and the mechanically gifted child, the talented and the untalented, are all pairs of unequals. Yet these inequalities are evidently themselves rather unequal, and have to be distinguished in at least two respects. One of these concerns the distinction between inequalities of natural capability and

---

[1] C. Meiners, *Geschichte der Ungleichheit der Stände unter den vornehmsten Europäischen Völkern* (Hanover, 1792), p. 41. [2] *Politics*, 1255a, 1254b, 1252b.

those of social position; the other requires a distinction between all those inequalities which do not involve any evaluative rank order and those which constitute a scale of superior and inferior positions. If we combine these two aspects, four types of inequality emerge, all of which we shall have to discuss. These are, in relation to the individual: (1) *natural differences of kind* between people's features, characters and interests, and (2) *natural differences of rank* between people's intelligence, talents and strength (leaving open the question of whether such differences do in fact exist). Correspondingly, in relation to society (and in the language of contemporary sociology) there are: (3) *social differentiation* of positions essentially equal in rank, and (4) *social stratification* according to reputation and wealth in terms of a rank order of social status.

Aristotle was concerned as we are here to examine the origin of the fourth type of inequality, social stratification. However, by trying to explain social stratification—as so many authors of antiquity, the Christian middle ages and modern times did after him—in terms of an assumption of natural differences of rank between men, he missed precisely that type of analysis which we should today describe as 'sociology'. In consequence, he surrenders a potentially sociological problem to assumptions which transcend the realm of social fact and defy the test of historical experience. That this attitude helped to delay the birth of sociology by more than twenty centuries is perhaps supportable. The political consequences of an explanation as unhistorical as this are certainly worse—and I believe that Rousseau was right, even in the sharpness of his polemic, when he argued that it did not make sense 'to investigate whether there might not be an essential connexion between the two inequalities [the natural and the social]. For it would mean that we must ask whether rulers are necessarily worth more than the ruled, and whether strength of body and mind, wisdom or virtue are always found in the same individuals, and found, moreover, in direct relation to their power or wealth; a question which it may be useful to discuss for slaves who think they are being overheard by their masters, but which is not appropriate for reasonable and free men searching for truth.'[1]

Such is Rousseau's argument in his prize essay of 1754 on the

[1] J.-J. Rousseau, *Du Contrat Social etc.* (Paris, n.d.), p. 39.

question of 'what is the origin of inequality among men and whether it is legitimated by natural law'. In contrast to his earlier essay of 1750 on the moral consequences of progress in the arts and sciences, Rousseau was not awarded the prize of Dijon Academy for this essay. I do not know why the judges in this case preferred the essay of a 'certain Abbé Talbert' (as one editor of Rousseau expresses it); but it is not inconceivable that they became worried about the radical implications of their own question. For the new meaning given by Rousseau and his contemporaries to the question of the origin of inequality involved a revolution in terms of politics as well as intellectual history.

The pivotal point of the Aristotelian argument—if I may use this formula as an abbreviation for all treatments of the problem before the eighteenth century—was the assumption that men are by nature unequal in rank, and that there is therefore a natural rank order among men. This presupposition collapsed in the face of the assumption of natural law that the natural rank of all men is equal. Politically, this meant that together with all other hierarchies the hierarchies of society also lost their undoubted stability. If men are equal by nature, then social inequalities cannot be established by nature or God; and if they are not so established, then they are subject to change, and the privileged of to-day may be the outcasts of to-morrow; it may then even be possible to abolish all inequalities. There is a straight road that leads from such reflections to the statement in the Declaration of the Rights of Man and Citizen of 1789: 'Men are born free and equal in their rights. Social differences can only be based on general utility.'

In terms of intellectual history, the same process means that the question of the origin of inequality was now phrased in a new and different, i.e. sociological manner. If men are by nature equal in rank, where do inequalities in society come from? If all men are born free and equal in rights—how can we explain that some are rich, others poor, some respected, others ignored, some powerful and others in subjection? In this form, only a sociological answer was possible to the question. We might therefore tend to agree with Sombart and others who looked for the beginnings of sociology in the works of those authors who first tried to give a sociological answer to this question—in particular, the French *philosophes*, the Scottish moral philosophers and political economists, and the thinkers of the German enlightenment in the second half of the eighteenth century.

The first sociological solution to the problem of the origin of inequality, however, remained disappointing, although for a century it reappeared in a succession of new forms. It consisted in a figure of thought which may be demonstrated by further reference to Rousseau's prize essay.

As we have seen, Rousseau sets out with the assumption of the natural equality of men. Following the style of his time, he then projects this assumption into history and constructs a pre-social original state in which there was complete equality of all, and nobody was superior to anybody else in terms of either rank or status. Thus the emergence of inequality came about in leaving the state of nature, a kind of original sin—and this Rousseau sees in the emergence of private property. How private property itself came into existence, Rousseau does not explain; instead, he confines himself to a statement as obscure as it is concrete: 'The first man who fenced in an area and said, "This is mine", and who found people sufficiently simple to believe him, was the real founder of civil society.'[1]

Not all of Rousseau's contemporaries, even among those who in general agreed with his assumptions, have followed him in the one-sidedness of his explanation, or in the evaluation of the process he described. Thus Adam Ferguson's *History of Civil Society* (1767) and John Millar's *Origin of the Distinction of Ranks* (1771) come quite close to Rousseau in that they too assume a natural state of equality and ascribe to property the crucial (Millar) or at least an important (Ferguson) part in breaking up this natural state. Both of them regard the fact that men have learnt 'to strive for riches and admire distinctions' and thus differentiate according to income and prestige, not as a curse but as a step towards the civilization of 'civil society'. Even further removed from Rousseau the romantic Utopian, is Schiller in his Jena lectures of 1789 entitled 'On the First Human Society', a clear, if implicit, reference to Kant's essay on the 'Probable Beginning of Human History', which in turn referred explicitly to Rousseau's essay.

Schiller praises the 'abolition of equality of status' as the

[1] Loc. cit., p. 66.

departure of man from the 'tranquil nausea of his paradise'.[1] But the assumption of an original state of equality, and the explanation of the origin of inequality in terms of private property, remained unchallenged from Rousseau to Lorenz von Stein and Marx.

For many authors between 1750 and 1850, and for their public, the explanation of inequality in terms of private property retained its political attraction. A society without private property is at least conceivable; and if the idea of equality is associated with this notion, the abolition of private property may become the supreme demand of political action. Indeed, it can be argued that two great revolutions have been fed to no small extent by Rousseau's dream of a re-establishment of the original, natural equality and by Marx's hope of a communist society—both of which were based on the association of inequality with private property. Nevertheless, although it may be attractive to some, and although it represents an undeniable methodological advance by comparison with the Aristotelian argument, the historical-sociological explanation of inequality in terms of property does not stand up to the test of historical experience.

There never existed, to be sure, a complete abolition of private property in the Soviet Union. Nevertheless, the disappointment of the Webbs and other Socialist visitors in the 1930s, caused by the evident inequalities of income and rank in the Soviet Union, may be taken as an experimental refutation of the thesis of Rousseau and Millar, Ferguson and Schiller, von Stein and Marx, and many others. In the Soviet Union, in Yugoslavia, in Israel, and wherever private property has been reduced to virtual insignificance, we still find social stratification. Even if such stratification cannot (as in the *kibbutzim* of Israel) for a short period manifest itself in differences of possessions and income, the undefinable yet effective force of prestige continues to create a noticeable order of rank. If social inequality were really based on private property, the abolition of private property would have to result in the elimination of inequality. Experience in propertyless and quasi-propertyless societies does not confirm this proposition. We may therefore regard it as falsified.

Lorenz von Stein and Marx are only marginal members of the group of authors who, by explaining the origin of stratification in terms of property, contributed to the emergence of sociology.

---

[1] *Werke*, ed. Goedeke (Stuttgart, 1872), V, pp. 600 ff.

Both Stein and Marx (and, to a lesser extent, Ferguson and several of the political economists of the late eighteenth century) mention a second factor, apart from property, a factor which came to dominate the discussion of the formation of classes, as our problem was now called, throughout the second half of the nineteenth and the beginning of the twentieth century. This factor was the division of labour.

As early as the 1870s Engels in his *Anti-Dühring* had developed a theory of class formation on the basis of the division of labour. The subsequent discussion, however, was associated with one name above all others: that of Gustav Schmoller. It began with the famous controversy between Schmoller and Treitschke about Schmoller's essay on 'The Social Question and the Prussian State'—a controversy which is of interest to us here because it raised once again the question of the possibility of a sociological science. Against Schmoller, Treitschke defended (one is tempted to say a century too late—if it were not this fact which characterized the whole of German history) the thesis of a congruence of natural differences of value and social inequality. Schmoller, on the other hand, tried (if with arguments often no less curious) to explain the formation of classes in terms of the division of labour.

Schmoller's essays on 'The Facts of the Division of Labour' and 'The Nature of the Division of Labour and the Formation of Classes', published in 1889 and 1890, prompted Karl Büchler's polemic in his Leipzig inaugural lecture of 1892 on *Division of Labour and Formation of Social Classes*, later extended and modified in his *Emergence of Economy*. This in turn was not only attacked by Schmoller, but taken up by Durkheim in his *Division of Labour in Society*. Durkheim also discussed at some length Simmel's work 'On Social Differentiation' which had appeared in 1890 in Schmoller's *Staatswissenschaftliche Forschungen*. Schmoller himself greeted Durkheim gladly in a review of his work, 'as one striving to the same end, although he has not convinced us altogether', and continued to pursue the subject and his thesis. After his death, however, in 1917, both the subject and Schmoller's position found few friends, apart from Fahlbeck and (with reservations) Oppenheimer and Schumpeter, before they were forgotten, without, of course, having been led to a satisfactory solution.

Many issues came up in the course of this prolonged discussion which we shall have to leave untouched here, either because they lead us away from our subject or because they are merely historical curiosities. The former holds above all for Simmel's and Durkheim's discussion of the relation between the division of labour and social integration, the latter for Schmoller's theory of the genetics of special abilities acquired by the progressive division of labour, to give one example. (This was a theory which Büchler rightly attacked repeatedly and violently without succeeding in forcing out of Schmoller more than very minor concessions.) Yet Schmoller's position, especially in his early papers of 1889 and 1890, contains elements of a theory of class formation that has to be taken quite seriously, if only because in a new (but not very different) form it seems to play a certain role in contemporary sociology.

According to this theory, class formation (that is, inequality of rank) is based on the fact that occupations are differentiated. However one may wish to explain the division of labour itself—Schmoller explains it in terms of the exchange principle, Büchler in terms of property (and neither regards it as universal)—in any case differentiation precedes the stratification of social positions. 'In the emergence of social classes, it is always a question in the first place of an advance in the division of labour within peoples and nations'.[1] Or even more clearly: 'The difference in social rank and property, in prestige and income, is merely a secondary consequence of social differentiation.'[2]

Schmoller later corrected and supplemented his own position without abandoning it in principle. It has to be admitted, however, that the crucial arguments against his attempt were not brought out in the literature of the time. In order to state them, we have to remember the distinction between social differentiation and social stratification introduced above.

Since we tend, particularly in modern society, to associate inequalities of social rank with people's occupational position, one might be led to suspect that differences of rank are in fact based on the differentiation of occupations. On the contrary, it must be emphasized that the notion of differentiation does not

[1] G. Schmoller, 'Das Wesen der Arbeitsteilung und der sozialen Klassenbildung', *Jahrbuch für Gesetzgebung, Verwaltung und Volkswirtschaft*, XIV (1890), p. 74.
[2] K. Büchler, *Arbeitsteilung und soziale Klassenbildung* (new edn., n.d., Frankfurt), p. 29.

in itself imply any distinctions of rank or value among the differentiated elements. From the point of view of the division of labour (the 'functional organization' of industrial sociology), there is no difference in rank between the director-general, the typist, the foreman, the fitter and the unskilled labourer of an enterprise: these are all partial activities equally indispensable for the attainment of the goal in question. If in fact we do associate a rank order (or 'scalar organization') with these partial activities, this is due to an additional act of evaluation which is neither caused nor explained by the division of labour; the same activities may be evaluated quite differently in different societies. Schmoller seems to have sensed this gap in his argument when, in later editions, he suddenly inserted a 'psychological fact' between the division of labour and the formation of classes: 'the necessity for human thought and feeling to bring all related phenomena of any kind into a sequence, and estimate and order them according to their value'.[1] However factual this fact may be, that Schmoller thought it necessary to introduce it may serve as further testimony to the argument that social differentiation and social stratification are not capable of explaining each other without some intermediate agency.

This conclusion is in itself one of the results of the third continuous discussion of the origin of inequality in the history of sociology: the American discussion of the theory of social stratification. Since Talcott Parsons first published his 'Analytical Approach to the Theory of Social Stratification' in 1940, the debate about the so-called 'functional' theory of social stratification has not ceased. Almost all major American sociologists have taken part in this debate which—unknown as it still is on the European continent—constitutes as a whole one of the more significant contributions of American sociology towards our understanding of social structures.

The immediate effect of Parsons' essay of 1940 was above all that American sociologists became aware of the subject of a theory of social stratification. The largely conceptual paper published by Parsons' disciple Kingsley Davis in 1942 was also mainly preparatory in character. The discussion proper was not opened until Davis and W. E. Moore published in 1945 their paper on 'Some Principles of Stratification'.[2] Both Rousseau

---

[1] Loc. cit., p. 78.   [2] *American Sociological Review*, X, 2 (1945).

and his successors and Schmoller and his adherents had regarded inequality as a historical phenomenon. For both, there was once a period of equality; for both, the elimination of inequality was conceivable. By contrast, Davis and Moore are trying to prove the universality of inequality by reference to its functional necessity for all human societies, i.e. its indispensability for the maintenance of any social structure whatever.

In the course of this demonstration, however, they develop an argument which (at least in its weaknesses) is not altogether dissimilar to that of Schmoller. It runs as follows: there are in every society different social positions. These positions—e.g. occupations—are neither equally pleasant nor are they equally important or difficult. In order to guarantee the complete and frictionless allocation of all positions, certain rewards have to be associated with them—namely, the very rewards which constitute the criteria of social stratification. In all societies, the importance of different positions to the society and the market value of the required qualifications determine the unequal distribution of income, prestige and power. Inequality is necessary because without it the differentiated (occupational) positions of societies cannot be adequately filled.

Several other authors, among them for example M. J. Levy and B. Barber, have adopted this theory more or less without modifications. But it has been subjected to severe criticism, and despite several thoughtful replies by the original authors some of the critical arguments seem to be gaining ground. The most persistent critic, M. Tumin, has presented two main arguments against Davis and Moore (in two essays published in 1953 and 1955).[1] The first argument is that the notion of 'functional importance' of positions is extremely imprecise, and that it probably implies the very differentiation of value that it allegedly explains; the second, that the assumptions of a harmony of stratification and distribution of talent as well as that of motivation by unequal incentives are theoretically problematical and empirically uncertain.

This second argument was confirmed in 1955 in an empirical investigation by R. Schwarz, who showed on the basis of an analysis of two Israeli communities that it is in fact possible to

---

[1] M. M. Tumin, 'Some Principles of Stratification: A Critical Analysis' and 'Rewards and Task-Orientations', *American Sociological Review*, XVIII, 4 (1953) and XX, 4 (1955).

fill positions adequately by means other than the inequality of social rewards.[1] W. Buckley charged Davis and Moore in 1958 with confusing differentiation and stratification; his legitimate objection to the evaluative undertones of the notion of 'functional importance' was, however, exaggerated into a not very promising terminological dispute. In 1959, D. Wrong, so far the last critic of Davis and Moore, took up the argument intimated earlier by Tumin that Davis and Moore had underestimated the 'dysfunctions' of social stratification, i.e. the disruptive consequences of social inequality.

But the significance of the American debate on stratification is only partly to be found in its manifest subject matter. In this respect, its main result would seem to be that social inequality has many functions and dysfunctions (that is, many consequences for the structure of societies), but that there cannot be a satisfactory functional explanation of the origin of inequality. This is because every such explanation is bound either to have recourse to dubious assumptions about human nature or to commit the *petitio principii* of explanation in terms of the object to be explained. Yet this discussion has—just like its historical predecessors—produced at several points propositions or mere remarks and intimations which turn out to be useful in the attempt to formulate a theory of social stratification which proves theoretically satisfactory and, above all, empirically fruitful.

The very first contribution to the American debate on stratification, the essay by Parsons, contained an idea which, although untenable in Parsons' form, may still advance our problem. Parsons tries to derive the necessity of a differentiated rank order from the existence of the concept of evaluation and its significance for social systems. This is a kind of ontological proof of stratification which is surprising rather than convincing—as Parsons himself seems to have felt, for in the revised version of his essay in 1953, he merely refers to the *probability*, not the necessity, of inequality because of the existence of a process of evaluation.[2] In fact, Parsons' thesis contains little more than the suggestion,

---

[1] R. D. Schwartz, 'Functional Alternatives to Inequality', *American Sociological Review*, XX, 4 (1955).
[2] 'An Analytical Approach to the Theory of Social Stratification', *American Journal of Sociology*, XLV (1940), p. 843; 'A Revised Analytical Approach to the Theory of Social Stratification' in R. Bendix and S. M. Lipset, edd., *Class, Status and Power* (Glencoe, Ill., 1953), p. 387.

formulated much more simply by Barber, that men tend to evaluate themselves and the things of their world differently.[1] This suggestion in turn refers back to Schmoller's 'psychological assumption' of a human tendency to produce evaluative rank orders, but it also refers—and here the relation between evaluation and stratification begins to be sociologically relevant—to Durkheim's famous proposition that 'every society is a moral community'. Durkheim rightly remarks that 'the state of nature of the eighteenth century philosophers is, if not immoral, at least amoral'.[2] The idea of the social contract is nothing but the idea of the emergence of society through the institution of norms which are obligatory in that they are equipped with sanctions. It is at this point that there arises the possibility of connecting the concept of human society with the problem of the origin of inequality—a possibility which is occasionally hinted at in the literature but which has not so far been realized.

Human society always means that people's behaviour is being removed from the randomness of chance and regulated by established and inescapable expectations. The obligatory character of these expectations or norms is based on the operation of sanctions, i.e. of rewards or punishments for conformist or deviant behaviour. If, however, every society is in this sense a moral community, it follows that there must always be at least that inequality of rank which results from the necessity of sanctioning behaviour according to whether it does or does not conform to established norms. Under whatever aspect given historical societies may introduce additional distinctions between their members, whatever symbols they may declare to be the outward signs of inequality, and whatever may be the precise content of their social norms, the hard core of social inequality can always be found in the fact that men are subject, according to their attitude to the expectations of their society, to sanctions which guarantee the obligatory character of these expectations.

Let me try to illustrate what I mean by some examples which, however different they may seem, are equally relevant. If the ladies of some city district are expected to exchange more or less interesting secrets and scandals with their near and distant neighbours, this norm will lead at the very least to a distinction be-

[1] B. Barber, *Social Stratification* (New York, 1957), p. 2.
[2] E. Durkheim, *De la division du travail social* (Paris, new edn., 1960), p. 394.

tween those held in high regard (who really enjoy gossip, and offer tea and cakes as well), those with average prestige, and the outsiders (who, whatever their reasons, take no part in the gossiping). If, in an industrial enterprise, a high individual output is expected from the workers and rewarded by piecework rates, there will be those who take home a relatively high and those who take home a relatively low pay-packet. If the citizens (or better, perhaps, subjects) of a state are expected to defend its official ideology as frequently and convincingly as possible, this will lead to a distinction between those who get ahead (becoming, say, civil servants or party secretaries), the mere followers, those who lead a quiet but somewhat anxious existence, and those who pay with their liberty or even their lives for their defiant behaviour.

One might think that individual, not social, inequalities are in fact established by the distinction between those who (as we must initially assume, and have assumed in the examples) for essentially personal reasons are either unprepared for or incapable of conformism and those who punctiliously fulfil every norm. For example: social stratification is always a rank order in terms of 'prestige' and not 'esteem', i.e. a rank order of positions ('worker', 'woman', 'resident of a certain area', etc.) which can be thought of independently of their individual incumbents. By contrast, attitudes to norms as governed by sanctions seem to be attitudes of individuals. There might therefore seem to be a link missing between the sanctioning of individual behaviour and the inequality of social positions. This missing link is, however, contained in the notion of social norm as we have used it so far.

It appears plausible to assume that the number of values capable of regulating human behaviour is unlimited. Our imagination permits the construction of an infinite number of customs and laws. Norms, that is socially established values, are therefore always a selection from the universe of possible established values. At this point, however, the further consideration which is relevant is that the selection of values for establishment as norms always involves an element of discrimination, not only against persons holding sociologically random moral convictions, but also against social positions which may debar their incumbents from conformity with established values.

Thus if gossip among neighbours becomes a norm, the professional woman necessarily becomes an outsider who cannot compete in prestige with ordinary housewives. If piecework rates are in operation in an industrial firm, the older worker is at a disadvantage by comparison with the younger ones, the woman by comparison with men. If it becomes the duty of the citizen to defend the ideology of the state, those who went to school before the establishment of this state cannot compete with those who have been born into it. Profession, woman, old man, young man, child of a given state are, however, all social positions which may be thought of independently of their individual human incumbents. Since every society discriminates in this sense against certain positions (and thereby all their incumbents, actual and potential), and since, moreover, every society uses sanctions to make such discrimination effective, social norms and sanctions are the basis not only of ephemeral individual rankings but also of lasting structures of social positions.

The origin of inequality is thus to be found in the existence in all human societies of norms of behaviour to which sanctions are attached. What we normally call the law, i.e. the system of laws and penalties, does not in ordinary usage comprise the whole range of the sociological notions of norm and sanction. If, however, we take the law in its widest sense as the epitome of all norms and sanctions, including those not codified, we may say that the law is both a necessary and a sufficient condition of social inequality. There is inequality because there is law; if there is law, there must also be inequality among men.

This is, of course, equally true in societies where equality before the law is recognized as a constitutional principle. If I may be allowed a somewhat flippant formulation which is nevertheless seriously meant, my proposed explanation of inequality means in the case of our own society that all men are equal *before* the law but they are no longer equal *after* it; i.e., after they have, as we put it, 'come in contact with' the law. So long as norms do not exist, and in so far as they do not effectively act upon people ('before the law'), there is no social stratification; once there are norms which impose inescapable requirements upon people's behaviour and once their actual behaviour is measured in terms of these norms ('after the law'), a rank order of social status is bound to emerge.

Important though it is to emphasize that by norms and sanctions we also mean laws and penalties in the sense of positive law.

the introduction of the legal system as an illustrative *pars pro toto* can itself be very misleading. Ordinarily, it is only the idea of punishment which we associate with legal norms as the guarantee of their obligatory character. The force of legal sanctions produces the distinction between the lawbreaker and those who succeed in never coming into conflict with any legal rule. Conformism in this sense is at best rewarded with the absence of penalties. Certainly, this crude division of 'conformists' and 'deviants' does constitute an element of social inequality, and it should be possible in principle to demonstrate in terms of legal norms the relation between legal sanctions and social stratification.

But an argument on these lines would reduce both concepts —sanction and stratification—to a rather feeble residual meaning. It is by no means necessary (although customary in ordinary language) to confine the concept of sanction to penalties. For the purpose of the present argument, at least, it is important on the contrary to recognize positive sanctions (rewards) in addition to negative sanctions (punishments) as mechanisms for enforcing conformity which are both equal in kind and similar in function. Only if we regard reward and punishment, incentive and threat as in this sense related instruments for the maintenance of social norms do we begin to see that the sanctioning of human behaviour in terms of social norms necessarily creates a system of inequality of rank and that social stratification is therefore an immediate result of the control of social behaviour by positive and negative sanctions. Apart from their immediate task of guaranteeing the normative patterns of social behaviour, sanctions always create almost unintentionally and as a by-product a rank order of prestige and wealth.

The presuppositions of this explanation are obvious. Using the concepts of the eighteenth century, one might describe them in terms of the social contract (*pacte d'association*) and the contract of government (*pacte de gouvernement*). The explanation sketched here presupposes that (1) every society is a moral community, and therefore recognizes norms which regulate the conduct of its members, and (2) there have to be sanctions connected with these norms which guarantee their obligatory character by acting as rewards for conformism and penalties for deviance.

It may perhaps be argued that by relating social stratification to these presuppositions we have removed our problem on to a

8

different level instead of explaining it. Indeed, it would seem necessary both from a philosophical and a sociological point of view, to ask some further questions. Where do the norms originate which regulate social behaviour? Under what conditions do these norms change in historical societies? Why must their obligatory character be enforced by sanctions? Is this in fact the case in all historical societies? I think, however, that independently of the solution of these questions, it constitutes a gain to have reduced social stratification to the existence of social norms backed by sanctions, since the derivative nature of the problem of inequality is thereby shown. In addition, the derivation suggested here has the advantage of leading back to presuppositions (the existence of norms and the necessity of sanctions) which at least in the context of sociological theory may be regarded as axiomatic, and which do not therefore require further analysis for the time being.

The origin of social inequality lies neither in human nature nor in dubious historical factors such as private property. It lies rather in certain features of all human societies which are, or can be conceived to be, necessary to them. Although the differentiation of social positions, the division of labour or, more generally, the multiplicity of roles, may be one such universal feature of all societies, it lacks the element of evaluation necessary for the explanation of distinctions of rank. Evaluative differentiation, the ordering of social positions and their incumbent scales of prestige or income, is effected only by the sanctioning of social behaviour in terms of normative expectations. Because there are norms and because sanctions are necessary to enforce conformity of human conduct, there has to be inequality of rank among men.

The explanation of inequality in terms of the necessity of enforcing the conformity of social behaviour to norms by the use of sanctions has certain consequences for the conceptual apparatus of sociological analysis. Social stratification in the sense in which I have used the term is above all a system of distributive status, i.e. a system of differential distribution of desired and scarce things. Honour and wealth, or, as we say to-day, prestige and income, may be the most general media of such differentiation of rank, but there is no reason to assume that it could not be effected according to entirely different criteria. As far as legitimate power is concerned, however, there is only one aspect from which it might be described as one of the differentiating characteristics of social stratification, namely patronage of offices or the distribution of power as a reward for certain qualities or merits. Thus the explanation of differences of rank in terms of the necessity of sanctions is not an explanation of the power structure of societies; it is, rather, an explanation of stratification in terms of the social structure of power and authority (using these terms to express Max Weber's distinction between *Macht* and *Herrschaft*). Logically, power and power structures precede—if the explanation of inequality attempted here is correct —the structures of social stratification.

It is an open and difficult question whether societies are conceivable whose system of norms and sanctions functions without an authority-structure to sustain it. Time and again, anthropologists have told us of 'tribes without rulers' and sociologists have invoked the notion of societies which can regulate themselves without power or authority. In opposition to such fantasies, I should tend with Max Weber to describe 'every order which is not based on the personal, free agreement of all involved' (i.e. every order that does not rest on the voluntary consensus of all its members) as 'enforced' (*oktroyiert*), i.e. based on authority and subordination.[1] Since a '*volonté de tous*' of this kind appears possible only in flights of fancy, we have to assume that a third fundamental category of sociological analysis belongs alongside the twin concepts of norm and sanction: that of institutionalized power. Society *means* that norms regulate human conduct; this regulation is guaranteed by the incentive or threat of sanctions; the possibility of imposing sanctions is the abstract core of all power. I am inclined to believe that all other categories of sociological analysis may be derived from the unequal but closely related trinity of norm, sanction and power. At any rate, this is true for the category of social stratification, which belongs therefore on a lower level of generality than that of power. All that is necessary to reveal the explosiveness of this analysis is to turn it into an empirical proposition: the system of inequality which we call social stratification is only a secondary consequence of the social structure of power.

The establishment of norms in a society means that conformity is rewarded and deviance punished. The sanctioning of con-

[1] Max Weber, *Wirtschaft und Gesellschaft* (Tübingen, 1956), I, p. 27.

formity and deviance in this sense means that the ruling groups of society have thrown their power on to the side of the maintenance of norms. Established norms are, in the last analysis, nothing but ruling norms, i.e. norms defended by the sanctioning agencies of society and those who control them. For the system of inequality, this means that the person who will be most favourably placed in society is the person who best succeeds in adapting himself to the ruling norms; and it also means, vice versa, that the established or ruling values of a society may be studied in their purest form by looking at its upper class. Whoever is not able or willing always to conform to the expectations of his society must not be surprised if the higher grades of prestige and income remain closed to him and if others overtake him who find it easier to conform. In this sense, every society honours the conformism which sustains it, i.e. its ruling groups; but by the same token, every society also produces within itself the resistance which leads to its supersession.

Naturally, the basic parallelism of conformist or deviant behaviour with high or low status is deflected and complicated in historical societies by many secondary factors (and in general, it must be emphasized that the explanation of inequality proposed here is not immediately intended to be an analysis of its history or its philosophy). Thus, the ascriptive character of the criteria determining social status in a given epoch (such as nobility or property) may bring about a kind of stratification lag, in the sense that status structures may lag behind changes in norms and power relations, so that the upper class of a bygone epoch may retain its status position for a while under new conditions. Yet normally we do not have to wait long for such processes as the '*déclassement* of the nobility' or the 'loss of function of property' which have occurred in several contemporary societies. If it is true—and there are good reasons to think so—that our own society is tending towards a period of 'meritocracy' as predicted by Michael Young, i.e. the rule of the possessors of diplomas and other entrance tickets issued by the educational system to the upper reaches of society, then the hypothesis of the stratification lag would suggest that in due course the members of the traditional upper strata (the nobility, the heirs to wealth and property) will have to worry about diplomas and academic titles in order to retain their position; for the ruling groups of every society have a tendency to try to adapt the existing system of social inequality to the established norms and values, i.e. their own. Nevertheless, despite this basic tendency we can never expect in historical societies full congruence between the scales of stratification and the structures of power.

The image of society which follows from the exceedingly general and abstract analysis intimated here is in two respects non-utopian and thereby anti-utopian as well. On the one hand, it differs from any explicit or concealed romanticism of a revolutionary Utopia á la Rousseau or Marx. If it is the case that inequalities among men follow from the very concept of societies as moral communities, then there cannot be, in the world of our experience, a society of absolute equals. Of course, equality before the law and equal suffrage, equal chances of education and other concrete equalities, are not only possible but in many countries real. But the idea of a society in which all distinctions of rank between men are abolished transcends what is sociologically possible and has its place in the sphere of poetic imagination alone. Wherever political programmes promise societies without classes or strata, a harmonious community of comrades who are all equals in rank, the reduction of all inequalities to functional differences, and the like, we have reason to be suspicious, if only because political promises are often merely a thin veil for the threat of terror and unfreedom. Wherever ruling groups or their ideologists try to tell us that in their society all men are in fact equals, we can rely on Orwell's suspicion that in this society 'some are more equal than others'.

The approach put forward here is in yet another sense a path out of Utopia. If we survey the explanations of inequality in recent American sociology—and this holds for Parsons and Barber as it does for Davis and Moore—we find that they betray a view of society from which there is no road leading to an understanding of the historical quality of social structures. In a less obvious sense this is also true, I think, of Rousseau and Marx; but it is more easily demonstrable by reference to recent sociological theory. The American functionalists tell us that we ought to look at societies as entities functioning without friction, and that therefore inequality among men (since it happens to exist) renders a contribution to this functioning. This point of view, however useful in other ways, may then lead to conclusions

like the following by Barber: 'Men have a sense of justice fulfilled and of virtue rewarded when they feel that they are fairly
ranked as superior and inferior by the value standards of their
own moral community.'[1] Even Barber's subsequent treatment
of the 'dysfunctions' of stratification cannot wipe out the impression that he is thinking of a society which does not need history
any more because everything has been settled in the best possible
way anyway: everybody, wherever he stands, is content with
his place in society, because a common value system unites all
men into a large and happy family.

It seems to me that an instrument of this kind may enable us
to understand Plato's Republic, but not a single real society in
history. Possibly, social inequality has some importance for the
integration of societies. But another consequence of its operation
seems rather more interesting. If the analysis sketched here
proves useful, inequality is closely related to that social constraint which grows out of sanctions and structures of power.
This would mean that the system of stratification, like sanctions
and structures of institutionalized power, always tends to its own
abolition. The assumption that those who are less favourably
placed in society will strive to realize a system of norms that
promises them a better rank is certainly more plausible and fruitful than the assumption that the poor in reputation and wealth
will also love their society for its justice. Since the 'value system'
of a society is common only in the sense of its universal validity,
and is in fact merely dominant, and since, therefore, the system
of social stratification is only a measure of the conformism in
behaviour of social groups, inequality becomes the sting that
serves to keep social structures alive. Inequality always means the
gain of one group at the expense of the others; thus every system
of social stratification carries protest against its principle and
seeds of its own supersession within itself. Since human society
without inequality is not realistically possible, and the complete
abolition of inequality is therefore excluded, the intrinsic explosiveness of every system of social stratification confirms the
general view that there cannot be an ideal, perfectly just and
therefore non-historical human society.

This is the place to recall once again Kant's critical remark
about Rousseau, that inequality is a 'rich source of much that is

[1] Barber, loc. cit., p. 7.

evil, but also of everything that is good'. There is certainly reason to regret that children are ashamed of their parents, that people are anxious and poor, that they suffer and are made unhappy and many other consequences of inequality. There are also many good reasons to strive against those historical and therefore, in an ultimate sense, arbitrary forces which erect insuperable barriers of caste or estate between men. That social inequality exists at all is, however, an impetus towards liberty because it guarantees the historical quality of societies. The perfectly egalitarian society is not only an unrealistic, it is also a terrible idea. Utopia is the home not of freedom, the for ever imperfect scheme for an uncertain future, but of the perfection either of terror or of absolute boredom.

6

THE IDEA OF EQUALITY

by Bernard Williams

THE idea of equality is used in political discussion both in statements of fact, or what purport to be statements of fact— that men *are* equal—and in statements of political principles or aims—that men *should be* equal, as at present they are not. The two can be, and often are, combined: the aim is then described as that of securing a state of affairs in which men are treated as the equal beings which they in fact already are, but are not already treated as being. In both these uses, the idea of equality notoriously encounters the same difficulty: that on one kind of interpretation the statements in which it figures are much too strong, and on another kind much too weak, and it is hard to find a satisfactory interpretation that lies between the two.[1]

To take first the supposed statement of fact: it has only too often been pointed out that to say that all men are equal in all those characteristics in respect of which it makes sense to say that men are equal or unequal, is a patent falsehood; and even if some more restricted selection is made of these characteristics, the statement does not look much better. Faced with this obvious objection, the defender of the claim that all men are equal is likely to offer a weaker interpretation. It is not, he may say, in their skill, intelligence, strength or virtue that men are equal, but merely in their being men: it is their common humanity that constitutes their equality. On this interpretation, we should not seek for some special characteristics in respect of which men are equal, but merely remind ourselves that they are all men. Now to this it might be objected that being men is not a respect in which men can strictly speaking be said to be *equal*; but, leaving that aside, there is the more immediate objection that if all that the statement does is to remind us that men are men, it does not do very much, and in particular does less than its proponents in

---

[1] For an illuminating discussion of this and related questions, see R. Wollheim and I. Berlin, *Equality*, Proceedings of the Aristotelian Society, Vol. LVI (1955-6), p. 281 seq.

political argument have wanted it to do. What looked like a
paradox has turned into a platitude.

I shall suggest in a moment that even in this weak form the
statement is not so vacuous as this objection makes it seem; but
it must be admitted that when the statement of equality ceases
to claim more than is warranted, it rather rapidly reaches the
point where it claims less than is interesting. A similar discomfiture tends to overcome the practical maxim of equality. It cannot be the aim of this maxim that all men should be treated alike
in all circumstances, or even that they should be treated alike as
much as possible. Granted that, however, there is no obvious
stopping point before the interpretation which makes the maxim
claim only that men should be treated alike in similar circumstances; and since 'circumstances' here must clearly include reference to what a man is, as well as to his purely external situation,
this comes very much to saying that for every difference in the
way men are treated, some general reason or principle of differentiation must be given. This may well be an important principle;
some indeed have seen in it, or in something very like it, an
essential element of morality itself.[1] But it can hardly be enough
to constitute the principle that was advanced in the name of
equality.¦ It would be in accordance with this principle, for
example, to treat black men differently from others just because
they were black, or poor men differently just because they were
poor, and this cannot accord with anyone's idea of equality.

In what follows I shall try to advance a number of considerations that can help to save the political notion of equality from
these extremes of absurdity and of triviality. These considerations are in fact often employed in political argument, but are
usually bundled together into an unanalysed notion of equality in
a manner confusing to the advocates, and encouraging to the
enemies, of that ideal. These considerations will not enable us
to define a distinct third interpretation of the statements which
use the notion of equality; it is rather that they enable us, starting
with the weak interpretations, to build up something that in
practice can have something of the solidity aspired to by the
strong interpretations. In this discussion, it will not be necessary
all the time to treat separately the supposedly factual application

[1] For instance, R. M. Hare: see his *Language of Morals*, Oxford: The Clarendon Press,
1952.

of the notion of equality, and its application in the maxim of action. Though it is sometimes important to distinguish them, and there are clear grounds for doing so, similar considerations often apply to both. The two go significantly together: on the one hand, the point of the supposedly factual assertion is to back up social ideals and programmes of political action; on the other hand—a rather less obvious point, perhaps—those political proposals have their force because they are regarded not as gratuitously egalitarian, aiming at equal treatment for reasons, for instance, of simplicity or tidiness, but as affirming an equality which is believed in some sense already to exist, and to be obscured or neglected by actual social arrangements.

1. *Common humanity.* The factual statement of men's equality was seen, when pressed, to retreat in the direction of merely asserting the equality of men as men; and this was thought to be trivial. It is certainly insufficient, but not, after all, trivial. That all men are human is, if a tautology, a useful one, serving as a reminder that those who belong anatomically to the species *homo sapiens*, and can speak a language, use tools, live in societies, can interbreed despite racial differences, etc., are also alike in certain other respects more likely to be forgotten. These respects are notably the capacity to feel pain, both from immediate physical causes and from various situations represented in perception and in thought; and the capacity to feel affection for others, and the consequences of this, connected with the frustration of this affection, loss of its objects, etc. The assertion that men are alike in the possession of these characteristics is, while indisputable and (it may be) even necessarily true, not trivial. For it is certain that there are political and social arrangements that systematically neglect these characteristics in the case of some groups of men, while being fully aware of them in the case of others; that is to say, they treat certain men as though they did not possess these characteristics, and neglect moral claims that arise from these characteristics and which would be admitted to arise from them.

Here it may be objected that the mere fact that ruling groups in certain societies treat other groups in this way does not mean that they neglect or overlook the characteristics in question. For, it may be suggested, they may well recognize the presence of these characteristics in the worse-treated group, but claim that in the case of that group, the characteristics do not give rise to any moral claim; the group being distinguished from other members of society in virtue of some further characteristic (for instance, by being black), this may be cited as the ground of treating them differently, whether they feel pain, affection, etc., or not.

This objection rests on the assumption, common to much moral philosophy that makes a sharp distinction between fact and value, that the question whether a certain consideration is *relevant* to a moral issue is an evaluative question: to state that a consideration is relevant or irrelevant to a certain moral question is, on this view, itself to commit oneself to a certain kind of moral principle or outlook. Thus, in the case under discussion, to say (as one would naturally say) that the fact that a man is black is, by itself, quite irrelevant to the issue of how he should be treated in respect of welfare, etc., would, on this view, be to commit to oneself to a certain sort of moral principle. This view, taken generally, seems to me quite certainly false. The principle that men should be differentially treated in respect of welfare merely on grounds of their colour is not a special sort of moral principle, but (if anything) a purely arbitrary assertion of will, like that of some Caligulan ruler who decided to execute everyone whose name contained three 'R's.

This point is in fact conceded by those who practice such things as colour discrimination. Few can be found who will explain their practice merely by saying, 'But they're black: and it is my moral principle to treat black men differently from others'. If any reasons are given at all, they will be reasons that seek to correlate the fact of blackness with certain other considerations which are at least candidates for relevance to the question of how a man should be treated: such as insensitivity, brute stupidity, ineducable irresponsibility, etc. Now these reasons are very often rationalizations, and the correlations claimed are either not really believed, or quite irrationally believed, by those who claim them. But this is a different point; the argument concerns what counts as a moral reason, and the rationalizer broadly agrees with others about what counts as such—the trouble with him is that his reasons are dictated by his policies, and not conversely. The Nazis' 'anthropologists' who tried to construct theories of Aryanism were paying, in very poor coin, the homage of irrationality to reason.

The question of relevance in moral reasons will arise again, in a different connexion, in this paper. For the moment its importance is that it gives a force to saying that those who neglect the moral claims of certain men that arise from their human capacity to feel pain, etc., are *overlooking* or *disregarding* those capacities; and are not just operating with a special moral principle, conceding the capacities to these men, but denying the moral claim. Very often, indeed, they have just persuaded themselves that the men in question have those capacities in a lesser degree. Here it is certainly to the point to assert the apparent platitude that these men are also human.

I have discussed this point in connexion with very obvious human characteristics of feeling pain and desiring affection. There are, however, other and less easily definable characteristics universal to humanity, which may all the more be neglected in political and social arrangements. For instance, there seems to be a characteristic which might be called 'a desire for self-respect'; this phrase is perhaps not too happy, in suggesting a particular culturally-limited, bourgeois value, but I mean by it a certain human desire to be identified with what one is doing, to be able to realize purposes of one's own, and not to be the instrument of another's will unless one has willingly accepted such a role. This is a very inadequate and in some ways rather empty specification of a human desire; to a better specification, both philosophical reflection and the evidences of psychology and anthropology would be relevant. Such investigations enable us to understand more deeply, in respect of the desire I have gestured towards and of similar characteristics, what it is to be human; and of what it is to be human, the apparently trivial statement of men's equality as men can serve as a reminder.

2. *Moral capacities.* So far we have considered respects in which men can be counted as all alike, which respects are, in a sense, negative: they concern the capacity to suffer, and certain needs that men have, and these involve men in moral relations as the recipients of certain kinds of treatment. It has certainly been a part, however, of the thought of those who asserted that men were equal, that there were more positive respects in which men were alike: that they were equal in certain things that they could do or achieve, as well as in things that they needed and could suffer. In respect of a whole range of abilities, from weight-

lifting to the calculus, the assertion is, as was noted at the beginning, not plausible, and has not often been supposed to be. It
has been held, however, that there are certain other abilities, both
less open to empirical test and more essential in moral connexions, for which it is true that men are equal. These are
certain sorts of moral ability or capacity, the capacity for virtue
or achievement of the highest kind of moral worth.

The difficulty with this notion is that of identifying any purely
moral capacities. Some human capacities are more relevant to
the achievement of a virtuous life than others: intelligence, a
capacity for sympathetic understanding, and a measure of
resoluteness would generally be agreed to be so. But these
capacities can all be displayed in non-moral connexions as well,
and in such connexions would naturally be thought to differ from
man to man like other natural capacities. That this is the fact
of the matter has been accepted by many thinkers, notably, for
instance, by Aristotle. But against this acceptance, there is a
powerful strain of thought that centres on a feeling of ultimate
and outrageous absurdity in the idea that the achievement of
the highest kind of moral worth should depend on natural
capacities, unequally and fortuitously distributed as they are; and
this feeling is backed up by the observation that these natural
capacities are not themselves the bearers of the moral worth,
since those that have them are as gifted for vice as for virtue.

This strain of thought has found many types of religious expression; but in philosophy it is to be found in its purest form in
Kant. Kant's view not only carries to the limit the notion that
moral worth cannot depend on contingencies, but also emphasizes, in its picture of the Kingdom of Ends, the idea of *respect*
which is owed to each man as a rational moral agent—and, since
men are equally such agents, is owed equally to all, unlike
admiration and similar attitudes, which are commanded unequally by men in proportion to their unequal possession of
different kinds of natural excellence. These ideas are intimately
connected in Kant, and it is not possible to understand his moral
theory unless as much weight is given to what he says about the
Kingdom of Ends as is always given to what he says about duty.

The very considerable consistency of Kant's view is bought at
what would generally be agreed to be a very high price. The
detachment of moral worth from all contingencies is achieved

only by making man's characteristic as a moral or rational agent a transcendental characteristic; man's capacity to will freely as a rational agent is not dependent on any empirical capacities he may have—and, in particular, is not dependent on empirical capacities which men may possess unequally—because, in the Kantian view, the capacity to be a rational agent is not itself an empirical capacity at all. Accordingly, the respect owed equally to each man as a member of the Kingdom of Ends is not owed to him in respect of any empirical characteristics that he may possess, but solely in respect of the transcendental characteristic of being a free and rational will. The ground of the respect owed to each man thus emerges in the Kantian theory as a kind of secular analogue of the Christian conception of the respect owed to all men as equally children of God. Though secular, it is equally metaphysical: in neither case is it anything empirical *about* men that constitutes the ground of equal respect.

This transcendental, Kantian conception cannot provide any solid foundation for the notions of equality among men, or of equality of respect owed to them. Apart from the general difficulties of such transcendental conceptions, there is the obstinate fact that the concept of 'moral agent', and the concepts allied to it such as that of responsibility, do and must have an empirical basis. It seems empty to say that all men are equal as moral agents, when the question, for instance, of men's responsibility for their actions is one to which empirical considerations are clearly relevant, and one which moreover receives answers in terms of different degrees of responsibility and different degrees of rational control over action. To hold a man responsible for his actions is presumably the central case of treating him as a moral agent, and if men are not treated as equally responsible, there is not much left to their equality as moral agents.

If, without its transcendental basis, there is not much left to men's equality as moral agents, is there anything left to the notion of the *respect* owed to all men? This notion of 'respect' is both complex and unclear, and I think it needs, and would repay, a good deal of investigation. Some content can, however, be attached to it; even if it is some way away from the ideas of moral agency. There certainly is a distinction, for instance, between regarding a man's life, actions or character from an æsthetic or technical point of view, and regarding them from a point of view which is concerned primarily with what it is *for him* to live that life and do those actions in that character. Thus from the technological point of view, a man who has spent his life in trying to make a certain machine which could not possibly work is merely a failed inventor, and in compiling a catalogue of those whose efforts have contributed to the sum of technical achievement, one must 'write him off': the fact that he devoted himself to this useless task with constant effort and so on, is merely irrelevant. But from a human point of view, it is clearly not irrelevant: we are concerned with him, not merely as 'a failed inventor', but as a man who wanted to be a successful inventor. Again, in professional relations and the world of work, a man operates, and his activities come up for criticism, under a variety of professional or technical titles, such as 'miner' or 'agricultural labourer' or 'junior executive'. The technical or professional attitude is that which regards the man solely under that title, the human approach that which regards him as *a man who has* that title (among others), willingly, unwillingly, through lack of alternatives, with pride, etc.

That men should be regarded from the human point of view, and not merely under these sorts of titles, is part of the content that might be attached to Kant's celebrated injunction 'treat each man as an end in himself, and never as a means only'. But I do not think that this is all that should be seen in this injunction, or all that is concerned in the notion of 'respect'. What is involved in the examples just given could be explained by saying that each man is owed an effort at identification: that he should not be regarded as the surface to which a certain label can be applied, but one should try to see the world (including the label) from his point of view. This injunction will be based on, though not of course fully explained by, the notion that men are conscious beings who necessarily have intentions and purposes and see what they are doing in a certain light. But there seem to be further injunctions connected with the Kantian maxim, and with the notion of 'respect', that go beyond these considerations. There are forms of exploiting men or degrading them which would be thought to be excluded by these notions, but which cannot be excluded merely by considering how the exploited or degraded men see the situation. For it is precisely a mark of extreme exploitation or degradation that those who suffer it do *not* see themselves differently from the way they are seen by the exploiters; either they do not see themselves as anything at all, or they acquiesce passively in the role for which they have been cast. Here we evidently need something more than the precept that one should respect and try to understand another man's consciousness of his own activities; it is also that one may not suppress or destroy that consciousness.

All these I must confess to be vague and inconclusive considerations, but we are dealing with a vague notion: one, however, that we possess, and attach value to. To try to put these matters properly in order would be itself to try to reach conclusions about several fundamental questions of moral philosophy. What we must ask here is what these ideas have to do with equality. We started with the notion of men's equality as moral agents. This notion appeared unsatisfactory, for different reasons, in both an empirical and a transcendental interpretation. We then moved, *via* the idea of 'respect', to the different notion of regarding men not merely under professional, social or technical titles, but with consideration of their own views and purposes. This notion has at least this much to do with equality: that the titles which it urges us to look behind are the conspicuous bearers of social, political and technical *inequality*, whether they refer to achievement (as in the example of the inventor), or to social roles (as in the example of work titles). It enjoins us not to let our fundamental attitudes to men be dictated by the criteria of technical success or social position, and not to take them at the value carried by these titles and by the structures in which these titles place them. This does not mean, of course, that the more fundamental view that should be taken of men is in the case of every man the same: on the contrary. But it does mean that each man is owed the effort of understanding, and that in achieving it, each man is to be (as it were) abstracted from certain conspicuous structures of inequality in which we find him.

These injunctions are based on the proposition that men are beings who are necessarily to some extent conscious of themselves and of the world they live in. (I omit here, as throughout the discussion, the clinical cases of people who are mad or mentally defective, who always constitute special exceptions to what is in general true of men.) This proposition does not assert that men are equally conscious of themselves and of their situation. It was precisely one element in the notion of exploitation considered above that such consciousness can be decreased by social action and the environment; we may add that it can similarly be increased. But men are at least potentially conscious, to an indeterminate degree, of their situation and of what I have called their 'titles', are capable of reflectively standing back from the roles and positions in which they are cast; and this reflective consciousness may be enhanced or diminished by their social condition.

It is this last point that gives these considerations a particular relevance to the political aims of egalitarianism. The mere idea of regarding men from 'the human point of view', while it has a good deal to do with politics, and a certain amount to do with equality, has nothing specially to do with political equality. One could, I think, accept this as an ideal, and yet favour, for instance, some kind of hierarchical society, so long as the hierarchy maintained itself without compulsion, and there was human understanding between the orders. In such a society, each man would indeed have a very conspicuous title which related him to the social structure; but it might be that most people were aware of the human beings behind the titles, and found each other for the most part content, or even proud, to have the titles that they had. I do not know whether anything like this has been true of historical hierarchical societies; but I can see no inconsistency in someone's espousing it as an ideal, as some (influenced in many cases by a sentimental picture of the Middle Ages) have done. Such a person would be one who accepted the notion of 'the human view', the view of each man as something more than his title, as a valuable ideal, but rejected the ideals of political equality.

Once, however, one accepts the further notion that the degree of man's consciousness about such things as his role in society is itself in some part the product of social arrangements, and that it can be increased, this ideal of a stable hierarchy must, I think, disappear. For what keeps stable hierarchies together is the idea of necessity, that it is somehow foreordained or inevitable that there should be these orders; and this idea of necessity must be eventually undermined by the growth of people's reflective consciousness about their role, still more when it is combined with the thought that what they and the others have always

9

thought about their roles in the social system was the product of the social system itself.

It might be suggested that a certain man who admitted that people's consciousness of their roles was conditioned in this way might nevertheless believe in the hierarchical ideal: but that in order to preserve the society of his ideal, he would have to make sure that the idea of the conditioning of consciousness did not get around to too many people, and that their consciousness about their roles did not increase too much. But such a view is really a very different thing from its naïve predecessor. Such a man, no longer himself 'immersed' in the system, is beginning to think in terms of compulsion, the deliberate *prevention* of the growth of consciousness, which is a poisonous element absent from the original ideal. Moreover, his attitude (or that of rulers similar to himself) towards the other people in the ideal society must now contain an element of condescension or contempt, since he will be aware that their acceptance of what they suppose to be necessity is a delusion. This is alien to the spirit of human understanding on which the original ideal was based. The hierarchical idealist cannot escape the fact that certain things which can be done decently without self-consciousness can, with self-consciousness, be done only hypocritically. This is why even the rather hazy and very general notions that I have tried to bring together in this section contain some of the grounds of the ideal of political equality.

3. *Equality in unequal circumstances.* The notion of equality is invoked not only in connexions where men are claimed in some sense all to be equal, but in connexions where they are agreed to be unequal, and the question arises of the distribution of, or access to, certain goods to which their inequalities are relevant. It may be objected that the notion of equality is in fact misapplied in these connexions, and that the appropriate ideas are those of fairness or justice, in the sense of what Aristotle called 'distributive justice', where (as Aristotle argued) there is no question of regarding or treating everyone as equal, but solely a question of distributing certain goods in proportion to men's recognized inequalities.

I think it is reasonable to say against this objection that there is some foothold for the notion of equality even in these cases. It is useful here to make a rough distinction between two different types of inequality, inequality of *need* and inequality of *merit*, with a corresponding distinction between goods—on the one hand, goods demanded by the need, and on the other, goods that can be earned by the merit. In the case of needs, such as the need for medical treatment in case of illness, it can be presumed for practical purposes that the persons who have the need actually desire the goods in question, and so the question can indeed be regarded as one of distribution in a simple sense, the satisfaction of an existing desire. In the case of merit, such as for instance the possession of abilities to profit from a university education, there is not the same presumption that everyone who has the merit has the desire for the goods in question, though it may, of course, be the case. Moreover, the good of a university education may be legitimately, even if hopelessly, desired by those who do not possess the merit; while medical treatment or unemployment benefit are either not desired, or not legitimately desired, by those who are not ill or unemployed, i.e. do not have the appropriate need. Hence the distribution of goods in accordance with merit has a competitive aspect lacking in the case of distribution according to need. For these reasons, it is appropriate to speak, in the case of merit, not only of the distribution of the good, but of the distribution of the opportunity of achieving the good. But this, unlike the good itself, can be said to be distributed equally to everybody, and so one does encounter a notion of *general* equality, much vaunted in our society to-day, the notion of equality of opportunity.

Before considering this notion further, it is worth noticing certain resemblances and differences between the cases of need and of merit. In both cases, we encounter the matter (mentioned before in this paper) of the relevance of reasons. Leaving aside preventive medicine, the proper ground of distribution of medical care is ill health: this is a necessary truth. Now in very many societies, while ill health may work as a necessary condition of receiving treatment, it does not work as a sufficient condition, since such treatment costs money, and not all who are ill have the money; hence the possession of sufficient money becomes in fact an additional necessary condition of actually receiving treatment. Yet more extravagantly, money may work as a sufficient condition by itself, without any medical need, in which case the reasons that actually operate for the receipt of this good are just

totally irrelevant to its nature; however, since only a few hypo-
chrondriacs desire treatment when they do not need it, this is,
in this case, a marginal phenomenon.

When we have the situation in which, for instance, wealth is
a further necessary condition of the receipt of medical treatment,
we can once more apply the notions of equality and inequality:
not now in connexion with the inequality between the well and
the ill, but in connexion with the inequality between the rich ill
and the poor ill, since we have straightforwardly the situation of
those whose needs are the same not receiving the same treatment,
though the needs are the ground of the treatment. This is an
irrational state of affairs.

It may be objected that I have neglected an important distinction here. For, it may be said, I have treated the ill health and
the possession of money as though they were regarded on the
same level, as 'reasons for receiving medical treatment', and this is
a muddle. The ill health is, at most, a ground of the *right* to receive medical treatment; whereas the money is, in certain circumstances, the causally necessary condition of securing the right,
which is a different thing. There is something in the distinction
that this objection suggests: there is a distinction between a man's
rights, the reasons why he should be treated in a certain way, and
his power to secure those rights, the reasons why he can in fact
get what he deserves. But this objection does not make it
inappropriate to call the situation of inequality an 'irrational'
situation: it just makes it clearer what is meant by so calling it.
What is meant is that it is a situation in which reasons are insufficiently *operative*; it is a situation insufficiently controlled by
reasons—and hence by reason itself. The same point arises with
another form of equality and equal rights, equality before the law.
It may be said that in a certain society, men have equal rights to
a fair trial, to seek redress from the law for wrongs committed
against them, etc. But if a fair trial or redress from the law can
be secured in that society only by moneyed and educated persons,
to insist that everyone *has* this right, though only these particular
persons can *secure* it, rings hollow to the point of cynicism: we
are concerned not with the abstract existence of rights, but with
the extent to which those rights govern what actually happens.

Thus when we combine the notions of the *relevance* of reasons,
and the *operativeness* of reasons, we have a genuine moral weapon,

which can be applied in cases of what is appropriately called unequal treatment, even where one is not concerned with the equality of people as a whole. This represents a strengthening of the very weak principle mentioned at the beginning of this paper, that for every difference in the way men are treated, a reason should be given: when one requires further that the reasons should be relevant, and that they should be socially operative, this really says something.

Similar considerations will apply to cases of merit. There is, however, an important difference between the cases of need and merit, in respect of the relevance of reasons. It is a matter of logic that particular sorts of needs constitute a reason for receiving particular sorts of good. It is, however, in general a much more disputable question whether certain sorts of merit constitute a reason for receiving certain sorts of good. For instance, let it be agreed, for the sake of argument, that the public school system provides a superior type of education, which it is a good thing to receive. It is then objected that access to this type of education is unequally distributed, because of its cost: among boys of equal promise or intelligence, only those from wealthy homes will receive it, and, indeed, boys of little promise or intelligence will receive it, if from wealthy homes; and this, the objection continues, is irrational.

The defender of the public school system might give two quite different sorts of answer to this objection; besides, that is, the obvious type of answer which merely disputes the facts alleged by the objector. One is the sort of answer already discussed in the case of need: that we may agree, perhaps, that boys of promise and intelligence have a right to a superior education, but in actual economic circumstances, this right cannot always be secured, etc. The other is more radical: this would dispute the premise of the objection that intelligence and promise are, at least by themselves, the grounds for receiving this superior type of education. While perhaps not asserting that wealth itself constitutes the ground, the defender of the system may claim that other characteristics significantly correlated with wealth are such grounds; or, again, that it is the purpose of this sort of school to maintain a tradition of leadership, and the best sort of people to maintain this will be people whose fathers were at such schools. We need not try to pursue such arguments here. The important point is that, while there can indeed be genuine disagreements about what constitutes the relevant sort of merit in such cases, such disagreements must also be disagreements about the nature of the good to be distributed. As such, the disagreements do not occur in a vacuum, nor are they logically free from restrictions. There is only a limited number of reasons for which education could be regarded as a good, and a limited number of purposes which education could rationally be said to serve; and to the limitations on this question, there correspond limitations on the sorts of merit or personal characteristic which could be rationally cited as grounds of access to this good. Here again we encounter a genuine strengthening of the very weak principle that, for differences in the way that people are treated, reasons should be given.

We may return now to the notion of equality of opportunity; understanding this in the normal political sense of equality of opportunity for *everyone in society* to secure certain goods. This notion is introduced into political discussion when there is question of the access to certain goods which, first, even if they are not desired by everyone in society, are desired by large numbers of people in all sections of society (either for themselves, or, as in the case of education, for their children), or would be desired by people in all sections of society if they knew about the goods in question and thought it possible for them to attain them; second, are goods which people may be said to earn or achieve; and third, are goods which not all the people who desire them can have. This third condition covers at least three different cases, however, which it is worth distinguishing. Some desired goods, like positions of prestige, management, etc., are *by their very nature* limited: whenever there are some people who are in command or prestigious positions, there are necessarily others who are not. Other goods are *contingently* limited, in the sense that there are certain conditions of access to them which in fact not everyone satisfies, but there is no intrinsic limit to the numbers who might gain access to it by satisfying the conditions: university education is usually regarded in this light nowadays, as something which requires certain conditions of admission to it which in fact not everyone satisfies, but which an indefinite proportion of people might satisfy. Third, there are goods which are *fortuitously* limited, in the sense that although everyone or large numbers of people satisfy the conditions of access to them, there is just not enough of them to go round; so some more stringent conditions or system of rationing have to be imposed, to govern access in an imperfect situation. A good can, of course, be both contingently and fortuitously limited at once: when, due to shortage of supply, not even the people who are qualified to have it, limited in numbers though they are, can in every case have it. It is particularly worth distinguishing those kinds of limitation, as there can be significant differences of view about the way in which a certain good is limited. While most would now agree that high education is contingently limited, a Platonic view would regard it as necessarily limited.

Now the notion of equality of opportunity might be said to be the notion that a limited good shall in fact be allocated on grounds which do not *a priori* exclude any section of those that desire it. But this formulation is not really very clear. For suppose grammar school education (a good perhaps contingently, and certainly fortuitously, limited) is allocated on grounds of ability as tested at the age of 11; this would normally be advanced as an example of equality of opportunity, as opposed to a system of allocation on grounds of parents' wealth. But does not the criterion of ability exclude *a priori* a certain section of people, viz. those that are not able—just as the other excludes *a priori* those who are not wealthy? Here it will obviously be said that this was not what was meant by *a priori* exclusion: the present argument just equates this with exclusion of anybody, i.e. with the mere existence of some condition that has to be satisfied. What then is *a priori* exclusion? It must mean exclusion on grounds *other* than those appropriate or rational for the good in question. But this still will not do as it stands. For it would follow from this that so long as those allocating grammar school education on grounds of wealth thought that such grounds were appropriate or rational (as they might in one of the ways discussed above in connexion with public schools), they could sincerely describe their system as one of equality of opportunity—which is absurd.

Hence it seems that the notion of equality of opportunity is more complex than it first appeared. It requires not merely that there should be no exclusion from access on grounds other than those appropriate or rational for the good in question, but that the grounds considered appropriate for the good should them-

selves be such that people from all sections of society have an
equal chance of satisfying them. What now is a 'section of
society'? Clearly we cannot include under this term sections of
the populace identified just by the characteristics which figure in
the grounds for allocating the good—since, once more, any
grounds at all must exclude some section of the populace. But
what about sections identified by characteristics which are
correlated with the grounds of exclusion? There are important
difficulties here: to illustrate this, it may help first to take an
imaginary example.

Suppose that in a certain society great prestige is attached to
membership of a warrior class, the duties of which require great
physical strength. This class has in the past been recruited from
certain wealthy families only; but egalitarian reformers achieve
a change in the rules, by which warriors are recruited from all
sections of the society, on the results of a suitable competition.
The effect of this, however, is that the wealthy families still provide virtually all the warriors, because the rest of the populace
is so under-nourished by reason of poverty that their physical
strength is inferior to that of the wealthy and well nourished.
The reformers protest that equality of opportunity has not really
been achieved; the wealthy reply that in fact it has, and that the
poor now have the opportunity of becoming warriors—it is just
bad luck that their characteristics are such that they do not pass
the test. 'We are not,' they might say, 'excluding anyone *for*
being poor; we exclude people for being weak, and it is unfortunate that those who are poor are also weak.'

This answer would seem to most people feeble, and even
cynical. This is for reasons similar to those discussed before in
connexion with equality before the law; that the supposed
equality of opportunity is quite empty—indeed, one may say
that it does not really exist—unless it is made more effective than
this. For one knows that it could be made more effective; one
knows that there is a causal connexion between being poor and
being undernourished, and between being undernourished and
being physically weak. One supposes further that something
could be done—subject to whatever economic conditions obtain
in the imagined society—to alter the distribution of wealth. All
this being so, the appeal by the wealthy to the 'bad luck' of the
poor must appear as disingenuous.

It seems then that a system of allocation will fall short of equality of opportunity if the allocation of the good in question in fact works out unequally or disproportionately between different sections of society, if the unsuccessful sections are under a disadvantage which could be removed by further reform or social action. This was very clear in the imaginary example that was given, because the causal connexions involved are simple and well known. In actual fact, however, the situations of this type that arise are more complicated, and it is easier to overlook the causal connexions involved. This is particularly so in the case of educational selection, where such slippery concepts as 'intellectual ability' are involved. It is a known fact that the system of selection for grammar schools by the '11+' examination favours children in direct proportion to their social class, the children of professional homes having proportionately greater success than those from working class homes. We have every reason to suppose that these results are the product, in good part, of environmental factors; and we further know that imaginative social reform, both of the primary educational system and of living conditions, would favourably effect those environmental factors. In these circumstances, this system of educational selection falls short of equality of opportunity.[1]

This line of thought points to a connexion between the idea of equality of opportunity, and the idea of equality of persons, which is stronger than might at first be suspected. We have seen that one is not really offering equality of opportunity to Smith and Jones if one contents oneself with applying the same criteria to Smith and Jones at, say, the age of 11; what one is doing there is to apply the same criteria to Smith as affected by favourable conditions and to Jones as affected by unfavourable but curable conditions. Here there is a necessary pressure to equal up the conditions: to give *Smith* and *Jones* equality of opportunity involves regarding their conditions, where curable, as themselves part of what is done to Smith and Jones, and not part of Smith and Jones themselves. Their identity, for these purposes, does not include their curable environment, which is itself unequal and a contributor of inequality. This abstraction of persons in themselves from unequal environments is a way, if not

[1] See on this C. A. R. Crosland, *Public Schools and English Education*, *Encounter*, July 1961.

of regarding them as equal, at least of moving recognizably in that direction; and is itself involved in equality of opportunity.

One might speculate about how far this movement of thought might go. The most conservative user of the notion of equality of opportunity is, if sincere, prepared to abstract the individual from some effects of his environment. We have seen that there is good reason to press this further, and to allow that the individuals whose opportunities are to be equal should be abstracted from more features of social and family background. Where should this stop? Should it even stop at the boundaries of heredity? Suppose it were discovered that when all curable environmental disadvantages had been dealt with, there was a residual genetic difference in brain constitution, for instance, which was cor-related with differences in desired types of ability; but that the brain constitution could in fact be changed by an operation.[1] Suppose further that the wealthier classes could afford such an operation for their children, so that they always came out top of the educational system; would we then think that poorer children did not have equality of opportunity, because they had no opportunity to get rid of their genetic disadvantages?

Here we might think that our notion of personal identity itself was beginning to give way; we might well wonder *who were* the people whose advantages and disadvantages were being dis-cussed in this way. But it would be wrong, I think, to try to solve this problem simply by saying that in the supposed circum-stances our notion of personal identity would have collapsed in such a way that we could no longer speak of the individuals involved—in the end, we could still pick out the individuals by spatio-temporal criteria, if no more. Our objections against the system suggested in this fantasy must, I think, be moral rather than metaphysical. They need not concern us here. What is interesting about the fantasy, perhaps, is that if one reached this state of affairs, the individuals would be regarded as in all respects equal in themselves—for in themselves they would be, as it were, pure subjects or bearers of predicates, everything else about them, including their genetic inheritance, being regarded as a fortuitous and changeable characteristic. In these circumstances, where

---

[1] A yet more radical situation — but one more likely to come about — would be that in which an individual's characteristics could be *pre-arranged* by interference with the genetic material. The dizzying consequences of this I shall not try to explore.

everything about a person is controllable, equality of opportunity and absolute equality seem to coincide; and this itself illustrates something about the notion of equality of opportunity.

I said that we need not discuss here the moral objections to the kind of world suggested in this fantasy. There is, however, one such point that is relevant to the different aspects of equality that have been discussed in this paper as a whole. One objection that we should instinctively feel about the fantasy world is that far too much emphasis was being placed on achieving high ability; that the children were just being regarded as locations of abilities. I think we should still feel this even if everybody (with results hard to imagine) was treated in this way; when not everybody was so treated, the able would also be more successful than others, and those very concerned with producing the ability would probably also be over-concerned with success. The moral objections to the excessive concern with such aims are, interestingly, not unconnected with the ideal of equality itself; they are connected with equality in the sense discussed in the earlier sections of this paper, the equality of human beings despite their differences, and in particular with the complex of notions considered in the second section under the heading of 'respect'.

This conflict within the ideals of equality arises even without resort to the fantasy world. It exists to-day in the feeling that a thorough-going emphasis on equality of opportunity must destroy a certain sense of common humanity which is itself an ideal of equality.[1] The ideals that are felt to be in conflict with equality of opportunity are not necessarily other ideals of equality —there may be an independent appeal to the values of community life, or to the moral worth of a more integrated and less competitive society. Nevertheless, the idea of equality itself is often invoked in this connexion, and not, I think, inappropriately.

If the idea of equality ranges as widely as I have suggested, this type of conflict is bound to arise with it. It is an idea which, on the one hand, is invoked in connexion with the distribution of certain goods, some at least of which are bound to confer on their possessors some preferred status or prestige. On the other hand, the idea of equality of respect is one which urges us to give less consideration to those structures in which people enjoy

[1] See, for example, Michael Young, *The Rise of the Meritocracy*, London: Thames and Hudson, 1958.

status or prestige, and to consider people independently of those goods, on the distribution of which equality of opportunity precisely focuses our, and their, attention. There is perhaps nothing formally incompatible in these two applications of the idea of equality: one might hope for a society in which there existed both a fair, rational and appropriate distribution of these goods, and no contempt, condescension or lack of human communication between persons who were more and less successful recipients of the distribution. Yet in actual fact, there are deep psychological and social obstacles to the realization of this hope; as things are, the competitiveness and considerations of prestige that surround the first application of equality certainly militate against the second. How far this situation is inevitable, and how far in an economically developed and dynamic society, in which certain skills and talents are necessarily at a premium, the obstacles to a wider realization of equality might be overcome, I do not think that we know: these are in good part questions of psychology and sociology, to which we do not have the answers.

When one is faced with the spectacle of the various elements of the idea of equality pulling in these different directions, there is a strong temptation, if one does not abandon the idea altogether, to abandon some of its elements: to claim, for instance, that equality of opportunity is the only ideal that is at all practicable, and equality of respect a vague and perhaps nostalgic illusion; or, alternatively, that equality of respect is genuine equality, and equality of opportunity an inegalitarian betrayal of the ideal— all the more so if it were thoroughly pursued, as now it is not. To succumb to either of these simplifying formulæ would, I think, be a mistake. Certainly, a highly rational and efficient application of the ideas of equal opportunity, unmitigated by the other considerations, could lead to a quite inhuman society (if it worked—which, granted a well-known desire of parents to secure a position for their children at least as good as their own, is unlikely). On the other hand, an ideal of equality of respect that made no contact with such things as the economic needs of society for certain skills, and human desire for some sorts of prestige, would be condemned to a futile Utopianism, and to having no rational effect on the distribution of goods, position and power that would inevitably proceed. If, moreover, as I have suggested, it is not really known how far, by new forms of social structure and of education, these conflicting claims might be reconciled, it is all the more obvious that we should not throw one set of claims out of the window; but should rather seek, in each situation, the best way of eating and having as much cake as possible. It is an uncomfortable situation, but the discomfort is just that of genuine political thought. It is no greater with equality than it is with liberty, or any other noble and substantial political ideal.

7

JUSTICE AS FAIRNESS[1]

by John Rawls

I

IT might seem at first sight that the concepts of justice and fairness are the same, and that there is no reason to distinguish them, or to say that one is more fundamental than the other. I think that this impression is mistaken. In this paper I wish to show that the fundamental idea in the concept of justice is fairness; and I wish to offer an analysis of the concept of justice from this point of view. To bring out the force of this claim, and the analysis based upon it, I shall then argue that it is this aspect of justice for which utilitarianism, in its classical form, is unable to account, but which is expressed, even if misleadingly, by the idea of the social contract.

To start with I shall develop a particular conception of justice by stating and commenting upon two principles which specify it, and by considering the circumstances and conditions under which they may be thought to arise. The principles defining this conception, and the conception itself, are, of course, familiar. It may be possible, however, by using the notion of fairness as a framework, to assemble and to look at them in a new way. Before stating this conception, however, the following preliminary matters should be kept in mind.

Throughout I consider justice only as a virtue of social institutions, or what I shall call practices.[2] The principles of justice are regarded as formulating restrictions as to how practices may define positions and offices, and assign thereto powers and liabilities, rights and duties. Justice as a virtue of particular actions or

---

[1] This article originally appeared in the *Philosophical Review*, 1958. Some footnotes have been omitted, others abbreviated, and the last paragraph of Section III has been revised.

[2] I use the word 'practice' throughout as a sort of technical term meaning any form of activity specified by a system of rules which defines offices, roles, moves, penalties, defences, and so on, and which gives the activity its structure. As examples one may think of games and rituals, trials and parliaments, markets and systems of property. I have attempted a partial analysis of the notion of a practice in a paper 'Two Concepts of Rules', *Philosophical Review*, LXIV (1955), 3–32.

of persons I do not take up at all. It is important to distinguish
these various subjects of justice, since the meaning of the concept
varies according to whether it is applied to practices, particular
actions, or persons. These meanings are, indeed, connected, but
they are not identical. I shall confine my discussion to the
sense of justice as applied to practices, since this sense is the
basic one. Once it is understood, the other senses should go
quite easily.

Justice is to be understood in its customary sense as representing
but *one* of the many virtues of social institutions, for these may be
antiquated, inefficient, degrading, or any number of other things,
without being unjust. Justice is not to be confused with an all-
inclusive vision of a good society; it is only one part of any such
conception. It is important, for example, to distinguish that sense
of equality which is an aspect of the concept of justice from that
sense of equality which belongs to a more comprehensive social
ideal. There may well be inequalities which one concedes are
just, or at least not unjust, but which, nevertheless, one wishes, on
other grounds, to do away with. I shall focus attention, then, on
the usual sense of justice in which it is essentially the elimination
of arbitrary distinctions and the establishment, within the structure of a practice, of a proper balance between competing claims.

Finally, there is no need to consider the principles discussed
below as *the* principles of justice. For the moment it is sufficient
that they are typical of a family of principles normally associated
with the concept of justice. The way in which the principles of
this family resemble one another, as shown by the background
against which they may be thought to arise, will be made clear
by the whole of the subsequent argument.

II

The conception of justice which I want to develop may be
stated in the form of two principles as follows: first, each person
participating in a practice, or affected by it, has an equal right
to the most extensive liberty compatible with a like liberty for all;
and second, inequalities are arbitrary unless it is reasonable to
expect that they will work out for everyone's advantage, and
provided the positions and offices to which they attach, or from
which they may be gained, are open to all. These principles

express justice as a complex of three ideas: liberty, equality, and reward for services contributing to the common good.[1]

The term 'person' is to be construed variously depending on the circumstances. On some occasions it will mean human individuals, but in others it may refer to nations, provinces, business firms, churches, teams, and so on. The principles of justice apply in all these instances, although there is a certain logical priority to the case of human individuals. As I shall use the term 'person', it will be ambiguous in the manner indicated.

The first principle holds, of course, only if other things are equal: that is, while there must always be a justification for departing from the initial position of equal liberty (which is defined by the pattern of rights and duties, powers and liabilities, established by a practice), and the burden of proof is placed on him who would depart from it, nevertheless, there can be, and often there is, a justification for doing so. Now, that similar particular cases, as defined by a practice, should be treated similarly as they arise, is part of the very concept of a practice; it is involved in the notion of an activity in accordance with rules. The first principle expresses an analogous conception, but as applied to the structure of practices themselves. It holds, for example, that there is a presumption against the distinctions and classifications made by legal systems and other practices to the extent that they infringe on the original and equal liberty of the persons participating in them. The second principle defines how this presumption may be rebutted.

It might be argued at this point that justice requires only an equal liberty. If, however, a greater liberty were possible for all without loss or conflict, then it would be irrational to settle on a lesser liberty. There is no reason for circumscribing rights unless their exercise would be incompatible, or would render the practice

---

[1] These principles are, of course, well known in one form or another and appear in many analyses of justice even where the writers differ widely on other matters. Thus if the principle of equal liberty is commonly associated with Kant (see *The Philosophy of Law*, tr. by W. Hastie, Edinburgh, 1887, pp. 56 f.), it may be claimed that it can also be found in J. S. Mill's *On Liberty* and elsewhere, and in many other liberal writers. Recently H. L. A. Hart has argued for something like it in his paper 'Are There Any Natural Rights?', *Philosophical Review*, LXIV (1955), 175–91. The injustice of inequalities which are not won in return for a contribution to the common advantage is, of course, widespread in political writings of all sorts. The conception of justice here discussed is distinctive, if at all, only in selecting these two principles in this form; but for another similar analysis, see the discussion by W. D. Lamont, *The Principles of Moral Judgment* (Oxford, 1946), ch. v.

defining them less effective. Therefore no serious distortion of the concept of justice is likely to follow from including within it the concept of the greatest equal liberty.

The second principle defines what sorts of inequalities are permissible; it specifies how the presumption laid down by the first principle may be put aside. Now by inequalities it is best to understand not *any* differences between offices and positions, but differences in the benefits and burdens attached to them either directly or indirectly, such as prestige and wealth, or liability to taxation and compulsory services. Players in a game do not protest against there being different positions, such as batter, pitcher, catcher, and the like, nor to there being various privileges and powers as specified by the rules; not do the citizens of a country object to there being the different offices of government such as president, senator, governor, judge, and so on, each with their special rights and duties. It is not differences of this kind that are normally thought of as inequalities, but differences in the resulting distribution established by a practice, or made possible by it, of the things men strive to attain or avoid. Thus they may complain about the pattern of honours and rewards set up by a practice (e.g. the privileges and salaries of government officials) or they may object to the distribution of power and wealth which results from the various ways in which men avail themselves of the opportunities allowed by it (e.g. the concentration of wealth which may develop in a free price system allowing large entre- preneurial or speculative gains).

It should be noted that the second principle holds that an inequality is allowed only if there is reason to believe that the practice with the inequality, or resulting in it, will work for the advantage of *every* party engaging in it. Here it is important to stress that *every* party must gain from the inequality. Since the principle applies to practices, it implies that the representative man in every office or position defined by a practice, when he views it as a going concern, must find it reasonable to prefer his condition and prospects with the inequality to what they would be under the practice without it. The principle excludes, therefore, the justification of inequalities on the grounds that the disad- vantages of those in one position are outweighed by the greater advantages of those in another position. This rather simple restriction is the main modification I wish to make in the utili-

10

tarian principle as usually understood. When coupled with the notion of a practice, it is a restriction of consequence, and one which some utilitarians, e.g. Hume and Mill, have used in their discussions of justice without realizing apparently its significance, or at least without calling attention to it. Why it is a significant modification of principle, changing one's conception of justice entirely, the whole of my argument will show.

Further, it is also necessary that the various offices to which special benefits or burdens attach are open to all. It may be, for example, to the common advantage, as just defined, to attach special benefits to certain offices. Perhaps by doing so the requisite talent can be attracted to them and encouraged to give its best efforts. But any offices having special benefits must be won in a fair competition in which contestants are judged on their merits. If some offices were not open, those excluded would normally be justified in feeling unjustly treated, even if they benefited from the greater efforts of those who were allowed to compete for them. Now if one can assume that offices are open, it is necessary only to consider the design of practices themselves and how they jointly, as a system, work together. It will be a mistake to focus attention on the varying relative positions of particular persons, who may be known to us by their proper names, and to require that each such change, as a once for all transaction viewed in isolation, must be in itself just. It is the system of practices which is to be judged, and judged from a general point of view: unless one is prepared to criticize it from the standpoint of a representative man holding some particular office, one has no complaint against it.

III

Given these principles one might try to derive them from *a priori* principles of reason, or claim that they were known by intuition. These are familiar enough steps and, at least in the case of the first principle, might be made with some success. Usually, however, such arguments, made at this point, are unconvincing. They are not likely to lead to an understanding of the basis of the principles of justice, not at least as principles of justice. I wish, therefore, to look at the principles in a different way.

Imagine a society of persons amongst whom a certain system of practices is *already* well established. Now suppose that by and large they are mutually self-interested; their allegiance to their established practices is normally founded on the prospect of self-advantage. One need not assume that, in all senses of the term 'person', the persons in this society are mutually self-interested. If the characterization as mutually self-interested applies when the line of division is the family, it may still be true that members of families are bound by ties of sentiment and affection and willingly acknowledge duties in contradiction to self-interest. Mutual self-interestedness in the relations between families, nations, churches, and the like, is commonly associated with intense loyalty and devotion on the part of individual members. Therefore, one can form a more realistic conception of this society if one thinks of it as consisting of mutually self-interested families, or some other association. Further, it is not necessary to suppose that these persons are mutually self-interested under all circumstances, but only in the usual situations in which they participate in their common practices.

Now suppose also that these persons are rational: they know their own interests more or less accurately; they are capable of tracing out the likely consequences of adopting one practice rather than another; they are capable of adhering to a course of action once they have decided upon it; they can resist present temptations and the enticements of immediate gain; and the bare knowledge or perception of the difference between their condition and that of others is not, within certain limits and in itself, a source of great dissatisfaction. Only the last point adds anything to the usual definition of rationality. This definition should allow, I think, for the idea that a rational man would not be greatly downcast from knowing, or seeing, that others are in a better position than himself, unless he thought their being so was the result of injustice, or the consequence of letting chance work itself out for no useful common purpose, and so on. So if these persons strike us as unpleasantly egoistic, they are at least free in some degree from the fault of envy.[1]

Finally, assume that these persons have roughly similar needs

---

[1] It is not possible to discuss here this addition to the usual conception of rationality. If it seems peculiar, it may be worth remarking that it is analogous to the modification of the utilitarian principle which the argument as a whole is designed to explain and justify. In the same way that the satisfaction of interests, the representative claims of which violate the principles of justice, is not a reason for having a practice (see sec. VII), unfounded envy, within limits, need not to be taken into account.

and interests, or needs and interests in various ways complementary, so that fruitful co-operation amongst them is possible;
and suppose that they are sufficiently equal in power and ability
to guarantee that in normal circumstances none is able to dominate the others. This condition (as well as the others) may seem
excessively vague; but in view of the conception of justice to
which the argument leads, there seems no reason for making it
more exact here.

Since these persons are conceived as engaging in their common
practices, which are already established, there is no question of
our supposing them to come together to deliberate as to how
they will set these practices up for the first time. Yet we can
imagine that from time to time they discuss with one another
whether any of them has a legitimate complaint against their
established institutions. Such discussions are perfectly natural
in any normal society. Now suppose that they have settled on
doing this in the following way. They first try to arrive at the
principles by which complaints, and so practices themselves, are
to be judged. Their procedure for this is to let each person
propose the principles upon which he wishes his complaints to be
tried with the understanding that, if acknowledged, the complaints of others will be similarly tried, and that no complaints
will be heard at all until everyone is roughly of one mind as to
how complaints are to be judged. They each understand further
that the principles proposed and acknowledged on this occasion
are binding on future occasions. Thus each will be wary of proposing a principle which would give him a peculiar advantage, in
his present circumstances, supposing it to be accepted. Each
person knows that he will be bound by it in future circumstances
the peculiarities of which cannot be known, and which might well
be such that the principle is then to his disadvantage. The idea
is that everyone should be required to make *in advance* a firm
commitment, which others also may reasonably be expected to
make, and that no one be given the opportunity to tailor the
canons of a legitimate complaint to fit his own special condition,
and then to discard them when they no longer suit his purpose.
Hence each person will propose principles of a general kind which
will, to a large degree, gain their sense from the various applications to be made of them, the particular circumstances of which
being as yet unknown. These principles will express the condi-

tions in accordance with which each is the least unwilling to
have his interests limited in the design of practices, given the
competing interests of the others, on the supposition that the
interests of others will be limited likewise. The restrictions which
would so arise might be thought of as those a person would keep
in mind if he were designing a practice in which his enemy were
to assign him his place.

The two main parts of this conjectural account have a definite
significance. The character and respective situations of the parties
reflect the typical circumstances in which questions of justice
arise. The procedure whereby principles are proposed and
acknowledged represents constraints, analogous to those of having
a morality, whereby rational and mutually self-interested persons
are brought to act reasonably. Thus the first part reflects the fact
that questions of justice arise when conflicting claims are made
upon the design of a practice and where it is taken for granted
that each person will insist, as far as possible, on what he considers
his rights. It is typical of cases of justice to involve persons who
are pressing on one another their claims, between which a fair
balance or equilibrium must be found. On the other hand, as
expressed by the second part, having a morality must at least
imply the acknowledgement of principles as impartially applying
to one's own conduct as well as to another's, and moreover
principles which may constitute a constraint, or limitation, upon
the pursuit of one's own interests. There are, of course, other
aspects of having a morality: the acknowledgement of moral
principles must show itself in accepting a reference to them as
reasons for limiting one's claims, in acknowledging the burden of
providing a special explanation, or excuse, when one acts contrary to them, or else in showing shame and remorse and a desire
to make amends, and so on. It is sufficient to remark here that
having a morality is analogous to having made a firm commitment in advance; for one must acknowledge the principles of
morality even when to one's disadvantage. A man whose moral
judgements always coincided with his interests could be suspected
of having no morality at all.

Thus the two parts of the foregoing account are intended to
mirror the kinds of circumstances in which questions of justice
arise and the constraints which having a morality would impose
upon persons so situated. In this way one can see how the accept-

ance of the principles of justice might come about, for given all these conditions as described, it would be natural if the two principles of justice were to be acknowledged. Since there is no way for anyone to win special advantages for himself, each might consider it reasonable to acknowledge equality as an initial principle. There is, however, no reason why they should regard this position as final; for if there are inequalities which satisfy the second principle, the immediate gain which equality would allow can be considered as intelligently invested in view of its future return. If, as is quite likely, these inequalities work as incentives to draw out better efforts, the members of this society may look upon them as concessions to human nature: they, like us, may think that people ideally should want to serve one another. But as they are mutually self-interested, their acceptance of these inequalities is merely the acceptance of the relations in which they actually stand, and a recognition of the motives which lead them to engage in their common practices. *They* have no title to complain of one another. And so provided that the conditions of the principle are met, there is no reason why they should not allow such inequalities. Indeed, it would be short-sighted of them to do so, and could result, in most cases, only from their being dejected by the bare knowledge, or perception, that others are better situated. Each person will, however, insist on an advantage to himself, and so on a common advantage, for none is willing to sacrifice anything for the others.

These remarks are not offered as a rigorous proof that persons conceived and situated as the conjectural account supposes, and required to adopt the procedure described, would settle on the two principles of justice. For such a proof a more elaborate and formal argument would have to be given: there remain certain details to be filled in, and various alternatives to be ruled out. The argument should, however, be taken as a proof, or a sketch of a proof; for the proposition I seek to establish is a necessary one, that is, it is intended as a theorem: namely, that when mutually self-interested and rational persons confront one another in typical circumstances of justice, and when they are required by a procedure expressing the constraints of having a morality to jointly acknowledge principles by which their claims on the design of their common practices are to be judged, they will settle on these two principles as restrictions governing the assignment of rights and duties, and thereby accept them as limiting their rights against one another. It is this theorem which accounts for these principles as principles of justice, and explains how they come to be associated with this moral concept. Moreover, this theorem is analogous to those about human conduct in other branches of social thought. That is, a simplified situation is described in which rational persons pursuing certain ends and related to one another in a definite way, are required to act subject to certain limitations; then, given this situation, it is shown that they will act in a certain manner. Failure so to act would imply that one or more of the assumptions does not obtain. The foregoing account aims to establish, or to sketch, a theorem in this sense; the aim of the argument is to show the basis for saying that the principles of justice may be regarded as those principles which arise when the constraints of having a morality are imposed upon rational persons in typical circumstances of justice.

IV

These ideas are, of course, connected with a familiar way of thinking about justice which goes back at least to the Greek Sophists, and which regards the acceptance of the principles of justice as a compromise between persons of roughly equal power who would enforce their will on each other if they could, but who, in view of the equality of forces amongst them and for the sake of their own peace and security acknowledge certain forms of conduct in so far as prudence seems to require. Justice is thought of as a pact between rational egoists the stability of which is dependent on a balance of power and a similarity of circumstances. While the previous account is connected with this tradition, and with its most recent variant, the theory of games, it differs from it in several important respects which, to forestall misinterpretations, I will set out here.

First, I wish to use the previous conjectural account of the background of justice as a way of analysing the concept. I do not want, therefore, to be interpreted as assuming a general theory of human motivation: when I suppose that the parties are mutually self-interested, and are not willing to have their (subtantial) interests sacrificed to others, I am referring to their conduct and motives as they are taken for granted in cases where questions of justice ordinarily arise. Justice is the virtue of practices where there are assumed to be competing interests and conflicting claims, and where it is supposed that persons will press their rights on each other. That persons are mutually self-interested in certain situations and for certain purposes is what gives rise to the question of justice in practices covering those circumstances. Amongst an association of saints, if such a community could really exist, the disputes about justice could hardly occur; for they would all work selflessly together for one end, the glory of God as defined by their common religion, and reference to this end would settle every question of right. The justice of practices does not come up until there are several different parties (whether we think of these as individuals, associations, or nations and so on, is irrelevant) who do press their claims on one another, and who do regard themselves as representatives of interests which deserve to be considered. Thus the previous account involves no general theory of human motivation. Its intent is simply to incorporate into the conception of justice the relations of men to one another which set the stage for questions of justice. It makes no difference how wide or general these relations are, as this matter does not bear on the analysis of the concept.

Again, in contrast to the various conceptions of the social contract, the several parties do not establish any particular society or practice; they do not covenant to obey a particular sovereign body or to accept a given constitution. Nor do they, as in the theory of games (in certain respects a marvellously sophisticated development of this tradition), decide on individual strategies adjusted to their respective circumstances in the game. What the parties do is to *jointly* acknowledge certain *principles* of appraisal relating to their common *practices* either as already established or merely proposed. They accede to standards of judgement, not to a given practice; they do not make any specific agreement, or bargain, or adopt a particular strategy. The subject of their acknowledgement is, therefore, very general indeed; it is simply the acknowledgement of certain principles of judgement, fulfilling certain general conditions, to be used in criticizing the arrangement of their common affairs. The relations of mutual self-interest between the parties who are similarly circumstanced mirror the conditions under which questions of justice arise, and the procedure by which the principles of judgement are proposed and acknowledged reflects the constraints of having a morality. Each aspect, then, of the preceding hypothetical account serves the purpose of bringing out a feature of the notion of justice. One could, if one liked, view the principles of justice as the 'solution' of this highest order 'game' of adopting, subject to the procedure described, principles of argument for all coming particular 'games' whose peculiarities one can in no way foresee. But this comparison, while no doubt helpful, must not obscure the fact that this highest order 'game' is of a special sort.[1] Its significance is that its various pieces represent aspects of the concept of justice.

Finally, I do not, of course, conceive the several parties as necessarily coming together to establish their common practices for the first time. Some institutions may, indeed, be set up *de novo*; but I have framed the preceding account so that it will apply when the full complement of social institutions already exists and represents the result of a long period of development. Nor is the account in any way fictitious. In any society where people reflect on their institutions they will have an idea of what principles of justice would be acknowledged under the conditions described, and there will be occasions when questions of justice are actually discussed in this way. Therefore if their practices do not accord with these principles, this will affect the quality of their social relations. For in this case there will be some recognized situations wherein the parties are mutually aware that one of them is being forced to accept what the other would concede is unjust. The foregoing analysis may then be thought of as representing the actual quality of relations between persons as defined by practices accepted as just. In such practices the parties will acknowledge the principles on which it is constructed, and the general recognition of this fact shows itself in the absence of resentment and in the sense of being justly treated. Thus one

---

[1] The difficulty one gets into by a mechanical application of the theory of games to moral philosophy can be brought out by considering among several possible examples, R. B. Braithwaite's study, *Theory of Games as a Tool for the Moral Philosopher* (Cambridge, 1955). What is lacking is the concept of morality, and it must be brought into the conjectural account in some way or other. In the text this is done by the form of the procedure whereby principles are proposed and acknowledged (Section III). If one starts directly with the particular case as known, and if one accepts as given and definitive the preferences and relative positions of the parties, whatever they are, it is impossible to give an analysis of the moral concept of fairness.

common objection to the theory of the social contract, its apparently historical and fictitious character, is avoided.

V

That the principles of justice may be regarded as arising in the manner described illustrates an important fact about them. Not only does it bring out the idea that justice is a primitive moral notion in that it arises once the concept of morality is imposed on mutually self-interested agents similarly circumstanced, but it emphasizes that, fundamental to justice, is the concept of fairness which relates to right dealing between persons who are co-operating with or competing against one another, as when one speaks of fair games, fair competition, and fair bargains. The question of fairness arises when free persons, who have no authority over one another, are engaging in a joint activity and amongst themselves settling or acknowledging the rules which define it and which determine the respective shares in its benefits and burdens. A practice will strike the parties as fair if none feels that, by participating in it, they or any of the others are taken advantage of, or forced to give in to claims which they do not regard as legitimate. This implies that each has a conception of legitimate claims which he thinks it reasonable for others as well as himself to acknowledge. If one thinks of the principles of justice as arising in the manner described, then they do define this sort of conception. A practice is just or fair, then, when it satisfies the principles which those who participate in it could propose to one another for mutual acceptance under the afore-mentioned circumstances. Persons engaged in a just, or fair, practice can face one another openly and support their respective positions, should they appear questionable, by reference to principles which it is reasonable to expect each to accept.

It is this notion of the possibility of mutual acknowledgement of principles by free persons who have no authority over one another which makes the concept of fairness fundamental to justice. Only if such acknowledgement is possible can there be true community between persons in their common practices; otherwise their relations will appear to them as founded to some extent on force. If, in ordinary speech, fairness applies more particularly to practices in which there is a choice whether to engage or not (e.g. in games, business competition), and justice to practices in which there is no choice (e.g. in slavery), the element of necessity does not render the conception of mutual acknowledgement inapplicable, although it may make it much more urgent to change unjust than unfair institutions. For one activity in which one can always engage is that of proposing and acknowledging principles to one another supposing each to be similarly circumstanced; and to judge practices by the principles so arrived at is to apply the standard of fairness to them.

Now if the participants in a practice accept its rules as fair, and so have no complaint to lodge against it, there arises a prima facie duty (and a corresponding prima facie right) of the parties to each other to act in accordance with the practice when it falls upon them to comply. When any number of persons engage in a practice, or conduct a joint undertaking according to rules, and thus restrict their liberty, those who have submitted to these restrictions when required have the right to a similar acquiescence on the part of those who have benefited by their submission. These conditions will obtain if a practice is correctly acknowledged to be fair, for in this case all who participate in it will benefit from it. The rights and duties so arising are special rights and duties in that they depend on previous actions voluntarily undertaken, in this case on the parties having engaged in a common practice and knowingly accepted its benefits.[1] It is not, however, an obligation which presupposes a deliberate performative act in the sense of a promise, or contract, and the like. An unfortunate mistake of proponents of the idea of the social contract was to suppose that political obligation does require some such act, or at least to use language which suggests it. It is sufficient that one has knowingly participated in and accepted the benefits of a practice acknowledged to be fair. This prima facie obligation may, of course, be overridden: it may happen, when it comes one's turn to follow a rule, that other considerations will justify not doing so. But one cannot, in general, be released from this obligation by denying the justice of the practice only when it falls on one to obey. If a person rejects a practice, he should, so far as possible, declare his inten-

---

[1] For the definition of this prima facie duty, and the idea that it is a special duty, I am indebted to H. L. A. Hart. See his paper 'Are There Any Natural Rights?', *Philosophical Review*, LXIV (1955), 185 f.

tion in advance, and avoid participating in it or enjoying its benefits.

This duty I have called that of fair play, but it should be admitted that to refer to it in this way is, perhaps, to extend the ordinary notion of fairness. Usually acting unfairly is not so much the breaking of any particular rule, even if the infraction is difficult to detect (cheating), but taking advantage of loop-holes or ambiguities in rules, availing oneself of unexpected or special circumstances which make it impossible to enforce them, insisting that rules be enforced to one's advantage when they should be suspended, and more generally, acting contrary to the intention of a practice. It is for this reason that one speaks of the sense of fair play: acting fairly requires more than simply being able to follow rules; what is fair must often be felt, or perceived, one wants to say. It is not, however, an unnatural extension of the duty of fair play to have it include the obligation which participants who have knowingly accepted the benefits of their common practice owe to each other to act in accordance with it when their performance falls due; for it is usually considered unfair if someone accepts the benefits of a practice but refuses to do his part in maintaining it. Thus one might say of the tax-dodger that he violates the duty of fair play: he accepts the benefits of government but will not do his part in releasing resources to it; and members of labour unions often say that fellow workers who refuse to join are being unfair: they refer to them as 'free riders', as persons who enjoy what are the supposed benefits of unionism, higher wages, shorter hours, job security, and the like, but who refuse to share in its burdens in the form of paying dues, and so on.

The duty of fair play stands beside other prima facie duties such as fidelity and gratitude as a basic moral notion; yet it is not to be confused with them. These duties are all clearly distinct, as would be obvious from their definitions. As with any moral duty, that of fair play implies a constraint on self-interest in particular cases; on occasion it enjoins conduct which a rational egoist strictly defined would not decide upon. So while justice does not require of anyone that he sacrifice his interests in that *general position* and procedure whereby the principles of justice are proposed and acknowledged. it may happen that in particular situations, arising in the context of engaging in a practice the duty of fair play will often cross his interests in the sense that he will be required to forgo particular advantages which the peculiarities of his circumstances might permit him to take. There is, of course, nothing surprising in this. It is simply the consequence of the firm commitment which the parties may be supposed to have made, or which they would make, in the general position, together with the fact that they have participated in and accepted the benefits of a practice which they regard as fair.

Now the acknowledgement of this constraint in particular cases, which is manifested in acting fairly or wishing to make amends, feeling ashamed, and the like, when one has evaded it, is one of the forms of conduct by which participants in a common practice exhibit their recognition of each other as persons with similar interests and capacities. In the same way that, failing a special explanation, the criterion for the recognition of suffering is helping one who suffers, acknowledging the duty of fair play is a necessary part of the criterion for recognizing another as a person with similar interests and feelings as oneself.[1] A person who never under any circumstances showed a wish to help others in pain would show, at the same time, that he did not recognize that they were in pain; nor could he have any feelings of affection or friendship for anyone; for having these feelings implies, failing special circumstances, that he comes to their aid when they are suffering. Recognition that another is a person in pain shows itself in sympathetic action; this primitive natural response of compassion is one of those responses upon which the various forms of moral conduct are built.

Similarly, the acceptance of the duty of fair play by participants in a common practice is a reflection in each person of the recognition of the aspirations and interests of the others to be realized by their joint activity. Failing a special explanation, their acceptance of it is a necessary part of the criterion for their recognizing one another as persons with similar interests and capacities, as the conception of their relations in the general position supposes them to be. Otherwise they would show no recognition of one

---

[1] I am using the concept of criterion here in what I take to be Wittgenstein's sense. That the response of compassion, under appropriate circumstances, is part of the criterion for whether or not a person understands what 'pain' means, is, I think, in the *Philosophical Investigations*. The view in the text is simply an extension of this idea. I cannot, however, attempt to justify it here.

another as persons with similar capacities and interests, and indeed, in some cases perhaps hypothetical, they would not recognize one another as persons at all, but as complicated objects involved in a complicated activity. To recognize another as a person one must respond to him and act towards him in certain ways; and these ways are intimately connected with the various prima facie duties. Acknowledging these duties in *some* degree, and so having the elements of morality, is not a matter of choice, or of intuiting moral qualities, or a matter of the expression of feelings or attitudes (the three interpretations between which philosophical opinion frequently oscillates); it is simply the possession of one of the forms of conduct in which the recognition of others as persons is manifested.

These remarks are unhappily obscure. Their main purpose here, however, is to forestall, together with the remarks in Section IV, the misinterpretation that, on the view presented, the acceptance of justice and the acknowledgement of the duty of fair play depends in every day life solely on there being a *de facto* balance of forces between the parties. It would indeed be foolish to underestimate the importance of such a balance in securing justice; but it is not the only basis thereof. The recognition of one another as persons with similar interests and capacities engaged in a common practice must, failing a special explanation, show itself in the acceptance of the principles of justice and the acknowledgement of the duty of fair play.

The conception at which we have arrived, then, is that the principles of justice may be thought of as arising once the constraints of having a morality are imposed upon rational and mutually self-interested parties who are related and situated in a special way. A practice is just if it is in accordance with the principles which all who participate in it might reasonably be expected to propose or to acknowledge before one another when they are similarly circumstanced and required to make a firm commitment in advance without knowledge of what will be their peculiar condition, and thus when it meets standards which the parties could accept as fair should occasion arise for them to debate its merits. Regarding the participants themselves, once persons knowingly engage in a practice which they acknowledge to be fair and accept the benefits of doing so, they are bound by the duty of fair play to follow the rules when it comes their turn to do so, and this implies a limitation on their pursuit of self-interest in particular cases.

Now one consequence of this conception is that, where it applies, there is no moral value in the satisfaction of a claim incompatible with it. Such a claim violates the conditions of reciprocity and community amongst persons, and he who presses it, not being willing to acknowledge it when pressed by another, has no grounds for complaint when it is denied; whereas he against whom it is pressed can complain. As it cannot be mutually acknowledged it is a resort to coercion; granting the claim is possible only if one party can compel acceptance of what the other will not admit. But it makes no sense to concede claims the denial of which cannot be complained of in preference to claims the denial of which can be objected to. Thus in deciding on the justice of a practice it is not enough to ascertain that it answers to wants and interests in the fullest and most effective manner. For if any of these conflict with justice, they should not be counted, as their satisfaction is no reason at all for having a practice. It would be irrelevant to say, even if true, that it resulted in the greatest satisfaction of desire. In tallying up the merits of a practice one must toss out the satisfaction of interests the claims of which are incompatible with the principles of justice.

VI

The discussion so far has been excessively abstract. While this is perhaps unavoidable, I should now like to bring out some of the features of the conception of justice as fairness by comparing it with the conception of justice in classical utilitarianism as represented by Bentham and Sidgwick, and its counterpart in welfare economics. This conception assimilates justice to benevolence and the latter in turn to the most efficient design of institutions to promote the general welfare. Justice is a kind of efficiency.

Now it is said occasionally that this form of utilitarianism puts no restrictions on what might be a just assignment of rights and duties in that there might be circumstances which, on utilitarian grounds, would justify institutions highly offensive to our ordinary sense of justice. But the classical utilitarian conception is not totally unprepared for this objection. Beginning with the notion that the general happiness can be represented by a social utility function consisting of a sum of individual utility functions with identical weights (this being the meaning of the maxim that each counts for one and no more than one), it is commonly assumed that the utility functions of individuals are similar in all essential respects. Differences between individuals are ascribed to accidents of education and upbringing, and they should not be taken into account. This assumption, coupled with that of diminishing marginal utility, results in a prima facie case for equality, e.g. of equality in the distribution of income during any given period of time, laying aside indirect effects on the future. But even if utilitarianism is interpreted as having such restrictions built into the utility function, and even if it is supposed that these restrictions have in practice much the same result as the application of the principles of justice (and appear, perhaps, to be ways of expressing these principles in the language of mathematics and psychology), the fundamental idea is very different from the conception of justice as fairness. For one thing, that the principles of justice should be accepted is interpreted as the contingent result of a higher order administrative decision. The form of this decision is regarded as being similar to that of an entrepreneur deciding how much to produce of this or that commodity in view of its marginal revenue, or to that of someone distributing goods to needy persons according to the relative urgency of their wants. The choice between practices is thought of as being made on the basis of the allocation of benefits and burdens to individuals (these being measured by the present capitalized value of their utility over the full period of the practice's existence), which results from the distribution of rights and duties established by a practice.

Moreover, the individuals receiving these benefits are not conceived as being related in any way: they represent so many different directions in which limited resources may be allocated. The value of assigning resources to one direction rather than another depends solely on the preferences and interests of individuals as individuals. The satisfaction of desire has its value irrespective of the moral relations between persons, say as members of a joint undertaking, and of the claims which, in the name of these interests, they are prepared to make on one another:[1]

---

[1] An idea essential to the classical utilitarian conception of justice. Bentham is firm in his statement of it. (*The Principles of Morals and Legislation*, ch. II, sec. iv. See also ch. X,

and it is this value which is to be taken into account by the (ideal) legislator who is conceived as adjusting the rules of the system from the centre so as to maximize the value of the social utility function.

It is thought that the principles of justice will not be violated by a legal system so conceived provided these executive decisions are correctly made. In this fact the principles of justice are said to have their derivation and explanation; they simply express the most important general features of social institutions in which the administrative problem is solved in the best way. These principles have, indeed, a special urgency because, given the facts of human nature, so much depends on them; and this explains the peculiar quality of the moral feelings associated with justice. This assimilation of justice to a higher order executive decision, certainly a striking conception, is central to classical utilitarianism; and it also brings out its profound individualism, in one sense of this ambiguous word. It regards persons as so many *separate* directions in which benefits and burdens may be assigned; and the value of the satisfaction or dissatisfaction of desire is not thought to depend in any way on the moral relations in which individuals stand, or on the kinds of claims which they are willing, in the pursuit of their interests, to press on each other.

VII

Many social decisions are, of course, of an administrative nature. Certainly this is so when it is a matter of social utility in what one may call its ordinary sense: that is, when it is a question of the efficient design of social institutions for the use of common means to achieve common ends. In this case either the benefits

sec. x, footnote 1.) The same point is made in *The Limits of Jurisprudence Defined*, pp. 115 f. Although much recent welfare economics, as found in such important works as I. M. D. Little, *A Critique of Welfare Economics*, 2nd ed. (Oxford, 1957) and K. J. Arrow, *Social Choice and Individual Values* (New York, 1951), dispenses with the idea of cardinal utility, and use instead the theory of ordinal utility as stated by J. R. Hicks, *Value and Capital*, 2nd ed. (Oxford, 1946), Pt. I, it assumes with utilitarianism that individual preferences have value as such, and so accepts the idea being criticized here. I hasten to add, however, that this is no objection to it as a means of analysing economic policy, and for that purpose it may, indeed, be a necessary simplifying assumption. Nevertheless it is an assumption which cannot be made in so far as one is trying to analyse moral concepts, expecially the concept of justice, as economists would, I think, agree. Justice is usually regarded as a separate and distinct part of any comprehensive criterion of economic policy. See, for example, Tibor Scitovsky, *Welfare and Competition* (London, 1952), pp. 59–69, and Little, op. cit., ch. VII.

11

and burdens may be assumed to be impartially distributed, or the question of distribution is misplaced, as in the instance of maintaining public order and security or national defence. But as an interpretation of the basis of the principles of justice, classical utilitarianism is mistaken. It *permits* one to argue, for example, that slavery is unjust on the grounds that the advantages to the slaveholder as slaveholder do not counterbalance the disadvantages to the slave and to society at large burdened by a comparatively inefficient system of labour. Now the conception of justice as fairness, when applied to the practice of slavery with its offices of slaveholder and slave, would not allow one to consider the advantages of the slaveholder in the first place. As that office is not in accordance with principles which could be mutually acknowledged, the gains accruing to the slaveholder, assuming them to exist, cannot be counted as in *any* way mitigating the injustice of the practice. The question whether these gains outweigh the disadvantages to the slave and to society cannot arise, since in considering the justice of slavery these gains have no weight at all which requires that they be overridden. Where the conception of justice as fairness applies, slavery is *always* unjust.

I am not, of course, suggesting the absurdity that the classical utilitarians approved of slavery. I am only rejecting a type of argument which their view allows them to use in support of their disapproval of it. The conception of justice as derivative from efficiency implies that judging the justice of a practice is always, in principle at least, a matter of weighing up advantages and disadvantages, each having an intrinsic value or disvalue as the satisfaction of interests, irrespective of whether or not these interests necessarily involve acquiescence in principles which could not be mutually acknowledged. Utilitarianism cannot account for the fact that slavery is always unjust, nor for the fact that it would be recognized as irrelevant in defeating the accusation of injustice for one person to say to another, engaged with him in a common practice and debating its merits, that nevertheless it allowed of the greatest satisfaction of desire. The charge of injustice cannot be rebutted in this way. If justice were derivative from a higher order executive efficiency, this would not be so.

But now, even if it is taken as established that, so far as the ordinary conception of justice goes, slavery is always unjust (that is, slavery by definition violates commonly recognized principles of justice), the classical utilitarian would surely reply that these principles, as other moral principles subordinate to that of utility, are only generally correct. It is simply for the most part true that slavery is less efficient than other institutions; and while common sense may define the concept of justice so that slavery is unjust, nevertheless, where slavery would lead to the greatest satisfaction of desire, it is not wrong. Indeed, it is then right, and for the very same reason that justice, as ordinarily understood, is usually right. If, as ordinarily understood, slavery is always unjust, to this extent the utilitarian conception of justice might be admitted to differ from that of common moral opinion. Still the utilitarian would want to hold that, as a matter of moral principle, his view is correct in giving no special weight to considerations of justice beyond that allowed for by the general presumption of effectiveness. And this, he claims, is as it should be. The everyday opinion is morally in error, although, indeed, it is a useful error, since it protects rules of generally high utility.

The question, then, relates not simply to the analysis of the concept of justice as common sense defines it, but the analysis of it in the wider sense as to how much weight considerations of justice, as defined, are to have when laid against other kinds of moral considerations. Here again I wish to argue that reasons of justice have a *special* weight for which only the conception of justice as fairness can account. Moreover, it belongs to the concept of justice that they do have this special weight. While Mill recognized that this was so, he thought that it could be accounted for by the special urgency of the moral feelings which naturally support principles of such high utility. But it is a mistake to resort to the urgency of feeling; as with the appeal to intuition, it manifests a failure to pursue the question far enough. The special weight of considerations of justice can be explained from the conception of justice as fairness. It is only necessary to elaborate a bit what has already been said as follows.

If one examines the circumstances in which a certain tolerance of slavery is justified, or perhaps better, excused, it turns out that these are of a rather special sort. Perhaps slavery exists as an inheritance from the past and it proves necessary to dismantle it piece by piece; at times slavery may conceivably be an advance on previous institutions. Now while there may be some excuse for slavery in special conditions, it is never an excuse for it that it is sufficiently advantageous to the slaveholder to outweigh the disadvantages to the slave and to society. A person who argues in this way is not perhaps making a wildly irrelevant remark; but he is guilty of a moral fallacy. There is disorder in his conception of the ranking of moral principles. For the slaveholder, by his own admission, has no moral title to the advantages which he receives as a slaveholder. He is no more prepared than the slave to acknowledge the principle upon which is founded the respective positions in which they both stand. Since slavery does not accord with principles which they could mutually acknowledge, they each may be supposed to agree that it is unjust: it grants claims which it ought not to grant and in doing so denies claims which it ought not to deny. Amongst persons in a general position who are debating the form of their common practices, it cannot, therefore, be offered as a reason for a practice that, in conceding these very claims that ought to be denied, it nevertheless meets existing interests more effectively. By their very nature the satisfaction of these claims is without weight and cannot enter into any tabulation of advantages and disadvantages.

Furthermore, it follows from the concept of morality that, to the extent that the slaveholder recognizes his position *vis-à-vis* the slave to be unjust, he would not choose to press his claims. His not wanting to receive his special advantages is one of the ways in which he shows that he thinks slavery is unjust. It would be fallacious for the legislator to suppose, then, that it is a ground for having a practice that it brings advantages greater than disadvantages, if those for whom the practice is designed, and to whom the advantages flow, acknowledge that they have no moral title to them and do not wish to receive them.

For these reasons the principles of justice have a special weight; and with respect to the principle of the greatest satisfaction of desire, as cited in the general position amongst those discussing the merits of their common practices, the principles of justice have an absolute weight. In this sense they are not contingent; and this is why their force is greater than can be accounted for by the general presumption (assuming that there is one) of the effectiveness, in the utilitarian sense, of practices which in fact satisfy them.

If one wants to continue using the concepts of classical utilitarianism, one will have to say, to meet this criticism, that at least the individual or social utility functions must be so defined that no value is given to the satisfaction of interests the representative claims of which violate the principles of justice. In this way it is no doubt possible to include these principles within the form of the utilitarian conception; but to do so is, of course, to change its inspiration altogether as a moral conception. For it is to incorporate within it principles which cannot be understood on the basis of a higher order executive decision aiming at the greatest satisfaction of desire.

It is worth remarking, perhaps, that this criticism of utilitarianism does not depend on whether or not the two assumptions, that of individuals having similar utility functions and that of diminishing marginal utility, are interpreted as psychological propositions to be supported or refuted by experience, or as moral and political principles expressed in a somewhat technical language. There are, certainly, several advantages in taking them in the latter fashion. For one thing, one might say that this is what Bentham and others really meant by them, as least as shown by how they were used in arguments for social reform. More importantly, one could hold that the best way to defend the classical utilitarian view is to interpret these assumptions as moral and political principles. It is doubtful whether, taken as psychological propositions, they are true of men in general as we know them under normal conditions. On the other hand, utilitarians would not have wanted to propose them merely as practical working principles of legislation, or as expedient maxims to guide reform, given the egalitarian sentiments of modern society. When pressed they might well have invoked the idea of a more or less equal capacity of men in relevant respects if given an equal chance in a just society. But if the argument above regarding slavery is correct, then granting these assumptions as moral and political principles makes no difference. To view individuals as equally fruitful lines for the allocation of benefits, even as a matter of moral principle, still leaves the mistaken notion that the satisfaction of desire has value in itself irrespective of the relations between persons as members of a common practice, and irrespective of the claims upon one another which the satisfaction of interests represents. To see the error of this idea one must give up the conception of justice as an executive decision altogether and refer to the notion of justice as fairness: that participants in a common practice be regarded as having an original and equal liberty and that their common practices be considered unjust unless they accord with principles which persons so circumstanced and related could freely acknowledge before one another, and so could accept as fair. Once the emphasis is put upon the concept of the mutual recognition of principles by participants in a common practice the rules of which are to define their several relations and give form to their claims on one another, then it is clear that the granting of a claim the principle of which could not be acknowledged by each in the general position (that is, in the position in which the parties propose and acknowledge principles before one another) is not a reason for adopting a practice. Viewed in this way, the background of the claim is seen to exclude it from consideration; that it can represent a value in itself arises from the conception of individuals as separate lines for the assignment of benefits, as isolated persons who stand as claimants on an administrative or benevolent largesse. Occasionally persons do so stand to one another; but this is not the general case, nor, more importantly, is it the case when it is a matter of the justice of practices themselves in which participants stand in various relations to be appraised in accordance with standards which they may be expected to acknowledge before one another. Thus however mistaken the notion of the social contract may be as history, and however far it may over-reach itself as a general theory of social and political obligation, it does express, suitably interpreted, an essential part of the concept of justice.

VIII

By way of conclusion I should like to make two remarks: first, the original modification of the utilitarian principle (that it require of practices that the offices and positions defined by them be equal unless it is reasonable to suppose that the representative man in *every* office would find the inequality to his advantage), slight as it may appear at first sight, actually has a different conception of justice standing behind it. I have tried to show how this is so by developing the concept of justice as fairness and by indicating how this notion involves the mutual acceptance, from a general position, of the principles on which a practice is founded, and how this in turn requires the exclusion from consideration of claims violating the principles of justice. Thus the slight alteration of principle reveals another family of notions, another way of looking at the concept of justice.

Second, I should like to remark also that I have been dealing with the *concept* of justice. I have tried to set out the kinds of principles upon which judgements concerning the justice of practices may be said to stand. The analysis will be successful to the degree that it expresses the principles involved in these judgements when made by competent persons upon deliberation and reflection.[1] Now every people may be supposed to have the concept of justice, since in the life of every society there must be at least some relations in which the parties consider themselves to be circumstanced and related as the concept of justice as fairness requires. Societies will differ from one another not in having or in failing to have this notion but in the range of cases to which they apply it and in the emphasis which they give to it as compared with other moral concepts.

A firm grasp of the concept of justice itself is necessary if these variations, and the reasons for them, are to be understood. No study of the development of moral ideas and of the differences between them is more sound than the analysis of the fundamental moral concepts upon which it must depend. I have tried, therefore, to give an analysis of the concept of justice which should apply generally, however large a part the concept may have in a given morality, and which can be used in explaining the course of men's thoughts about justice and its relations to other moral concepts. How it is to be used for this purpose is a large topic which I cannot, of course, take up here. I mention it only to emphasize that I have been dealing with the concept of justice itself and to indicate what use I consider such an analysis to have.

[1] For a further discussion of the idea expressed here, see my paper, 'Outline of a Decision Procedure for Ethics', in the *Philosophical Review*, LX (1951), 177–97. For an analysis, similar in many respects but using the notion of the ideal observer instead of that of the considered judgement of a competent person, see Roderick Firth, 'Ethical Absolutism and the Ideal Observer', *Philosophy and Phenomenological Research*, XII (1952), 317–45. While the similarities between these two discussions are more important than the differences, an analysis based on the notion of a considered judgement of a competent person, as it is based on a kind of judgement, may prove more helpful in understanding the features of moral judgement than an analysis based on the notion of an ideal observer, although this remains to be shown. A man who rejects the conditions imposed on a considered judgement of a competent person could no longer profess to *judge* at all. This seems more fundamental than his rejecting the conditions of observation, for these do not seem to apply, in an ordinary sense, to making a moral judgement.

8

PROLEGOMENON TO THE PRINCIPLES OF PUNISHMENT[1]

by H. L. A. Hart

I

INTRODUCTORY

THE main object of this paper is to provide a framework for the discussion of the mounting perplexities which now surround the institution of criminal punishment, and to show that any morally tolerable account of this institution must exhibit it as a compromise between radically distinct and partly conflicting principles.

General interest in the topic of punishment has never been greater than it is at present and I doubt if the public discussion of it has ever been more confused. The interest and the confusion are both in part due to relatively modern scepticism about two elements which have figured as essential parts of the traditionally opposed 'theories' of punishment. On the one hand, the old Benthamite confidence in fear of the penalties threatened by the law as a powerful deterrent has waned with the growing realization that the part played by calculation of any sort in anti-social behaviour has been exaggerated. On the other hand, a cloud of doubt has settled over the keystone of 'Retributive' theory. Its advocates can no longer speak with the old confidence that statements of the form 'This man who has broken the law could have kept it' had a univocal or agreed meaning; or where scepticism does not attach to the *meaning* of this form of statement, it has shaken the confidence that we are generally able to distinguish the cases where this form of statement is true from those where it is not.[2]

Yet quite apart from the uncertainty engendered by these

---

[1] This paper was read as the presidential address of the Aristotelian Society in 1959, and published in the Society's *Proceedings* for 1959–60.

[2] See Barbara Wootton, *Social Science and Social Pathology* for a clear and most comprehensive modern statement of these doubts.

fundamental doubts, which seem to call in question the accounts given of the efficacy and the morality of punishment by all the old competing theories, the public utterances of those who conceive themselves to be expounding, as plain men for other plain men, orthodox or common-sense principles, untouched by modern psychological doubts, are uneasy. Their words often sound as if the authors had not fully grasped their meaning or did not intend the words to be taken quite literally. A glance at the parliamentary debates or the *Report of the Royal Commission on Capital Punishment* shows that many are now troubled by the suspicion that the view that there is just one supreme value or objective (e.g. Deterrence, Retribution or Reform) in terms of which *all* questions about the justification of punishment are to be answered, is somehow wrong: yet, from what is said on such occasions no clear account can be extracted of what the different values or objectives are, or how they fit together in the justification of punishment.[1]

No one expects judges or statesmen occupied in the business of sending people to the gallows or prison, or in making (or unmaking) laws which enable this to be done, to have much time for philosophical discussion of the principles which make it morally tolerable to do these things. A judicial bench is not and should not be a professorial chair. Yet what is said in public debates about punishment by those specially concerned with it as judges or legislators is important. Few are likely to be more circumspect, and if what they say seems, as it often does, unclear, one-sided and easily refutable by pointing to some aspect of things which they have overlooked, it is likely that in our inherited ways of talking or thinking about punishment there is some persistent drive towards an over-simplification of multiple issues which require separate consideration. To counter this drive what is most needed is *not* the simple admission that instead of a single value or aim (Deterrence, Retribution, Reform or any other) a plurality of different values and aims should be given

---

[1] In the Lords debate in July 1956 the Lord Chancellor agreed with Lord Denning that 'the ultimate justification of any punishment is not that it is a deterrent but that it is the emphatic denunciation of the committing of a crime' yet also said that 'the real crux of the question at issue is whether capital punishment is a uniquely effective deterrent'. See 198 *H. L. Deb* (5th July), 576, 577, 596 (1956). In his article 'An Approach to the Problems of Punishment' (*Philosophy*, 1958) Mr. S. I. Benn rightly observes of Lord Denning's view that denunciation does not imply the deliberate imposition of suffering which is the feature needing justification (325 n. 1).

as a conjunctive answer to some *single* question concerning the
justification of punishment. What is needed is the realization
that different principles (each of which may in a sense be called a
'justification') are relevant at different points in any morally
acceptable account of punishment. What we should look for
are answers to a number of different questions such as: What
justifies the general practice of punishment? To whom may
punishment be applied? How severely may we punish? In
dealing with these and other questions concerning punishment
we should bear in mind that in this, as in most other social
institutions, the pursuit of one aim may be qualified by or
provide an opportunity, not to be missed, for the pursuit of others.
Till we have developed this sense of the complexity of punishment (and this prolegomenon aims only to do this) we shall be in
no fit state to assess the extent to which the whole institution has
been eroded by or needs to be adapted to new beliefs about the
human mind.

II

JUSTIFYING AIMS AND PRINCIPLES OF DISTRIBUTION

There is, I think, an analogy worth considering between the
concept of Punishment and that of Property. In both cases we
have to do with a social institution of which the centrally important form is a structure of *legal* rules, though it would be dogmatic
to deny the names of Punishment or Property to the similar
though more rudimentary rule-regulated practices within groups
such as a family, or a school, or in customary societies whose
customs may lack some of the standard or salient features of law
(e.g. legislation, organized sanctions, courts). In both cases we
are confronted by a complex institution presenting different
inter-related features calling for separate explanation; or, if the
morality of the institution is challenged, for separate justification.
In both cases failure to distinguish separate questions or attempting to answer them all by reference to a single principle ends in
confusion. Thus in the case of Property we should distinguish
between the question of the *definition* of Property, the question
why and in what circumstance it is a *good* institution to maintain,
and the questions in what ways individuals may become *entitled* to
property and *how much* they should be allowed to acquire. These
we may call questions of *Definition*, *General Justifying Aim*, and

Distribution with the last subdivided into questions of *Title* and *Amount*. It is salutary to take some classical exposition of the idea of Property, say Locke's Chapter 'Of Property' in the *Second Treatise*,[1] and to observe how much darkness is spread by the use of a single notion (in this case 'the labour of (a man's) body and the work of his hands') to answer all these different questions which press upon us when we reflect on the institution of Property. In the case of Punishment the beginning of wisdom (though by no means its end) is to distinguish similar questions and confront them separately.

(a) Definition

Here I shall simply draw upon the recent admirable work scattered through English philosophical[2] journals and add to it only an admonition of my own against the abuse of definition in the philosophical discussion of punishment. So with Mr. Benn and Professor Flew I shall define the standard or central case of 'punishment' in terms of five elements:

   (i) It must involve pain or other consequences normally considered unpleasant.
  (ii) It must be for an offence against legal rules.
 (iii) It must be of an actual or supposed offender for his offence.
 (iv) It must be intentionally administered by human beings other than the offender.
  (v) It must be imposed and administered by an authority constituted by a legal system against which the offence is committed.

In calling this the standard or central case of punishment I shall relegate to the position of sub-standard or secondary cases the following among many other possibilities:

  (a) Punishments for breaches of legal rules imposed or administered otherwise than by officials (decentralized sanctions).
  (b) Punishments for breaches of non-legal rules or orders (punishments in a family or school).

[1] Chapter IV.
[2] K. Baier, 'Is Punishment Retributive?' *Analysis*, 16, p. 26 (1955). A. Flew, 'The Justification of Punishment', *Philosophy*, 1954, pp. 291–307. S. I. Benn, op. cit., pp. 325–6.

(c) Vicarious or collective punishment of some member of a social group for actions done by others without the former's authorization, encouragement, control or permission.

(d) Punishment of persons (otherwise than under (c)) who are neither in fact nor supposed to be offenders.

The chief importance of listing these sub-standard cases is to prevent the use of what I shall call the 'definitional stop' in discussions of punishment. This is an abuse of definition especially tempting when use is made of conditions (ii) and (iii) of the standard case against the utilitarian claim that the practice of punishment is justified by the beneficial consequences resulting from the observance of the laws which it secures. Here the stock 'retributive' argument[1] is: If *this* is the justification of punishment, why not apply it when it pays to do so to those innocent of any crime chosen at random, or to the wife and children of the offender? And here the wrong reply is: That, by definition, would not be 'punishment' and it is the justification of punishment which is in issue.[2] Not only will this definitional stop fail to satisfy the advocate of 'Retribution'; it would prevent us from investigating the very thing which modern scepticism most calls in question: namely the rational and moral status of our preference for a system of punishment under which measures painful to individuals are to be taken against them only when they have committed an offence. Why do we prefer this to other forms of social hygiene which we might employ instead to prevent anti-social behaviour and which we do employ in special circumstances sometimes with reluctance? No account of punishment can afford to dismiss this question with a definition.

(b) The nature of an offence

Before we reach any question of justification we must identify a preliminary question to which the answer is so simple that the question may not appear worth asking; yet it is clear that some curious 'theories' of punishment gain their only plausibility from

---

[1] Ewing, *The Morality of Punishment*, D. J. B. Hawkins, *Punishment and Moral Responsibility* (The King's Good Servant, p. 92), J. D. Mabbott, 'Punishment', *Mind*, 1939, p. 153.

[2] Mr. Benn seemed to succumb at times to the temptation to give 'The short answer to the critics of utilitarian theories of punishment—that they are theories of *punishment* not of any sort of technique involving suffering' (op. cit., p. 322). He has since told me that he does not now rely on the definitional stop.

ignoring it, and others from confusing it with other questions. This question is: Why are certain kinds of action forbidden by law and so made crimes or offences? The answer is: To announce to society that these actions are not to be done and to secure that fewer of them are done. These are the common immediate aims of making any conduct a criminal offence, and until we have laws made with these primary aims we shall lack the notion of a 'crime' and so of a 'criminal'. Without recourse to the simple idea that the criminal law sets up, in its rules, standards of behaviour to encourage certain types of conduct and discourage others we cannot distinguish a punishment in the form of a fine from a tax on a course of conduct.[1] This indeed is one grave objection to those theories of law which in the interests of simplicity or uniformity obscure the distinction between primary laws setting standards for behaviour and secondary laws specifying what officials must or may do when they are broken. Such theories insist that all legal rules are 'really' directions to officials to exact 'sanctions' under certain conditions, e.g. if people kill.[2] Yet only if we keep alive the distinction (which such theories thus obscure) between the primary objective of the law in encouraging or discouraging certain kinds of behaviour and its merely ancillary sanction or remedial steps can we give sense to the notion of a crime or offence.

It is important however to stress the fact that in thus identifying the immediate aims of the criminal law we have not reached the stage of justification. There are indeed many forms of undesirable behaviour which it would be foolish because ineffective or too costly to attempt to inhibit by use of the law and some of these may be better left to educators, trade unions, churches, marriage guidance councils or other non-legal agencies. Conversely there are some forms of conduct which we believe cannot be effectively inhibited without use of the law. But it is only too plain that in fact the law may make activities criminal which it is morally important to promote and the suppression

---

[1] This generally clear distinction may be blurred. Taxes may be imposed to discourage the activities taxed though the law does not announce this as it does when it makes them criminal. Conversely fines payable for some criminal offences because of a depreciation of currency became so small that they are cheerfully paid and offences are frequent. They are then felt to be mere taxes because the sense is lost that the rule is meant to be taken seriously as a standard of behaviour.

[2] Cf. Kelsen, *General Theory of Law and State*, 30–3, 33–4, 143–4 (1946). 'Law is the primary norm which stipulates the sanction. . . .' (id. 61).

of these may be quite unjustifiable. Yet confusion between the simple immediate aim of any criminal legislation and the justification of punishment seems to be the most charitable explanation of the claim that punishment is justified as an 'emphatic denunciation by the community of a crime'. Lord Denning's[1] dictum that this is the ultimate justification of punishment can be saved from Mr. Benn's criticism, noted above, only if it is treated as a blurred statement of the truth that the aim not of punishment but of criminal legislation is indeed to denounce certain types of conduct as something not to be practised. Conversely the immediate aim of criminal legislation cannot be any of the things which are usually mentioned as justifying punishment: for until it is settled what conduct is to be legally denounced and discouraged we have not settled from what we are to *deter* people, or who are to be considered *criminals* from whom we are to exact *retribution*, or on whom we are to wreak *vengeance*, or whom we are to *reform*.

Even those who look upon human law as a mere instrument for enforcing 'morality as such' (itself conceived as the law of God or Nature) and who at the stage of justifying punishment wish to appeal not to socially beneficial consequences but simply to the intrinsic value of inflicting suffering on wrongdoers who have disturbed by their offence the moral order, would not deny that the aim of criminal legislation is to set up types of behaviour (in this case conformity with a pre-existing moral law) as legal standards of behaviour and to secure conformity with them. No doubt in all communities certain moral offences, e.g. killing, will always be selected for suppression as crimes and it is conceivable that this may be done not to protect human beings from being killed but to save the potential murderer from sin; but it would be paradoxical to look upon the law as designed not to prevent murder at all (even conceived as sin rather than harm) but simply to extract the penalty from the murderer.

(c) General Justifying Aim

I shall not here criticize the intelligibility or consistency or adequacy of these theories that are united in denying that the

---

[1] In evidence to the Royal Commission on Capital Punishment, Cmd. 8932, Section 53 (1953). *Supra*, p. 3, n. 2.

practice of a system of punishment is justified by its beneficial consequences and claim instead that the main justification of the practice lies in the fact that when breach of the law involves moral guilt the application to the offender of the pain of punishment is itself a thing of value. A great variety of claims of this character designating 'Retribution' or 'Expiation' or 'Reprobation' as the justifying aim, fall in spite of differences under this rough general description. Though in fact I agree with Mr. Benn[1] in thinking that these all either avoid the question of justification altogether or are in spite of their protestations disguised forms of Utilitarianism, I shall assume that Retribution, defined simply as the application of the pains of punishment to an offender who is morally guilty, may figure among the conceivable justifying aims of a system of punishment. Here I shall merely insist that it is one thing to use the word Retribution *at this point* in an account of the principle of punishment in order to designate the General Justifying Aim of the system, and quite another to use it to secure that to the question 'To whom may punishment be applied?' (the question of Distribution) the answer given is 'Only to an offender for an offence'. Failure to distinguish Retribution as a General Justifying Aim from retribution as the simple insistence that only those who have broken the law—and voluntarily broken it—may be punished may be traced in many writers even perhaps in Mr. J. D. Mabbott's[2] otherwise most illuminating essay. We shall distinguish the latter from Retribution in General Aim as 'retribution in Distribution'. Much confusing shadow-fighting between Utilitarians and their opponents may be avoided if it is recognized that it is perfectly consistent to assert *both* that the General Justifying Aim of the practice of punishment is its beneficial consequences and that the pursuit of this general aim should be qualified or restricted out of deference to principles of Distribution which require that punishment should be only of an offender for an offence. Conversely it does not in the least follow from the admission of the latter principle of retribution in Distribution that the General Justifying Aim of punishment is Retribution, though of course Retribution in General Aim entails retribution in Distribution.

---

[1] Op. cit., pp. 326–35.
[2] Op. cit. It is not always quite clear what he considers a 'retributive' theory to be.

We shall consider later the principles of justice lying at the root of retribution in Distribution. Meanwhile it is worth observing that both the most old fashioned Retributionist (in General Aim) and the most modern sceptic often make the same and, I think, wholly mistaken assumption that sense can only be made of the restrictive principle that punishment be applied only to an offender for an offence if the General Justifying Aim of the practice of punishment is Retribution. The sceptic consequently imputes to all systems of punishment (when they are restricted by the principle of retribution in Distribution) all the irrationality he finds in the idea of Retribution as a General Justifying Aim; conversely the advocates of the latter think the admission of retribution in Distribution is a refutation of the utilitarian claim that the social consequences of punishment are its Justifying Aim.

The most general lesson to be learnt from this extends beyond the topic of punishment. It is, that in relation to any social institution, after stating what general aim or value its maintenance fosters we should enquire whether there are any and if so what principles limiting the unqualified pursuit of that aim or value. Just because the pursuit of any single social aim always has its restrictive qualifier our main social institutions always possess a plurality of features which can only be understood as a compromise between partly discrepant principles. This is true even of relatively minor legal institutions like that of a contract. In general this is designed to enable individuals to give effect to their wishes to create structures of legal rights and duties and so to change, in certain ways, their legal position. Yet at the same time there is need to protect those who, in good faith, understand a verbal offer made to them to mean what it would ordinarily mean and accept it, and then act on the footing that a valid contract has been concluded. As against them, it would be unfair to allow the other party to say that the words he used in his verbal offer or the interpretation put on them did not express his real wishes or intention. Hence principles of 'estoppel' or doctrines of the 'objective sense' of a contract are introduced to prevent this and to qualify the principle that the law enforces contracts in order to give effect to the joint wishes of the contracting parties.

(d) Distribution

This as in the case of property has two aspects, (i) Liability (Who may be punished?) and (ii) Amount. In this section I shall chiefly be concerned with the first of these.[1]

From the foregoing discussions two things emerge. First, though we may be clear as to what value the practice of punishment is to promote, we have still to answer as a question of Distribution 'Who may be punished?' Secondly, if in answer to this question we say 'only an offender for an offence', this admission of retribution in Distribution is not a principle from which anything follows as to the severity or amount of punishment; in particular it neither licenses nor requires, as Retribution in General Aim does, more severe punishments than deterrence or other utilitarian criteria would require.

The root question to be considered is however why we attach the moral importance which we do to retribution in Distribution. Here I shall consider the efforts made to show that restriction of punishment to offenders is a simple consequence of whatever principles (Retributive or Utilitarian) constitute the Justifying Aim of punishment.

The standard example used by philosophers to bring out the importance of retribution in Distribution is that of a wholly innocent person who has not even unintentionally done anything which the law punishes if done intentionally. It is supposed that in order to avert some social catastrophe officials of the system fabricate evidence on which he is charged, tried, convicted and sent to prison or death. Or it is supposed that without resort to any fraud more persons may be deterred from crime if wives and children of offenders were punished vicariously for their crimes. In some forms this kind of thing may be ruled out by a consistent sufficiently comprehensive utilitarianism.[2] Certainly expedients involving fraud or faked charges might be very difficult to justify on utilitarian grounds. We can of course imagine that a negro might be sent to prison or executed on a false charge of rape in order to avoid widespread lynching of many others; but a *system* which openly empowered authorities to do this kind of thing, even if it succeeded in averting specific

---

[1] Amount is considered below in Section III (in connexion with Mitigation) and Section V.

[2] See J. Rawls, 'Two Concepts of Rules', *Philosophical Review*, 1955, pp. 4–13.

12

evils like lynching, would awaken such apprehension and insecurity that any gain from the exercise of these powers would by any utilitarian calculation be offset by the misery caused by their existence. But official resort to this kind of fraud on a particular occasion in breach of the rules and the subsequent indemnification of the officials responsible might save many lives and so be thought to yield a clear surplus of value. Certainly vicarious punishment of an offender's family might do so and legal systems have occasionally though exceptionally resorted to this. An example of it is the Roman *Lex Quisquis* providing for the punishment of the children of those guilty of *majestas*.[1] In extreme cases many might still think it right to resort to these expedients but we should do so with the sense of sacrificing an important principle. We should be conscious of choosing the lesser of two evils, and this would be inexplicable if the principle sacrificed to utility were itself only a requirement of utility.

Similarly the moral importance of the restriction of punishment to the offender cannot be explained as merely a consequence of the principle that the General Justifying Aim is Retribution for immorality involved in breaking the law. Retribution in the Distribution of punishment has a value quite independent of Retribution as Justifying Aim. This is shown by the fact that we attach importance to the restrictive principle that only offenders may be punished even where breach of this law might not be thought immoral: indeed even where the laws themselves are hideously immoral as in Nazi Germany, e.g. forbidding activities (helping the sick or destitute of some racial group) which might be thought morally obligatory, the absence of the principle restricting punishment to the offender would be a further *special* iniquity; whereas admission of this principle would represent some residual respect for justice though in the administration of morally bad laws.

III

JUSTIFICATION, EXCUSE AND MITIGATION

What is morally at stake in the restrictive principle of Distribution cannot, however, be made clear by these simple examples of its violation by faked charges or vicarious punishment. To make

---

[1] Constitution of emperors Arcadius and Honorius.

it clear we must allot to their place the appeals to matters of Justification, Excuse and Mitigation made in answer to the claim that someone should be punished. The first of these depends on the General Justifying Aim; the last two are different aspects of the principles of Distribution of punishment.

(a) Justification and Excuse

English lawyers once distinguished between 'excusable' homicide (e.g. accidental non-negligent killing) and 'justifiable' homicide (e.g. killing in self-defence or the arrest of a felon) and different legal consequences once attached to these two forms of homicide. To the modern lawyer this distinction has no longer any legal importance: he would simply consider both kinds of homicide to be cases where some element, negative or positive, required in the full definition of criminal homicide (murder or manslaughter) was lacking. But the distinction between these two different ways in which actions may fail to constitute a criminal offence is still of great moral importance. Killing in self-defence is an exception to a general rule making killing punishable; it is admitted because the policy or aims which in general justify the punishment of killing (e.g. protection of human life) do not include cases such as this. In the case of 'justification' what is done is regarded as something which the law does not condemn or even welcomes.[1] But where killing (e.g. accidental) is excused, criminal responsibility is excluded on a different footing. What has been done is something which is deplored, but the psychological state of the agent when he did it exemplified one or more of a variety of conditions which are held to rule out the public condemnation and punishment of individuals. This is a requirement of fairness or of justice to individuals independent of whatever the General Aim of punishment is, and remains a value whether the laws are good, morally indifferent or iniquitous.

The most prominent of these excusing conditions are those forms of lack of knowledge which make action unintentional: lack of muscular control which make it involuntary, subjection to gross forms of coercion by threats, and types of mental abnor-

---

[1] In 1811 Mr. Purcell of Co. Cork, a septuagenarian, was knighted for killing four burglars with a carving knife. Kenny, *Outlines of Criminal Law*, 5th ed., p. 103, n. 3.

mality, which are believed to render the agent incapable of choice or of carrying out what he has chosen to do. Not all these excusing conditions are admitted by all legal systems for all offenders. Nearly all penal systems make some compromise at this point as we shall see with other principles; but most of them are admitted to some considerable extent in the case of the most serious crimes. Actions done under these excusing conditions are in the misleading terminology of Anglo-American law done without 'mens rea';[1] and most people would say of them that they were 'not voluntary' or 'not wholly voluntary'.

(b) Mitigation

Justification and Excuse though different from each other are alike in that if either is made out then conviction and punishment are excluded. In this they differ from the idea of Mitigation which presupposes that someone is convicted and liable to be punished and the question of the severity of his punishment is to be decided. It is therefore relevant to that aspect of Distribution which we have termed Amount. Certainly the severity of punishment is in part determined by the General Justifying Aim. A utilitarian will for example exclude in principle punishments the infliction of which is held to cause more suffering than the offence unchecked, and will hold that if one kind of crime causes greater suffering than another then a greater penalty may be used to repress it. He will also exclude degrees of severity which are useless in the sense that they do no more to secure or maintain a higher level of law-observance or any other valued result than less severe penalties. But in addition to restrictions on the severity of punishment which follow from the aim of punishing special limitations are imported by the idea of Mitigation. These, like the principle of Distribution restricting liability to punishment to offenders, have a status which is independent of the general Aim. It is characteristic of the idea of Mitigation that a reason for administering a less severe penalty is made out if the situation or mental state of the convicted criminal is such that he was exposed to an unusual or specially great temptation, or his ability to control his actions is thought to have been impaired or weakened

---

[1] Misleading because it suggests moral guilt is a necessary condition of criminal responsibility.

otherwise than by his own action, so that conformity to the law which he has broken was a matter of special difficulty for him as compared with normal persons normally placed.

The special features of the idea of Mitigation are however often concealed by the various legal techniques which make it necessary to distinguish between what may be termed 'informal' and 'formal' Mitigation. In the first case the law fixes a maximum penalty and leaves it to the judge to give such weight as he thinks proper in selecting the punishment to be applied to a particular offender to (among other considerations) mitigating factors. It is here that the barrister makes his 'plea in mitigation'. Sometimes however legal rules provide that the presence of a mitigating factor shall always remove the offence into a separate category carrying a lower maximum penalty. This is 'formal' mitigation and the most prominent example of it is Provocation which in English law is operative only in relation to homicide. It is not a matter of Justification or Excuse for it does not exclude conviction or punishment; but 'reduces' the charges from murder to manslaughter and the possible maximum penalty from death to life imprisonment. It is worth stressing that not every provision reducing the maximum penalty can be thought of as 'Mitigation': the very peculiar provisions of s. 5 of the Homicide Act 1957 which (*inter alia*) restricted the death penalty to types of murder not including, for example, murder by poisoning, did not in doing this recognize the use of poison as a 'mitigating circumstance'. Only a reduction of penalty made in view of the individual criminal's personal history or his special difficulties in keeping the law which he has broken is so conceived.

Though the central cases are distinct enough the border lines between Justification, Excuse and Mitigation are not. There are many features of conduct which can be and are thought of in more than one of these ways. Thus, though little is heard of it, duress (coercion by threat of serious harm) is in English law in relation to some crimes an Excuse excluding responsibility. Where it is so treated the conception is that since B has committed a crime only because A has threatened him with gross violence or other harm, B's action is not the outcome of a 'free' or independent choice; B is merely an instrument of A who has 'made him do it'. Nonetheless B is not an instrument in the same sense that he would have been had he been pushed by A against a window and broken it: unless he is literally paralysed by fear of the threat, we may believe that B could have refused to comply. If he complies we may say '*coactus voluit*' and treat the situation not as one making it intolerable to punish at all, but as one calling for mitigation of the penalty as gross provocation does. On the other hand, if the crime which A requires B to commit is a petty one compared with the serious harm threatened (e.g. death) by A there would be no absurdity in treating A's threat as a Justification for B's conduct though few legal systems overtly do this. If this line is taken coercion merges into the idea of 'Necessity'[1] which appears on the margin of most systems of criminal law as an exculpating factor.

In view of the character of modern sceptical doubts about criminal punishment it is worth observing that even in English law the relevance of mental disease to criminal punishment is not always as a matter of Excuse though exclusive concentration on the M'Naghten rules relating to the criminal responsibility of the mentally diseased encourages the belief that it is. Even before the Homicide Act 1957 a statute[2] provided that if a mother murdered her child under the age of 12 months 'while the balance of her mind was disturbed' by the processes of birth or lactation she should be guilty only of the felony of infanticide carrying a maximum penalty of life imprisonment. This is to treat mental abnormality as a matter of (formal) Mitigation. Similarly in other cases of homicide the M'Naghten rules relating to certain types of insanity as an Excuse no longer stand alone; now such abnormality of mind as 'substantially impaired the mental responsibility'[3] of the accused is a matter of formal mitigation, which like provocation reduces the homicide to the category of manslaughter which does not carry the death penalty.

IV

THE RATIONALE OF EXCUSES

The admission of excusing conditions as a feature of the Distribution of punishment is required by distinct principles of Justice which restrict the extent to which general social aims may be pursued at the cost of individuals. The moral importance

---

[1] I.e. when breaking the law is held justified as the lesser of two evils.
[2] Infanticide Act, 1938.   [3] Homicide Act, 1957, sec. 2.

attached to these in punishment distinguishes it from other measures which pursue similar aims (e.g. the protection of life, wealth or property) by methods which like punishment are also often unpleasant to the individuals to whom they are applied, e.g. the detention of persons of hostile origin or association in war time, or of the insane, or the compulsory quarantine of persons suffering from infectious disease. To these we resort to avoid damage of a catastrophic character.

Every penal system in the name of some other social value compromises over the admission of excusing conditions and no system goes as far (particularly in cases of mental disease) as many would wish. But it is important (if we are to avoid a superficial but tempting answer to modern scepticism about the meaning or truth of the statement that a criminal could have kept the law which he has broken) to see that our moral preference for a system which does recognize such excuses cannot, any more than our reluctance to engage in the cruder business of false charges or vicarious punishment, be explained by reference to the General Aim which we take to justify the practice of punishment. Here, too, even where the laws appear to us morally iniquitous or where we are uncertain as to their moral character so that breach of law does not entail moral guilt, punishment of those who break the law unintentionally would be an added wrong and refusal to do this some sign of grace.

Retributionists (in General Aim) have not paid much attention to the rationale of this aspect of punishment; they have usually (wrongly) assumed that it has no status except as a corollary of Retribution in General Aim. But Utilitarians have made strenuous, detailed efforts to show that the restriction on the use of punishment to those who have voluntarily broken the law is explicable on purely utilitarian lines. Bentham's efforts are the most complete, and their failure is an instructive warning to contemporaries.

Bentham's argument was a reply to Blackstone who in expounding the main excusing conditions recognized in the criminal law of his day,[1] claimed that 'all the several pleas and excuses which protect the committer of a forbidden act from punishment which is otherwise annexed thereunto reduce to this single consideration: the want or defect of will' . . . [and to the

[1] *Commentaries*, Book IV, Chap. 11.

principle] 'that to constitute a crime . . . there must be first a vitious will'. In the Principles of Morals and Legislation[1] under the heading 'Cases unmeet for punishment' Bentham sets out a list of the main excusing conditions similar to Blackstone's; he then undertakes to show that the infliction of punishment on those who have done what the law forbids while in any of these conditions 'must be inefficacious: it cannot act so as to prevent the mischief'. All Blackstone's talk about want or defect of will or lack of a 'vitious' will is, he says, 'nothing to the purpose', except so far as it implies the reason (inefficacy of punishment) which he himself gives for recognizing these excuses.

Bentham's argument is in fact a spectacular *non-sequitur*. He sets out to prove that to *punish* the mad, the infant child or those who break the law unintentionally or under duress or even under 'necessity' must be inefficacious; but all that he proves (at the most) is the quite different proposition that the *threat* of punishment will be ineffective so far as the class of persons who suffer from these conditions is concerned. Plainly is it possible that the actual *infliction* of punishment on those persons, though (as Bentham says) the *threat* of punishment could not have operated on them, may secure a higher measure of conformity to law on the part of normal persons than is secured by the admission of excusing conditions. If this is so and if Utilitarian principles only were at stake, we should, without any sense that we were sacrificing any principle of value or were choosing the lesser of two evils, drop from the law the restriction on punishment entailed by the admission of excuses; unless, of course, we believed that the terror or insecurity or misery produced by the operation of laws so Draconic was worse than the lower measure of obedience to law secured by the law which admits excuses.

This objection to Bentham's rationale of excuses is not merely a fanciful one. Any increase in the number of conditions required to establish criminal liability increases the opportunity for deceiving courts or juries by the pretence that some condition is not satisfied. When the condition is a psychological factor the chances of such pretence succeeding are considerable. Quite apart from the provision made for mental disease, the cases where an accused person pleads that he killed in his sleep or accidentally

[1] Chap. XIII.

or in some temporary abnormal state of unconsciousness show that deception is certainly feasible. From the Utilitarian point of view this may lead to two sorts of 'losses'. The belief that such deception is feasible may embolden persons who would not otherwise risk punishment to take their chance of deceiving a jury in this way. Secondly, a murderer who actually succeeds in this deception will be left at large, though belonging to the class which the law is concerned to incapacitate. Developments in Anglo-American law since Bentham's day have given more concrete form to the objection to this argument. There are now offences (known as offences of 'strict liability') where it is not necessary for conviction to show that the accused either intentionally did what the law forbids or could have avoided doing it by use of care: selling liquor to an intoxicated person, possessing an altered passport, selling adulterated milk[1] are examples out of a range of 'strict liability' offences where it is no defence that the accused did not offend intentionally, or through negligence, e.g. that he was under some mistake against which he had no opportunity to guard. Two things should be noted about them. First, the justification of this form of criminal liability can only be that if proof of intention or lack of care were required guilty persons would escape. Secondly, 'strict liability' is generally viewed with great odium and admitted as an exception to the general rule with the sense that an important principle has been sacrificed to secure a higher measure of conformity and conviction of offenders. Thus Bentham's argument curiously ignores both the two possibilities which have been realized. First, actual punishment of those who act unintentionally or in some other normally excusing condition may have a utilitarian value in its effects on others; and secondly, that when because of this probability, strict liability is admitted and the normal excuses are excluded, this may be done with the sense that some other principle has been overriden.

On this issue modern extended forms of Utilitarianism fare no better than Bentham's whose main criterion here of 'effective' punishment was deterrence of the offender or of others by example. Sometimes the principle that punishment should be restricted to those who have voluntarily broken the law is de-

---

[1] See Glanville Williams, *The Criminal Law*, Chap. 7, p. 238, for a discussion of and protest against strict liability.

fended not as a principle which is rational or morally important in itself but as something so engrained in popular conceptions of justice[1] in certain societies, including our own, that not to recognize it would lead to disturbances, or to the nullification of the criminal law since officials or juries might refuse to co-operate in such a system. Hence to punish in these circumstances would either be impracticable or would create more harm than could possibly be offset by any superior deterrent force gained by such a system. On this footing, a system should admit excuses much as, in order to prevent disorder or lynching, concessions might be made to popular demands for more savage punishment than could be defended on other grounds. Two objections confront this wider pragmatic form of Utilitarianism. The first is the factual observation that even if a system of strict liability for all or very serious crime would be unworkable, a system which admits strict liability only for relatively minor offences is not only workable but an actuality which we have, though many object to it or admit it with reluctance. The second objection is simply that we do not dissociate ourselves from the principle that it is wrong to punish the hopelessly insane or those who act unintentionally, etc., by treating it as something merely embodied in popular *mores* to which concessions must be made sometimes. We condemn legal systems where they disregard this principle; whereas we try to educate people out of their preference for savage penalties, even if we might in extreme cases of threatened disorder concede them.

It is therefore impossible to exhibit the principle by which punishment is excluded for those who act under the excusing conditions merely as a corollary of the general Aim—Retributive or Utilitarian—justifying the practice of punishment. Can anything positive be said about this principle except that it is one to which we attach moral importance as a restriction on the pursuit of any aim we have in punishing?

It is clear that like all principles of Justice it is concerned with the adjustment of claims between a multiplicity of persons. It incorporates the idea that each individual person is to be protected against the claim of the rest for the highest possible measure of security, happiness or welfare which could be got at his expense

---

[1] Wechsler and Michael, 'A Rationale of the Law of Homicide', 37, *Columbia Law Review*, 701, esp. pp. 752–7, and Rawls, op. cit.

by condemning him for the breach of the rules and punishing him. For this a moral licence is required in the form of proof that the person punished broke the law by an action which was the outcome of his free choice, and the recognition of excuses is the most we can do to ensure that the terms of the licence are observed. Here perhaps the elucidation of this restrictive principle should stop. Perhaps we (or I) ought simply to say that it is a requirement of Justice, and Justice simply consists of principles to be observed in adjusting the competing claims of human beings which (i) treat all alike as persons by attaching special significance to human voluntary action and (ii) forbid the use of one human being for the benefit of others except in return for his voluntary actions against them. I confess however to an itch to go further; though what I have to say may not add to these principles of Justice. There are, however, three points which, even if they are restatements from different points of view of the principles already stated, may help us to identify what we now think of as values in the practice of punishment and what we may have to reconsider in the light of modern scepticism.

(*a*) We may look upon the principle that punishment must be reserved for voluntary offences from two different points of view. The first is that of the rest of society considered as *harmed* by the offence (either because one of its members has been injured or because the authority of the law essential to its existence has been challenged or both). The principle then appears as one securing that the suffering involved in punishment is a return for the harm done to others: this is valued, not as the Aim of punishment, but as the only fair terms on which the General Aim (protection of society, maintenance of respect for law, etc.) may be pursued.

(*b*) The second point of view is that of society concerned not as harmed by the crime but as *offering* individuals including the criminal the protection of the laws on terms which are fair, because they not only consist of a framework of reciprocal rights and duties, but because within their framework each individual is given a *fair* opportunity to choose between keeping the law required for society's protection or paying the penalty. From the first point of view the actual punishment of a criminal appears not merely as something useful to society (General Aim) but as justly extracted from the criminal as a return for harm done;

from the second it appears as a price justly extracted because the criminal had a fair opportunity beforehand to avoid liability to pay.

(c) Criminal punishment, as an attempt to secure desired behaviour, differs by taking a risk from the manipulative techniques of the Brave New World (conditioning propaganda, etc.) and from the simple incapacitation of those with anti-social tendencies. It defers action till harm has been done; its primary operation consists simply in announcing certain standards of behaviour and attaching penalties for deviation, making it less eligible, and then leaving individuals to choose. This is a method of social control which maximizes individual freedom within the coercive framework of law in a number of different ways, or perhaps, different senses. First, the individual has an option between obeying or paying. The worse the laws are, the more valuable the possibility of exercising this choice becomes in enabling an individual to decide how he shall live. Secondly, this system not only enables individuals to exercise this choice but increases the power of individuals to identify beforehand periods when the law's punishments will not interfere with them and to plan their lives accordingly. This very obvious point is often overshadowed by the other merits of restricting punishment to offences voluntarily committed, but is worth separate attention. Where punishment is not so restricted individuals will be liable to have their plans frustrated by punishments for what they do unintentionally, in ignorance, by accident or mistake. Such a system of strict liability for all offences, even if logically possible,[1] would not only vastly increase the number of punishments, but would diminish the individual's power to identify beforehand particular periods during which he will be free from them. This is so because we can have very little grounds for confidence that during a particular period we will not do something unintentionally, accidentally, etc.; whereas from their own knowledge of themselves many can say with justified confidence that for some period ahead they are not likely to engage intentionally in crime and can plan their lives from point to point in confidence that they will be left free during that period. Of course the confidence justified does not amount to certainty though drawn

---

[1] Some crimes, e.g. demanding money by menaces, cannot (logically) be committed unintentionally.

from knowledge of ourselves. My confidence that I will not during the next 12 months intentionally engage in any crime and will be free from punishment, may turn out to be misplaced; but it is both greater and better justified than my belief that I will not do unintentionally any of the things which our system punishes if done intentionally.

V

REFORM AND THE INDIVIDUALIZATION OF PUNISHMENT

The idea of Mitigation incorporates the conviction that though the amount or severity of punishment is primarily to be determined by reference to the General Aim, yet Justice requires that those who have special difficulties to face in keeping the law which they have broken should be punished less. Principles of Justice however are also widely taken to bear on the amount of punishment in at least two further ways. The first is the somewhat hazy requirement that 'like cases be treated alike'. This is certainly felt to be infringed at least when the ground for different punishment for those guilty of the same crime is neither some personal characteristic of the offender connected with the commission of the crime nor the effect of punishment on him. If because at a given time a certain offence is specially prevalent a Judge passes a heavier sentence than on previous offenders ('as a warning'), some sacrifice of justice to the safety of society is involved though it is often acceptable to many as the lesser of two evils.

The further principle that different kinds of offence of different gravity (however that is assessed) should not be punished with equal severity is one which like other principles of Distribution may qualify the pursuit of our General Aim and is not deducible from it. Long sentences of imprisonment might effectually stamp out car parking offences, yet we think it wrong to employ them; *not* because there is for each crime a penalty 'naturally' fitted to its degree of iniquity (as some Retributionists in General Aim might think); nor because we are convinced that the misery caused by such sentences (which might indeed be slight because they would need to be rarely applied) would be greater than that caused by the offences unchecked (as a Utilitarian might argue). The guiding principle is that of a proportion within a system of penalties between those imposed for different offences where these have a distinct place in a common-sense scale of gravity. This scale itself no doubt consists of very broad judgements both of relative moral iniquity and harmfulness of different types of offence: it draws rough distinctions like that between parking offences and homicide, or between 'mercy killing' and murder for gain, but cannot cope with any precise assessment of an individual's wickedness in committing a crime (who can?). Yet maintenance of proportion of this kind may be important: for where the legal gradation of crimes expressed in the relative severity of penalties diverges sharply from this rough scale, there is a risk of either confusing common morality or flouting it and bringing the law into contempt.

The ideals of Reform and Individualization of punishment (e.g. corrective training, preventive detention) which have been increasingly accepted in English penal practice since 1900 plainly run counter to the second if not to both of these principles of Justice or proportion. Some fear, and others hope, that the further intrusion of these ideals will end with the substitution of 'treatment' by experts for judicial punishment. It is, however, important to see precisely what the relation of Reform to punishment is because its advocates too often mis-state it. 'Reform' as an objective is no doubt very vague; it now embraces any strengthening of the offender's disposition and capacity to keep within the law which is intentionally brought about by human effort otherwise than through fear of punishment. Reforming methods include the inducement of states of repentance or recognition of moral guilt or greater awareness of the character and demands of society, the provision of education in a broad sense, vocational training and psychological treatment. Many seeing the futility and indeed harmful character of much traditional punishment speak as if Reform could and should be the General Aim of the whole practice of punishment or the dominant objective of the criminal law:

The corrective theory based upon a conception of multiple causation and curative rehabilitative treatment should clearly predominate in legislation and in judicial and administrative practices.[1]

Of course this is a possible ideal but is not an ideal for punish-

[1] Hall and Gluck, *Cases on Criminal Law and its Enforcement*, 8 (1951).

ment. Reform can only have a place within a system of punishment as an exploitation of the opportunities presented by the conviction or compulsory detention of offenders. It is not an alternative General Justifying Aim of the practice of punishment but something the pursuit of which within a system of punishment qualifies or displaces altogether recourse to principles of justice or proportion in determining the amount of punishment. This is where both Reform and individualized punishment have run counter to the customary morality of punishment.

There is indeed a paradox in asserting that Reform should 'predominate' in a system of Criminal Law, as if the main purpose of providing punishment for murder was to reform the murderer, not to prevent murder; and the paradox is greater where the legal offence is not a serious moral one: e.g. infringing a state monopoly of transport. The objection to assigning to Reform this place in punishment is not merely that punishment entails suffering and Reform does not; but that Reform is essentially a remedial step for which *ex hypothesi* there is an opportunity only at the point where the criminal law has failed in its primary task of securing society from the evil which breach of the law involves. Society is divisible at any moment into two classes, (i) those who have actually broken a given law and (ii) those who have not yet broken it but may. To take Reform as the dominant objective would be to forego the hope of influencing the second and—in relation to the more serious offences—numerically much greater class. We should thus subordinate the prevention of first offences to the prevention of recidivism.

Consideration of what conditions or beliefs would make this appear a reasonable policy brings us to the topic to which this paper is a mere prolegomenon: modern sceptical doubt about the whole institution of punishment. If we believed that nothing was achieved by announcing penalties or by the example of their infliction, either because those who do not commit crimes would not commit them in any event or because the penalties announced or inflicted on others are not among the factors which influence them in keeping the law, then some dramatic change concentrating wholly on actual offenders would be necessary. Just because at present we do not entirely believe this we have a dilemma and an uneasy compromise. Penalties which we believe are required as a threat to maintain conformity to law at its maximum may convert the offender to whom they are applied into a hardened enemy of society; while the use of measures of Reform may lower the efficacy and example of punishment on others. At present we compromise on this relatively new aspect of punishment as we do over its main elements. What makes this compromise seem tolerable is the belief that the influence which the threat and example of punishment exerts is often independent of the severity of the punishment and is due more to the disgrace attached to conviction for crime or to the deprivation of freedom which many reforming measures in any case involve.

9

THE HISTORY OF POLITICAL THOUGHT:
A METHODOLOGICAL ENQUIRY

by J. G. A. Pocock

IN this article I shall attempt to make a theoretical statement of what it is we study when we claim to be studying the history of political thought, and to draw from this statement some inferences about how the study thus defined might be undertaken.

The history of political thought is an established and flourishing discipline, but the terms on which it is established and flourishes appear to be conventional and traditional. At the level of academic enquiry, it is often useful to submit a tradition to examination and make it yield some theoretical account of itself; and it may happen that a tradition of thought is shown to contain some vaguenesses and inconsistencies, whose removal could have been achieved in no other way. When I suggest that certain improvements could be carried out in this discipline if a more precise theoretical formulation were adopted of its subject-matter and methods, I shall not be suggesting that this, or any other, formulation is the only basis on which the discipline can be effectively carried on. But a political scientist may further be interested in the relations between the political activities, institutions and traditions of a society and the terms in which that political complex is from time to time expressed and commented on, and in the uses to which those terms are put; in short, in the functions within a political society of what may be called its language (or languages) of politics.

When I say that the history of political thought is at present a traditional form of study, I mean that it consists of the study of such thinkers about politics as have become and remained the objects of historical attention; and that our reasons for studying them, and the character of the attention we pay them, are such as have grown up in the course of our historical experience. These men and their ideas do not form the subject-matter of a single consistent science. Simply, there is a body of thinkers to whom we have grown into the habit of paying attention, and a number of viewpoints from which they appear interesting to us. These thinkers, from these viewpoints—now from one, now from another—we study; doing so is a traditional piece of behaviour, and they and their study form a tradition, or part of a tradition, which, in Oakeshott's parlance,[1] we get to know.

Since it can be accepted that there is no one set of assumptions from which alone it is proper to approach the history of political thought, there must consequently be an indefinite number of approaches which we may make; and what these are is determined less by ourselves, independently choosing a line of enquiry, than by the social and intellectual traditions in which we conduct our thinking. The traditionalist attitude consists in accepting (1) the indefinite variety of these possible approaches, (2) that there is no *a priori* reason for preferring any one of them to others, (3) that we can never hope to rid ourselves entirely of the simultaneous presence in our thoughts of more than one of the different sets of assumptions and interests on which they are founded. In this field as in others, the traditionalist acknowledges that the subject-matter of his study forms a tradition in which he is involved, and that his own approach to it is determined by this and other traditions; he settles down to conduct his thinking from within a pattern of inheritance over which he has not perfect control.

This situation is one in which reasonably satisfactory intellectual activity can be carried on. But to say that a historian does his thinking within a tradition is to say that he does it within an inheritance of intellectual positions which can never be reduced to a single pattern of coherence and cannot even be completely distinguished from one another. The more fully we accept this, the clearer should the necessity become to distinguish between the various positions of which our tradition consists with as great a degree of precision as can be managed—meaning by the term 'precision' that precision which knows the limits of its own preciseness. To accept that our position is a traditional one is to accept that there are and must be limits on our power to clarify our proceedings, but it obviously does not mean that we should not clarify what we are trying to do at any given moment

[1] See Michael Oakeshott, *Political Education*, in *Philosophy, Politics and Society* (1st Series). 1956.

to the limits of our ability, or seek for means of pushing those limits back. The defect of the traditionalist definition of an intellectual enquiry, however, is that it says nothing about the means by which this clarification may be attempted. If means of doing this are not found, confusions will occur which may lead, paradoxically enough, as easily in the direction of intellectual vagueness and pretension as in that of the conservative and empirical caution which it is generally the design of the traditionalist definition to produce.

This is peculiarly the case with the tradition of thought we call the history of political ideas, because that tradition is a tradition of intellectualizing; and there is a two-way relationship between confusions of thought about how other men did their thinking and confusions of thought about why and how we are thinking about them. To define what I mean by 'a tradition of intellectualizing', I shall adopt the Burkean-Oakeshottian characterization of political theorizing as an activity of 'abstraction, or abridgment, from a tradition'. In this usage 'tradition' now refers to a 'tradition of behaviour', meaning the whole complex of ways of behaving, talking and thinking in politics which we inherit from a social past. From this 'tradition of behaviour' political thought forms a series of 'abstractions' or 'abridgments'; the sense in which it is desirable to define this series as itself a 'tradition' has been given earlier and does not for the present concern us. From a 'tradition of behaviour', then, men perform acts of abstraction; the study of political thought is the study of what takes place when they do this.

There are at least two approaches to this study. Political thought may be regarded as an aspect of social behaviour, of the ways in which men behave towards each other and towards the institutions of their society; or it may be regarded as an aspect of intellectuality, of men's attempts to gain understanding of their experience and environment. Abstractions are made for a medley of purposes, varying between the rhetorical and the scientific. Indeed, in political as in other forms of social thought, it is never possible to isolate one of the two functions of abstraction decisively from the other. To solve a theoretical problem may have practical implications and, conversely, to state and solve a practical problem may raise new problems of wider generality. However much the conservative may deplore the fact, the human mind does pursue implications from the theoretical to the practical and from the practical to the theoretical; and no man knows where the process of abstraction may lead, which he is beginning (perhaps) with a clear and limited purpose in view.

Abstractions point to further abstractions and the level of thought shifts constantly between the theoretical and the practical. The same piece of thought may be viewed, simultaneously, as an act of political persuasion and as an incident in the pursuit of understanding; and arguments and concepts are repeated, after very short intervals, for purposes more theoretical or more practical than those for which they were just now employed. A philosophy reappears as an ideology; a party slogan as a heuristic device of high scientific value. It becomes important, then, that we do not make *a priori* assumptions about the character of political thought—as we do when we dismiss a piece of theoretical writing by representing it as a piece of persuasion on behalf of a group—and that we possess means of distinguishing between the different functions which political thought may be performing, and of following the history of concepts and abstractions as they move from one employment to another.

It may therefore be expected that the political thought appearing in a given society over a period—and the same may well be true of the political thought of a given individual—will prove on inspection to exist on a number of different levels of abstraction, varying with the character of the problems which it is intended to solve. This will confront the historian with no insoluble conundrum. It is perfectly possible, by the ordinary methods of historical reconstruction, to determine the level of abstraction on which a particular piece of thinking took place. But it does mean that the only assumptions we can make *in advance* about that level will be selective ones. We can choose to concern ourselves only with political thought at a certain level of abstraction; we cannot assume in advance that political thought in actual fact took place only at that level. The strictly historical task before us is plainly that of determining by investigation on what levels of abstraction thought did take place.

But the historian of political thought is all too often diverted from carrying out this task, and what diverts him may be termed the indefinite rationality of his subject. The act of disengagement, of 'abstraction from a tradition', is simultaneously an act of intellectual re-organization, and the men whose thought he studies had all, in varying degrees, a tendency to become philosophers—that is, to organize their thought towards higher states of rational coherence. To this process, once embarked upon, there is no known end, and our effort to understand the philosopher's thought must be an effort not only to follow it, but actually to assist it, in its indefinite progress towards higher states of organization. Consequently, the historian of political thought finds himself engaged both in strictly historical re-construction and in a kind of philosophical reconstruction—he seeks to understand past political thought by raising it to ever higher levels of generality and abstraction.

As a result, the history of political thought has a constant tendency to become philosophy. The historian has a further professional motive pressing him in this direction: the need to find a narrative theme around which to organize the piece of history which he is studying. He may be writing a history of political thought in a certain period, embracing a number of thinkers who developed their political ideas in the attempt to deal with a number of problems at a number of different levels of abstraction; and he desires to make a single coherent story out of it all. He has already, as we have seen, a tendency to study each thinker at a high level of abstraction; and by interpreting all their thought at a high common level, he discovers certain general assumptions which all adopted, or by their attitude towards which each can be interpreted.

The history of political thought in his period now becomes the history of these assumptions: of the various consequences that were deduced from them, of the various attitudes that were adopted towards them, and of the various modifications that were introduced into them, so that perhaps by the end of his period they are shown to have become significantly unlike what they were at its beginning. The history of political thought —in this no doubt resembling that of other forms of organized thought—has in this way a tendency to become the history of mutations in the cardinal assumptions (perhaps unconscious ones) on which it can be shown to have been based. If the term 'philosophy' may be used for thought which leads to the establishment or modification of cardinal assumptions, the history being written will be philosophical history; and if the set of assumptions whose history is being traced can be shown to have been cardinal not only to the political thought of an age but to all or several of its modes of organized thought, they may properly be termed its *Weltanschauung* and the history being written will be *Weltanschauungsgeschichte*.

In this way, the tradition which is the object of study has been condensed into a single narrative, taking place at a high level of abstraction. It must next be asked whether the process described furnishes valid historical explanations. The answer must depend on the criteria we adopt; but a good test of the value of a piece of history expressed in highly abstract terms is to ask whether its abstractions correspond to realities actually experienced, to things which some identifiable Alcibiades really did or suffered. If the assumptions on which changes in thought are supposed to rest, are represented as such that nobody was aware of making them, it will be difficult to submit the model to verification. But if it can independently be shown that these assumptions were consciously formulated from time to time, then what was an explanatory model will begin to appear a history of events which actually occurred. We may write the history of thought in terms of abstractions at any level of generality, no matter how high, so long as we can provide independent verification that the abstractions we employ were employed in the relevant field, at the relevant time, by thinkers included in our story. We may write in terms of mutations occurring in the *Weltanschauung*, of a continuing dialogue between more or less stable systems of philosophy or cardinal ideas in a stable vocabulary of political theory; and whenever the explanations we construct are found to be historically valid, historical understanding will be enriched.

Yet it is impossible to be wholly satisfied with the process of thought so far described. If political thought is 'abstraction from a tradition', that abstraction may be carried to many different levels of theoretical generality; and we have so far depicted a historian capable of verifying whether political thought did in fact take place at the level of abstraction at which he has chosen to explain it, but not of starting his enquiries by empirically ascertaining the level at which it was taking place. His choice of a level of abstraction is determined by his need to give as completely rational an explanation as possible of the piece of thought with which he is concerned; the level he chooses will therefore tend to be high, and to rise. He selects the assumptions on the basis of which the piece of thought can be explained with maximum rational coherence, and then seeks to show that they were in use at the relevant period and were employed by the thinker or thinkers he is studying.

If this is the only method he is capable of adopting, he may be at a loss when confronted with the possibility that the piece of thought in question may be as well or better explained on assumptions which do not endow it with maximum rational coherence. There are passages in the writings of Burke (let us suppose) which can be explained by assuming them to be based on presumptions which are to be found explicit in the writings of Hume. Our historian embraces this mode of explanation, with the consequence that he presents Burke's thought in these passages as being systematic political philosophy of the same order as the relevant passages from Hume. His method predisposes him to accept the idea that Burke's political thought can best be explained as political philosophy. But now let it be suggested that the same passages in Burke can be no less plausibly explained as grounded on assumptions of a different order of generality—assumptions made by lawyers about institutions and practice, for example, rather than assumptions made by philosophers about thought and action; and let it be further suggested that though this explanation does not provide Burke's thought with maximum rational coherence, it is capable of a higher degree of historical verification than the explanation which does.

The historian we have hitherto imagined is poorly placed for taking part in this discussion, because he is not yet capable of adopting a method which recognizes that there are different levels of abstraction at which thought takes place and different degrees of rational coherence with which it can be explained; still less one which permits him to discriminate between these levels as a matter of historical enquiry. He is as yet the prisoner of a method which condemns him to explain political thought only in so far as it can be presented as systematic political theory or philosophy. When he writes of political thinking as a series of events taking place in history, he will treat them as taking place in, and explicable only by reference to, a context of events consisting of the thinking of theorists or philosophers. In the case we have been supposing,[1] he will present Burke's thinking as he did as the effect, or in some other way the historical consequence, of Hume's thinking as *he* did; and the political thought of a society over a given period will appear historically intelligible only as a sequence of thought-patterns exchanged among its political theorists or philosophers.

There seems to be general agreement that political thought, at whatever level of abstraction or systematization, is a mode of discussing certain aspects of social experience. If this is so, it becomes important to distinguish between the approaches made to this subject by the philosopher and the historian. The philosopher is interested in the thought produced in so far as it can be explained in strict rationality, and in establishing the limits within which this can be done. The historian is interested in men thinking about politics as he is interested in them fighting or farming or doing anything else, namely as individuals behaving in a society, whose recorded behaviour can be studied, by the method of historical reconstruction, in order to show what manner of world they lived in and why they behaved in it as they did. He is concerned with the relation between experience and thought, between the tradition of behaviour in a society and the abstraction from it of concepts which are used in attempts to understand and influence it; but he may easily fail to pursue his proper function by confusing it with that of the philosopher.

If the historian attempts to explain thought only by endowing it with the highest attainable rational coherence, he is condemned to study it only at the highest attainable level of abstraction from the traditions, or transmitted experience, of the society in which it went on; he is not well placed to study the actual process of abstraction which produced it. In short, if thought be defined as a series of abstractions from experience, or from a tradition, thinking may be defined as the activity of producing and using those abstractions, and it is this activity of thinking which the historian who confuses himself with the philosopher is disqualifying himself from studying properly. To put it in another

---

[1] Which may be located in empirical reality; see F. Meinecke, *Die Enstehung des Historismus* (2nd ed., Munich, 1946), Part 1, ch. VI, and G. H. Sabine, *A History of Political Theory* (New York, 1945), ch. XXIX.

way, he is disqualifying himself from studying the relations between thinking and experience.

We may now see why he is vulnerable to the attacks of those who deny that there is any significant relation between political activity and political theory—between the tradition of behaviour and the concepts abstracted from it. This kind of attack, though frequently launched, is not always easy to understand precisely. In many cases, of course, what is intended is a piece of conservative polemic. The launcher of the attack presupposes that he is in the presence of an opponent who takes a more sanguine—and therefore more dangerous—view than he does of the extent to which political concepts can be used to criticize and modify the tradition of behaviour from which they have been abstracted; he therefore sets out to emphasize the limitations on the extent to which they can be so used.

The situation becomes more complex, however, when the attack is launched in the course of a debate between historians. Here the argument appears, at least initially, to be concerned with motivation and causation. One historian will accuse another of exaggerating the extent to which men's actions in a political context are motivated by the theories which they have formed from that context and the extent to which these theories, even supposing that they motivate men's actions, in fact determine the course which they take. He will ask whether the individual's actions must not be understood 'more' by reference to the determining influence of the historical situation in which they were carried out than by reference to the theoretical principles on which they were said to be founded.

Now many arguments between historians, as to whether one historical factor was 'more important' than another, are undeniably meaningless. If $5 \times 3 = 15$, it is vain to contend that 5 is 'more important' than 3 in making 15 on the grounds that 5 is greater than 3. The only question worth discussing is whether it is possible to construct a satisfactory explanation of the process without taking the factor in question into account. It is unlikely that this will be impossible. If one constructs an explanation of a political action in such a way as to lay all the emphasis on the situational factors determining it, one can easily explain it in such a way as to make no reference necessary to any theoretical principles which may have been expressed during its course. One may even succeed in refuting in this way any explanation which supposes that they either motivated its inception or determined its outcome.

It is still perfectly possible that expressions of principle were frequently put forward in the course of the action, and absorbed much of the time and energy of those engaged in bringing it to completion. At this point we shall find them spoken of as 'propaganda', 'rationalizations', 'myths' and so forth—vaguely dismissive language designed to indicate that, whatever part they played in the story, it is not worth considering. But from what standpoint is it not worth considering? One or more explanations of the action may be constructed without taking it into account, and a historian may legitimately say that he is interested only in those aspects of the action which can be explained in this way. But the expressions of principle happened; they form part of the action and modify by their presence its total character. They must have borne some relation to its course, and though a historian may not wish to explore that relation and may be satisfied with an explanation of the action that omits it, he is not entitled to say that there was no such relation or that his explanation may not be modified by the construction of an explanation which includes it.[1]

What historiography requires at this point is the ability to explore the different possible relations which theorizing may bear to experience and action. But the anti-ideological interpreter tends to suppose that when he has refuted the suggestion that theory stands in a certain relation to action, he has refuted the suggestion that there is any relation between the two at all. As a historian he can be convicted of methodological naivety. Employing, in none too sophisticated a manner, the concepts of motive and cause, he refutes the suggestion that theory was, by itself, a sufficient motive to explain the inception of an action or a sufficient cause to explain its outcome, and supposes that he has deprived it of any place in the story whatever. Men in politics, he asserts, learn from experience 'and not' from theory—as if their theoretical formulations of experience could be pronounced

---

[1] It can be contended that the word 'explanation' should be used only when an account of the action is constructed in purely causal terms. If this is so, and if all mention of the role of ideas is omitted, then an account of the action which included ideas only in some other capacity—e.g. that of bringing out the subjective significance of the action to those taking part in it—would have to be called by some name other than 'explanation'.

in advance to play no part whatever in the way they learn from it. As a political theorist, he is oversimplifying the thesis of conservative empiricism, which is designed to refute, and does refute, any theory of politics contending that the concepts abstracted from a tradition suffice either to justify men in seeking to annul and replace that tradition or to explain the actions which they take within it. To deny that concepts may be isolated and shown to play a determining role in politics is not to deny that they play any role whatever; yet the anti-ideological interpreter not only supposes that it is, but often has difficulty in believing that the student of ideas in the political process is not, automatically, assigning a determining role to them.[1]

His error—that of supposing that theory can bear only one relation to action, so that if it does not bear this relation it does not bear any—is only the counterpart of the error earlier assigned to the historian of political thought: that of supposing that theory could only be studied at the highest attainable level of abstraction from experience. If the latter insisted on studying thought, as it accompanied experience and action, only in the form of systematic theory and philosophy, the former was hardly to blame for supposing that thought could accompany the activity of politics only in the detached role of a normative and programmatic guide. When he had, understandably, rejected this account of its behaviour, no alternative was offered him, and it was not his fault if his relations with the historian of ideas degenerated into a scholastic comedy of cross-purposes.

If this is the situation in which the historiography of political thought largely finds itself at the present time, it is not, as has been demonstrated, incompatible with the gaining of valid and valuable results in countless particular investigations. It does mean, however, that confusions and frustrations may arise, and efforts be misdirected and wasted, because there is an area of enquiry over which we have not adequate methodological control. Our capacities might be increased, then, if our methods were to be refined; and for this purpose it would seem that we

[1] The present writer once published a study of some aspects of English political controversy in the 1680s and pointed out that there was a logical connexion between certain views of certain writers and certain defences of the Revolution of 1688. A reviewer accused him of exaggerating the role of the former ideas in *causing* the Revolution—and, being challenged, refused to withdraw; apparently because he was unable to conceive that any other assertion could be made about them.

need means of discriminating between the different relations
which concepts abstracted from a tradition of behaviour may
bear (*a*) to that tradition, (*b*) to the behaviour, stemming from it,
with which they are associated.

There are two distinguishable fields of study here: what takes
place when concepts are abstracted from a tradition; and what
takes place when they are employed in action within that tradition. In the former, we are concerned with an activity of thinking, i.e. abstracting; in the latter, with an activity of political
action. It may be asserted that the historian of thought is concerned with the activity of thinking rather than that of action,
and that consequently some modification is required of the
demand, often put forward, that the political thought of a
Bodin or a Burke should be studied in the context of practical
activity in which it took shape and which it was designed to
influence. Certainly, much (though not all) political thinking
does take shape in an immediate practical context, and when this
is the case it must be studied accordingly.

But there is an evident difference between the intellectual
content of a piece of thinking, and the role it was designed to play,
or actually did play, in influencing political action. We must not
confuse the motive behind an idea with its source, or suppose
that when we have found the intention with which a particular
piece of thought was constructed, we have adequately explained
it. A man may wish to justify a particular action, to persuade
others to adopt or approve it, and this will doubtless do much to
determine the content of his argument. But it is an error, not
uncommon among historians, to suppose that men are at entire
liberty to find and put forward exactly the rationalizations they
need. How a man justifies his actions is determined by factors
not at his command, and what they are must be ascertained by
studying both the situation in which he is placed and the tradition
within which he acts. And this is a distinguishable enquiry from
that entailed in the study of how the arguments he advances
affect the situation which they are intended to influence.

As a rough division of labour, then, it is for the historian of
action to investigate how ideas, beliefs and arguments help us
to understand the actions of men in particular situations; for the
historian of thought to study the activity of thinking, of con-
ceptualizing, of abstracting ideas from particular situations and

traditions. (The historian of Bodin or Burke, of course, may need to cast himself in both these roles; all the more reason why they should not be confused.) The historian of thought will be perpetually interested in thought as it takes shape under the pressure of immediate events, but this interest will not be exclusive. He is more likely to take as his main concern the relatively stable concepts which are regularly employed in the political thought of relatively stable societies, and to spend most of his time studying how these are abstracted from traditions of behaviour, employed to criticize them and finally incorporated in them. Once he has taken this turn, he will tend to be concerned with thought as the language of tradition, rather than with action, though as he moves towards studying how traditional concepts are employed and modified in particular situations of action, he will approach the point where his work shades into that of the historian of action as it is modified by thought. On the whole, however, he will tend to approach the history of political thought through studying the regular employment of relatively stable concepts; and it may seem as though this entailed the arbitrary choice of a certain level of abstraction from experience and tradition. But because he is investigating the process of abstraction itself, he is in a position to judge of the level to which it has been carried and to relate it to the social and traditional context from which it began; his choice is not an arbitrary one.

Any stable and articulate society possesses concepts with which to discuss its political affairs, and associates these to form groups or languages. There is no reason to suppose that a society will have only one such language; we may rather expect to find several, differing in the departments of social activity from which they originate, the uses to which they are put and the modifications which they undergo. Some originate in the technical vocabulary of one of society's institutionalized modes of regulating public affairs. Western political thought has been conducted largely in the vocabulary of law, Confucian Chinese in that of ritual. Others originate in the vocabulary of some social process which has become relevant to politics: theology in an ecclesiastical society, land tenure in a feudal society, technology in an industrial society.

As such vocabularies are increasingly used out of their original contexts, there may grow up corresponding languages of theory, designed to explain and defend their use in their new setting and relate them to terms of other origin similarly employed, and even languages of philosophy, designed to defend or criticize the ethical and logical intelligibility of the use of all these terms. But the advent of, say, a vocabulary of legal philosophy need not supersede the use in political discussion of the vocabulary of institutional law which the former was developed to defend; some political argument will be conducted at an institutional, some at a philosophical, level of abstraction. A comparable development occurs with the concepts used to denote the sources of legitimacy in a society, or to express the society's sense of its continuity with those sources; but here the process of abstraction produces different results. The criticism of a traditional account of society's continuity results in the writing of history. We reach a point at which a society possesses both a body of political theory and a manner of interpreting its history, yet where its traditions continue to be related, perhaps on more than one level of critical sophistication, as means of defending or denying the legitimacy of political behaviour, and thus figure among the modes in which its political thought is conducted.[1]

A society's political thought is built up largely in this way, by the adoption of technical vocabularies from different aspects of its social and cultural traditions and by the development of specialized languages in which to explain and defend the use of the former as means of discussing politics. We might call the former traditional languages, the latter theoretical languages, and it is tempting to add that political philosophy is never more than a theoretical language of a special kind, a second-order mode of discussing the intelligibility of all the other languages which may be in use. To say this, however, would be—from the historian's point of view—to underestimate the significance of political philosophy in the classical sense, which is found when a thinker mobilizes the principal moral and metaphysical ideas known to him with the intention of bringing political experience under their control and explaining it by their means.

Analysts may, indeed, hold that philosophers of this kind achieve no more than a critique and restatement of the political

---

[1] See further Pocock, 'The Origins of Study of the Past—a Comparative Approach', in *Comparative Studies in Society and History*, IV, II (1962).

ideas traditional in their societies. But the historian must stress, first, that a tradition of this kind of philosophizing may provide a society with one of its languages of political discussion, secondly, that it does not originate simply in the attempt to make existing languages more intelligible. A tradition of moral and metaphysical thinking may originate independently of political discussion and then be applied to it. Here, then, are at least two ways in which a language may develop capable of making statements about politics of greater generality than can normally be achieved by the simple adaptation of terms from other departments of social activity.

Once such languages have developed, thought about politics may become an autonomous theoretical activity and assume such forms as political philosophy or political science; and it may be supposed that the historian of political thought is the historian of these forms of autonomous theory. But once we define political thought as the language of political discussion, this cannot be so. For the practical and the theoretical are not separable, and the same political question may be discussed, at one and the same time, in a vocabulary adapted from social tradition and a vocabulary specialized for making universal statements about political association as such. When vocabularies of the latter kind appear, their claims may be investigated by the relevant methodologists, and it may be necessary to conduct this investigation historically—i.e. by tracing the development of their claims to elucidate certain types of problem. But the historian we are supposing is not a methodologist and there is no reason why he should confine himself to those branches of political thought which have been said to be autonomous theoretical sciences. A mode of political discussion for which this claim can be made is not intrinsically more interesting to him than one for which it cannot. He is interested in the presence of both in the vocabulary of a certain society, and in the relation of both to that society's traditions and developing experience.

Such a historian might approach the political thought of a society by observing, first, what modes of criticizing or defending the legitimacy of political behaviour were in existence, to what symbols or principles they referred, and in what language and by what forms of argument they sought to achieve their purposes. In late seventeenth-century England, for example, political behaviour could be discussed by reference to events which had occurred in three historical areas. First there was English constitutional history, whose authority as a guide in present affairs rested on certain ideas about legal continuity, themselves derived from the structure of English law and landed property. Then there was Old and New Testament history, deriving its authority from the ideas and procedures of the Christian Church. Finally there was Greco-Roman history, whose authority arose from the ideas of Latin humanism. In addition to all these there was a body of classical political theory and philosophy, common to the thinkers of Western Europe generally, deriving its vocabulary from civilian and scholastic sources and from the arguments of this tradition's more recent critics. In studying the possession and use by Englishmen of these four distinctive modes of political argument, a historian would be doing work akin to that of Raymond Firth when he studies the use made by Tikopia of the traditions belonging to their several lineages, and the part these play in maintaining social solidarity or furthering social conflict.[1]

He would be studying the elements of its social structure and cultural traditions which a society chooses to keep in mind for purposes of validating social behaviour, and the language and ideas which are employed to see that these purposes are achieved. In studying the conceptualization of elements from a tradition, he would be conducting a systematic exploration in historical terms of what we have been meaning by 'abstraction from a tradition'—for merely to repeat, negatively, that political thought can only be such a form of abstraction is, in the last analysis, no more than conservative polemic. This historian is analysing the vague and compendious term 'tradition' into some of its elements, and noting which of them give rise to articulate languages which are themselves transmitted and used for purposes of discussion. No doubt, much of what a tradition most effectively transmits is inarticulate and unorganized, and it will be proper for the historian who so desires to follow Oakeshott in emphasizing the importance of the unspoken in shaping the tradition on which thought is a commentary. But the business of the historian of thought is to study the emergence and the role of the organizing

[1] Firth, *Tikopia Tradition and History* (Wellington, 1961).

concepts employed by society, and the knowledge that this role has necessary limitations need not deter him.

At this point in his studies, he is investigating how the ideas, in which consciousness of a tradition becomes articulate, are abstracted from that tradition, and is particularly concerned with the relationship between thought and the structure of society. Knowing of what elements in that structure men were conscious, and in what terms their consciousness was expressed, he is in a position to criticize the not uncommon fallacies which are committed when historians, assuming that political thought must be the 'reflection' of a social structure or political situation, construct a model of that structure or situation and proceed to explain the thought as in accordance with the model, though often unable to offer more than a vague congruency or parallelism in support of their claims. Our historian may agree that thought 'reflects' society and its interests. But he has made it his business to see how the process of 'reflection' takes place, and how far language is from a simple mirror of unmediated experience or aspiration.

He is, to put it in other terms, investigating the stereotypes of various elements in its structure and traditions with which a society conducts its political thinking. All stereotypes are, more or less, obsolete or otherwise inadequate; the historian gets used to the fact that the models of itself with which a society does its thinking often seem wholly unconvincing to a historian like himself, seeking to understand that society from the standpoint of a later time. Eighteenth-century England was not governed by corruption and parties, but eighteenth-century Englishmen—and not only political propagandists—regularly talked and wrote as if it was. Why were these assumptions generally accepted? There is a gap between thinking and experience; but it is the business of the historian of political ideas to inhabit that gap and try to understand its significance. All stereotypes are, more or less, satisfactory as means to understanding and action; but we do not know why until we understand their history.

But not all the concepts used in a society's political discussion, or the languages based upon them, consist of simple stereotypes abstracted direct from society's structure and traditions. We have seen that the process of abstraction is a complex one, and that languages of increasing theoretical generality are built up from older traditional languages or intruded into the tradition from other sources. This is how a society's political thought comes to be conducted on more than one level of abstraction and to consist of languages of more than one degree of theoretical generality. The historian we are imagining has to cope with the situation that results and do his best to render it intelligible; and this is the point at which, as we saw earlier, he encounters the temptation to search for underlying assumptions of the utmost theoretical generality on which all the varying languages in use can with equal satisfactoriness be explained. Given that this is a dangerous procedure—unless he can provide independent verification that these assumptions were in use as widely as his interpretation implies—we must now show how our ideal historian may escape adopting it.

To begin with, since he has grown familiar with the different languages of discussion that were in use, and the different levels of abstraction which they normally implied, he will be able to ascertain in which language and on which level a given controversy was conducted or a given thinker developed his ideas. He will be able to join Burke and Macaulay in considering whether the Revolution of 1688 was justified more in terms of historical precedent or of abstract political theory, and to consider whether Burke's traditionalism was based on a common lawyer's vision of immemorial custom or a German romantic's vision of the unfolding national *Geist*. It is of some importance to be able to interpret thought by placing it in the tradition of discourse to which it rightfully belongs; and this is so for two reasons. In the first place, it enables us to interpret thought as social behaviour, to observe the mind acting with relation to its society, that society's traditions and its fellow-inhabitants of that society. In the second place, it is of assistance in rendering thought intelligible to be able to identify the concepts which the thinker was handling and the language in which he was communicating with his fellow-men; what he was talking about and what he was taken to mean.

But as the language employed in political discussion comes to be of increasing theoretical generality, so the persuasive success of the thinker's arguments comes to rest less on his success in invoking traditional symbols than on the rational coherence of the statements he is taken to be making in some field of political discourse where statements of wide theoretical generality are taken to be possible. Here, sooner or later, our historian must abandon his role of a student of thought as the language of a society, and become a student of thought as philosophy—i.e. in its capacity for making intelligible general statements. The advantage at this point of the approach we have supposed him to adopt is this. Being familiar with the language of discussion which the thinker is employing he knows—he has 'got to know' —how it is normally employed and the degree of theoretical generality of the assumptions which it normally implies. Now, either by some technique of analysis or by some acquired familiarity with the way in which a particular theorist's mind works, he may attempt a reconstruction of the latter's thought to the extent to which it possesses rational completeness. In this way he may form an estimate of the degree and kind of theoretical generality with which the traditional language is being employed by the thinker he is studying—as well as of the problem the thinker is using it to solve and the prepossessions with which he is approaching the problem. The historian can now consider the level of abstraction on which the thinker's language tends to make him operate, and the level of abstraction on which the thinker's preoccupations tend to make him use his language. He can now give some precision of meaning to the vague phrase —every thinker operates within a tradition; he can study the demands which thinker and tradition make upon each other.

If the traditional language which the thinker employs is one specialized for use upon the highest attainable level of generality, and the thinker's preoccupations impel him to operate on a similarly high level, then the historian's problems will be few and the method by which he interprets his subject's thought will be close to that by which a philosopher might interpret it. But it is implicit in the picture of political thought which has been given here, and in the definition of such thought as 'abstraction from a tradition', that this will not always happen and cannot be expected to go on happening for long. There may be a tradition of philosophical discussion of politics in a society; this tradition may be self-developing and need not be regarded as a mere analytical commentary on other modes of discussing politics. But in any complex society it is probable that politics will be discussed in too many languages and on too many levels of abstraction, and will raise too many problems directing thought to some particular language and level, to make it safe to predict that even the philosopher will succeed, any more than we ourselves do, in keeping his thought at any one level of theoretical generality. To the extent that this is so, it will be found desirable to study political philosophy in the context of a tradition, consisting of a number of languages used in a given society for the discussion of politics; and the only alternative to anatomizing that tradition in the socio-linguistic way that has been suggested, seems to be the attempt to study it by converting it into a philosophy that has probably grown out of it or grown up in it.

10

SOCIAL STRATIFICATION AND THE POLITICAL COMMUNITY[1]

by Reinhard Bendix

IN the developing areas of the world new class-relations emerge, as one after another country adopts democratic institutions and initiates industrial growth. In the 'developing areas' of Europe a comparable process took place after the French Revolution and during much of the nineteenth century. This essay seeks to enhance our understanding of the modern problem by a re-examination of the European experience with special reference to the relation of social stratification and the political community in the nation-state.[2]

This re-examination has a theoretical purpose. The social and political changes of European societies provided the context in which the concepts of modern sociology were formulated. As we turn to-day to the developing areas of the non-Western world, we employ concepts that have a Western derivation. In so doing one can proceed in one of two ways: by formulating a new set of categories applying to all societies or by rethinking the categories familiar to us in view of the transformation and diversity of the Western experience itself. This study adopts the second alternative in the belief that the insights gained in the past should not be discarded lightly and that a reassessment of the Western experience may aid our understanding of the developing areas of the non-Western world.

[1] This article originally appeared in the *European Journal of Sociology*, 1960. The footnotes have been considerably abbreviated.

[2] The two terms used in the title of this paper were chosen in preference to the more conventional terms 'society' and 'state', although the latter are used in the text as well. My reason is that 'social stratification' emphasizes (as 'society' does not) the division of individuals into social ranks which provide the basis of group-formation that is of interest here. The term is used in this very general sense with the understanding that individuals who differ from one another are united into groups by a force that overrides the differences existing between them, as T. H. Marshall put it in his definition of 'class'. 'Political community' in turn emphasizes the consensus between governors and governed within the framework of a polity while the term 'state' puts the emphasis upon the administrative aspect of government, at any rate in English usage. Both aspects must be considered together, but I did not wish to emphasize the latter in the title.

The problem before us is the transformation of Western Europe from the estate-societies of the Middle Ages to the absolutist regimes of the eighteenth century and thence to the class-societies of plebiscitary democracy in the nation-states of the twentieth century. In the course of this transformation new class-relations emerged, the functions and powers of centralized national governments increased and all adult citizens acquired formal legal and (at a later time) political equality. Attempts to understand this transformation gave rise to social theories that were necessarily a part of the society they sought to comprehend. Though their scientific value is independent of this fact, our understanding is aided when we learn how men come to think as they do about the society in which they live. Such self-scrutiny can protect us against the unwitting adoption of changing intellectual fashions; it can alert us to the limitations inherent in any theoretical framework. Since the present essay deals with social stratification in relation to the political community, a critical assessment of some of the assumptions implicit in studies of this relationship constitutes a part of our enquiry.

A glance at the history of social thought since the Renaissance suggests that this relation has been viewed in terms of three perspectives: that society is an object of government, that politics and government are a product of society, and thirdly that society and government are partly interdependent and partly autonomous spheres of social life.[1]

Inevitably, this division of social theories since the Renaissance is arbitrary. Each of the three orientations can be traced back much farther; and there are many linkages among these orientations which blur the distinctions between them. But it is also true that these perspectives have recurred in the history of social theory and that they provide us with useful benchmarks for the

---

[1] For easy identification it would be desirable to label these three approaches, but it is awkward to do so since every label has misleading connotations. 'Society as an object of state-craft' may be considered a Machiavellian approach, but this perspective is also characteristic of the social-welfare state which is not 'Machiavellian' in the conventional meaning of that term. Government considered as a 'product of society' might be called the sociological perspective, but this is also characteristic of Marxism which should not be identified with sociology, and then there are sociologists like Max Weber and Robert MacIver who do not adhere to this view. The theory of a partial dualism between society and government is a characteristic feature of European liberalism, but to call it the 'liberal orientation' carries overtones of a specific political theory which need not be associated with this approach. In view of such difficulties I have decided to avoid convenient labels and repeat the three phrases mentioned in the text.

reconsideration of 'society and the state' which is the particular purpose of this essay.

I

The idea that society is an object of state-craft goes back in the Western tradition to the mediæval tracts containing 'advice to princes'. From an education of character designed for the sons of rulers this idea was developed into an instrument of state council by Machiavelli. In the eighteenth century Montesquieu drew upon this tradition in his theory of law in which he combined the old precepts of state-craft by a personal ruler with an analysis of the social and physical conditions which would facilitate or hinder the exercise of authority under different systems of rule. A view of society as an object of state-craft was closely related to the rise of absolutism in Europe, as Friedrich Meinecke has shown in his study of ideas concerning 'reasons of state' and the rights and duties of rulers.[1] In this intellectual perspective a high degree of passivity on the part of society had been presupposed. The masses of the people were excluded from all political participation and became an object of governmental attention primarily as a source of tax revenue and military recruitment. Accordingly, this intellectual perspective lost its appeal wherever absolutism declined and political participation on the part of the people at large increased, although in inchoate form it has come back into fashion through the growth of the welfare-state.

As attention came to be focused on the conditions facilitating or hindering the ruler's purpose, 'Machiavellism' gradually blended with the second perspective, the idea that politics and government are products of society. In post-Renaissance Europe this idea came to the fore in the attacks of the Enlightenment philosophers on the established privileges of the Church and the aristocracy. These privileges were seen as unjust usurpations arising from the vested interests of established institutions, while politics appeared as a by-product of established prerogatives. If this orientation tended to sociologize politics, its application to the past politicized history. With unabashed forthrightness

---

[1] See Friedrich Meinecke, *Die Idee der Staatsräson* (München, R. Oldenbourg, 1925), *passim*. The work is available in English translation under the title *Machiavellism*.

writers like Voltaire surveyed and judged past events in terms of the eighteenth-century concept of a universal human nature and its inherent morality. By distributing praise or blame among contestants of the past they made history appear as a story of ever-changing conflicts among vested interests, suggesting that all governments are mere by-products of contemporary partisanship.

During the eighteenth century such judgements were made in the belief that 'man' was endowed by God with certain universal moral attributes. During the nineteenth century this belief and the theory of natural law were replaced increasingly by attempts to develop a scientific study of human nature and the political community. A key figure in this transition was Henri de Saint-Simon who proposed to make morals and politics into a 'positive science' by basing both on the study of physiology which concerned the truly universal properties of man. In this way speculation would be replaced by precise knowledge with the result that political problems would be solved as simply as questions of hygiene. The outstanding feature of this approach was the tendency to reduce the manifest diversity of social and political life to some underlying, basic element, that presumably could be understood with scientific precision. During the nineteenth century ever new elaborations of this reductionist approach were advanced, from proposals of a 'sociology' based upon biological facts through various explanations in terms of climate, race and the struggle for survival to Marx's theory of history as ultimately determined by the imperative that men 'must be able to live, if they are to "make history".' Many of these theories of society accepted the scientific optimism of the nineteenth century and assumed that a knowledge of the 'underlying' forces of society or nature provided the clue to human power and that in one way or another such knowledge could be translated into action.

The third intellectual perspective, that society and government are partly interdependent and partly autonomous spheres of social life, deserves more extended consideration, since it reflects (and provides insight into) the structural transformation of Western societies which is the focus of this essay. Here again we may begin with the Enlightenment, especially with those philosophers who emphasized the cleavage between bourgeois *society* and the *state*. That cleavage existed as long as each man's private concerns were at variance with his duties as a citizen. It was towards a solution of this problem that Rousseau made his many attempts to reconcile man in the 'state of nature' whose virtues and sentiments were as yet unspoiled by civilization, and man as a citizen who must subordinate himself to the community but without doing violence to his dignity as a man. This speculative contrast between man's potential morality and his actual conduct, and this effort to base the political community on the first rather than the second, were replaced in the nineteenth century by explanations which accounted for man's ethical capacities *and* his actual behaviour in terms of human nature in society.

An outstanding example of such an explanation is found in the work of Emile Durkheim, which illuminates both the theoretical perspective of liberalism and the transformation of Western society which is examined below. As a sociologist Durkheim wished to study morality empirically, as a phenomenon arising 'naturally' from the group-affiliations of the individual. But as a political liberal Durkheim also knew that such group-affiliation would obliterate the personality of the individual, unless the state intervened to guarantee his freedom. It will be seen that in this way Durkheim altered and continued the tradition of the Enlightenment; for him society itself was the 'state of nature' for each individual, but as such it was also differentiated from the legal order and representative government of the 'civil state'.

From the beginning of his work Durkheim was concerned with a scientific analysis of the moral problems raised by the Enlightenment. He praised Rousseau for developing a construct of the *civil state* or society that was superimposed on the 'state of nature' *without doing violence to the latter*. But he also criticized Rousseau's conception of the individual person as isolated, which made it difficult to see how any society was possible. Durkheim applied a similar criticism to the utilitarian doctrine, which indeed he regarded as inferior to the Enlightenment tradition in that it made the social nexus entirely dependent upon the exchange relationship on the market while abandoning the earlier concern with the moral pre-conditions of the civil state. The supposition underlying these approaches, that a basic conflict existed between 'man in nature' and 'man in society', appeared to Durkheim to be factually incorrect. By a study of the exterior social constraints which compel individuals to act alike regardless of personal motivation he proceeded to demonstrate that society was possible because man was naturally social. In a series of studies of suicide, the family, crime, religion and the division of labour he showed that the moral norms governing individual behaviour originated in each person's group-affiliation and hence that Rousseau had been wrong in postulating a conflict between man in a 'state of nature' and man in society. In other words, Durkheim 'solved' Rousseau's problem by making the individual completely subordinate to society.

> Every society is despotic, at least if nothing from without supervenes to restrain its despotism. Still, I would not say that there is anything artificial in this despotism: it is natural because it is necessary, and also because, in certain conditions, societies cannot endure without it. Nor do I mean that there is anything intolerable about it: on the contrary, the individual does not feel it any more than we feel the atmosphere that weighs on our shoulders. From the moment the individual has been raised in this way by the collectivity, he will naturally desire what it desires and accept without difficulty the state of subject to which he finds himself reduced.[1]

Thus, if society is jeopardized, this is due not to a hypothetical conflict between society and the individual, but to a state of *anomie* in which his group-affiliations no longer provide the individual with norms regulating his conduct in a stable fashion. Where such group-norms are weakening as in modern society, the social order can be rebuilt only on the basis of strengthened group-norms. Accordingly, Durkheim concluded his studies with the proposal of a new corporatism, based on modern occupational groups, so that 'the individual is not to be alone in the face of the State and live in a kind of alternation between anarchy and servitude'.[2]

As these studies progressed Durkheim continued to espouse the 'moral existence of the individual'. As a life-long liberal he was not willing to postpone this humanistic component to the indefinite future, as Marx had done. And as a sociologist he had demonstrated both man's fundamentally social nature and the seemingly inevitable tendency of increasing 'individual variations' as the division of labour increased and the 'common conscience'

---

[1] Emile Durkheim, *Professional Ethics and Civic Morals* (Glencoe, The Free Press, 1958), p. 61. Published for the first time in 1950 in a Turkish edition of the French manuscript, these lectures were delivered by Durkheim in 1898, 1899 and 1900 at Bordeaux and in 1904 and 1912 at the Sorbonne.

[2] I take this telling phrase from Marcel Mauss's introduction to Emile Durkheim, *Socialism and Saint-Simon* (Yellow Springs, The Antioch Press, 1958), p. 2.

of the group became more general and permissive. But if individualism is inevitable sociologically, why be concerned with safeguarding it politically? This combination of a sociological determinism with political liberalism arose, because like Tocqueville, Durkheim became concerned with the *secular transformation of group-constraint*. The associational ties of the province, the parish and the municipality one after another lost their significance for the individual. 'In the structure of European societies', he observed, a 'great gap' had been created between the state and the individual.[1] Durkheim's proposal to bridge this 'gap' by a new corporatism did not provide a political solution to the problem, as he himself recognized. The individual would be saved in this way from anomie and loneliness *vis-à-vis* the state, but he would also be oppressed by the secondary group to which he belonged.

Durkheim's answer to this question deserves extensive quotation, since it is not generally familiar.

In order to prevent this happening, and to provide a certain range for individual development, it is not enough for a society to be on a big scale; the individual must be able to move with some degree of freedom over a wide field of action. He must not be curbed and monopolized by the secondary groups, and these groups must not be able to get a mastery over their members and mould them at will. There must therefore exist above these local, domestic —in a word, secondary—authorities, some overall authority which makes the law for them all: it must remind each of them that it is but a part and not the whole and that it should not keep for itself what rightly belongs to the whole. The only means of averting this collective particularism and all it involves for the individual, is to have a special agency with the duty of representing the overall collectivity, its rights and its interests, *vis-à-vis* these individual collectivities [...]

Let us see why and how the main function of the State is to liberate the individual personalities. It is solely because, in holding its constituent societies in check, it prevents them from exerting the repressive influences over the individual that they would otherwise exert. So there is nothing inherently tyrannical about State intervention in the different fields of collective life; on the contrary, it has the object and the effect of alleviating tyrannies that do exist. It will be argued, might not the State in turn become despotic? Undoubtedly, provided there were nothing to counter that trend [...] The inference to be drawn from this comment, however, is simply that if that collective force, the State, is to be the liberator of the individual, it has itself need of some counter-balance; it must be restrained by other collective forces,

[1] Emile Durkheim, *The Division of Labor in Society* (Glencoe, The Free Press, 1947), pp. 27–8, 218–19, 283 ff.

that is, by those secondary groups [...] *And it is out of this conflict of social forces that individual liberties are born.*[1]

For these reasons Durkheim defined the political society as 'one formed by the coming together of a rather large number of secondary social groups, subject to the same one authority which is not itself subject to any other superior authority duly constituted'.

Durkheim's sociological theories do not prepare us for this political solution of his problem. The emancipation of the individual from the 'despotism of the group' appears in the bulk of his work as a result of the increasing division of labour and the related attenuation of custom and law. Though as a political liberal Durkheim valued this 'range of individual development', as a social philosopher he feared its consequences for social morality where these consisted in the isolation of the individual and the loss of regulative norms of conduct (anomie). Accordingly he sought to safeguard the individual against the dangers of anomie by his re-integration in the 'secondary groups' of society (corporations based on the occupational division of labour). Yet at the same time he called on the aid of the state to preserve individual liberties against the 'despotism' with which these groups would seek to control the individual. Implicit in this approach is, therefore, a 'dualism' whereby man's psychological and moral attributes are explained in terms of his membership in the society, while the society as a whole is characterized by an overall process (the increasing division of labour), which accounts among other things for man's capacity to alter these attributes through state-intervention in the interest of justice.

This incongruity between Durkheim's sociological and political theories was symptomatic of the liberal tradition in the nineteenth century. Even the classic formulation of this tradition contained, as Elie Halévy has shown, two contradictory principles. Arising from the division of labour in a market-economy man's 'propensity to truck, barter and exchange one thing for another' tended to reveal a 'natural identity of interests' which enhanced unaided the general interest of society. Yet the quantity of subsistence is insufficient to allow all men to live in abundance and this insufficiency is aggravated by the failure of men voluntarily to limit their numerical increase. Hence it follows, by an excep-

---

[1] Emile Durkheim, *Professional Ethics and Civic Morals*, pp. 61–3. My italics.

tion to the first principle, that the state should protect the property of the rich against the poor as well as educate the latter so that they will restrain their instinct of procreation. In this way the state acts to ensure the 'artificial identification of interests'.

Thus, the liberal tradition in its classic or its Durkheimian version is characterized by a 'dualism' according to which society and government constitute two interdependent, but partially autonomous spheres of thought and action. From a theoretical standpoint this tradition is unsatisfactory because it constantly shifts from the empirical level, as in the analysis of market-behaviour or the individual's group-affiliation, to the ethical and political level, as in the demand that the state should act to prevent the undesired consequences of market-behaviour or group-affiliation. Still, historically, this perspective can be explained by the unquestioned fact that the societies of nineteenth- and twentieth-century Europe witnessed a juxtaposition between society as an aggregate of interrelated groups and the nation-state with its identifiable culture and institutional structure.

II

In turning now from theoretical perspectives to problems of social structure it will prove useful to begin, however sketchily, with the pre-conditions of representative government in the West. In the problematic relations between the 'estates' and the power of royal government, say since the eleventh and twelfth centuries, we have to do with group-formations in society and the exercise of legitimate authority and hence with the relation between society and government which was discussed above in theoretical terms.

Characteristic of the political communities of this early period was the fundamental assumption that the personal ruler of a territory is a leader who exercises his authority in the name of God and with the consent of the 'people'.[1] Because he is the

---

[1] The quotation marks refer to the ineradicable ambiguity of this term in medieval society. The 'people' were objects of government who took no part in political life. Yet kings and estates frequently couched their rivalries in terms of some reference to the 'people' they claimed to represent. In fact, 'consent of the people' referred to the secular and clerical notables whose voice was heard in the councils of government. See the discussion of this issue in Otto Gierke, *Political Theories of the Middle Ages* (Boston, Beacon Press, 1958), pp. 37–61. It may be added that this ambiguity is not confined to the Middle Ages, since all government is based in some degree on popular consent and

consecrated ruler and represents the whole community, the 'people' are obliged to obey his commands; but he in turn is also responsible to the community. This idea of a reciprocal obligation between ruler and ruled was part of an accepted tradition; it can be traced back to ancient Roman and Germanic practices, was greatly strengthened by Christian beliefs, but became formal law only very gradually.

These characteristics of medieval kingship were closely related to the political conditions of royal administration. Each ruler possessed a domain of his own which he governed as the head of a very large household. On the basis of the economic resources derived from this domain, and in principle, on the basis of his consecrated claim to legitimate authority, each ruler then faced as his major political task the extension of his authority over a territory beyond his domain. In their efforts to solve this task secular rulers necessarily had to rely upon those elements of the population which by virtue of their possessions and local authority were in a position to aid the ruler financially and militarily, both in the extension of his territory and the exercise of his rule over its inhabitants. From a pragmatic political standpoint this was a precarious expedient, since such aid of local notables could enhance their own power as well as that of the ruler.

As a result, secular rulers typically sought to offset the drive towards local autonomy by a whole series of devices which were designed to increase the personal and material dependence of such notables on the ruler and his immediate entourage.[1] This typical antinomy of the pre-modern political community in Western Europe became manifest with every demand by secular rulers for

---

since even in the most democratic form of government the 'people' are excluded from political life in greater or lesser degree. These differences of degree, as well as the qualities of consent and participation are all-important, of course, even though it may be impossible to do more than formulate proximate typologies.

[1] In his analysis of traditional domination Max Weber distinguished patrimonial from feudal administration, i.e. the effort of rulers to extend their authority and retain control by the use of 'household officials' or by their 'fealty-relationship' with aristocratic notables of independent means. These two devices are by no means mutually exclusive, since 'household officials' were usually of noble birth and in territories of any size demanded autonomy, while 'feudal' notables despite their independence frequently depended upon the ruler for services of various kinds. Contractual obligations as well as elaborate ideologies buttressed the various methods of rule under these complementary systems. For an exposition of Weber's approach cf. R. Bendix, *Max Weber, An Intellectual Portrait* (Garden City, Doubleday and Co., 1960), pp. 334–79, which is based on Weber, *Wirtschaft und Gesellschaft* (Tübingen, J. C. B. Mohr, 1925), II, pp. 679–752. These sections are not available in translation.

increased revenue and military service. And to the extent that such demands were followed up by administrative measures, local notables typically responded by uniting into estates that could exact further guarantees or increases of their existing privileges by way of compensating for the greater services demanded of them.

A second characteristic of medieval political life was, therefore, that certain persons and groups were exempted from direct obedience to the commands issued by, or in the name of, the ruler. This 'immunity' guaranteed that within the delimited sphere of their authority these persons and groups were entitled to exercise the legal powers of government. This institution goes back to the privileged legal position of the royal domains in Imperial Rome, a privilege which was subsequently transferred to the possessions of the church, the secular local rulers (i.e. the landed nobility under feudalism) and during the eleventh and twelfth centuries to the municipalities. This system of negative and positive privileges (which may be called 'immunities' and 'autonomous jurisdiction') became the legal foundation of representative government in Western Europe, because it accorded positive, public rights to particular persons and groups within the political community. This institution of public rights on the part of certain privileged subjects is more or less unique to Western Europe. Perhaps the most important factor contributing to this development was the fundamental influence of the church, which through its consecration of the ruler and through the autonomy of its organization restrained the power of secular rulers and re-enforced the political autonomy of the secular estates.

In this setting a political life in the modern sense could not exist. Rather, the political community consisted of an aggregate of more or less autonomous jurisdictions, firmly or precariously held together by a king to whom all lords and corporate bodies owed allegiance, and under whose strong or nominal rule they fought or bargained with him and with each other over the distribution of fiscal and administrative preserves. Consequently, politics at the 'national' level consisted for the most part of a species of 'international' negotiations among more or less autonomous jurisdictions, within the confines of a country that sometimes possessed only a precarious cultural and political unity. In such a community the coalescence of interests among individuals was not based on voluntary acts, but on rights and obligations determined by birth, such that each man was—at least in principle—bound to abide by the rules pertaining to his group lest he impair the privileges of his fellows. Classes or status-groups in the modern sense could not exist, because joint action occurred as a result of common rights and obligations imposed on each group by law, custom or special edict. Thus, every group or social rank encompassed the rights and obligations of the individual person. Under these conditions a man could modify the personal and corporate rule to which he was subject only by an appeal to the established rights of his rank and to the benevolence of his lord, although these rights might be altered collectively in the course of conflicts and adjustments with competing jurisdictions. As Max Weber has stated,

the individual carried his *professio juris* with him wherever he went. Law was not a *lex terrae,* as the English law of the King's court became soon after the Norman Conquest, but rather the privilege of the person as a member of a particular group. Yet this principle of 'personal law' was no more consistently applied at that time than its opposite principle is to-day. All volitionally formed associations always strove for the application of the principle of personal law on behalf of the law created by them, but the extent to which they were successful in this respect varied greatly from case to case. At any rate, the result was the coexistence of numerous 'law communities', the autonomous jurisdictions of which overlapped, the compulsory, political association being only one such autonomous jurisdiction in so far as it existed at all [...].[1]

In Western Europe this medieval political structure of more or less loosely united congeries of jurisdictions was superseded gradually by absolutist regimes marked by a relative concentration of power in the hands of the king and his officials and by a gradual transformation of the king's relation to the privileged estates. The variety and fluidity of conditions under these absolutist regimes were as great as under the feudal political structure. For example, the nation-wide powers of the king developed much earlier in England than on the Continent, partly as a legacy of the Norman conquest. However, the insular condition with its relative ease of communication together with legal tradition antedating the conquest both in Normandy and in England also made for an early and effective growth of 'countervailing' powers. None of the Continental countries achieved a similar balance with the result that their absolutist political

[1] Max Weber, *Law in Economy and Society* (Harvard University Press, 1954), p. 143.

structures revealed either a greater concentration of royal power and correspondingly a greater destruction of the estates as in France or an ascendance of many principalities with some internal balance between king and estates but at the expense of overall political unity, as in Germany. Still, by the eighteenth century, most European societies were characterized by absolutist regimes in which the division of powers between the king and oligarchic estates as represented by various 'constituted bodies' was at the centre of the political struggle.

The French Revolution with its Napoleonic aftermath destroyed this system of established privileges and initiated the mass democracies of the modern world. We can best comprehend this major transformation of the relation between society and the state if we leave the complicated transitional phenomena to one side and focus attention on the contrast between medieval political life and the modern political community which has emerged in the societies of Western civilization. To do so, it will prove useful to take the work of Tocqueville as our guide.

Tocqueville's analysis has power because it covered a very long time-period, because the French Revolution unquestionably marked a transition despite all equally unquestioned continuities, and because in his admittedly speculative fears about a tyranny of the future he used a 'logic of possibilities' that enabled him to cope intellectually with contingencies he could not predict. By extending the scope of his analysis he made sure that he was dealing with genuine distinctions between different patterns of social relations and political institutions at the beginning and the end of the time-span he chose to consider.

In his famous study of the French Revolution Tocqueville showed how the *ancien régime* had destroyed the centuries-old pattern of medieval political life by concentrating power in the hands of the king and his officials and by depriving the various autonomous jurisdictions of their judicial and administrative functions. In pointed contrast to Burke's great polemic against the French Revolution Tocqueville demonstrated that in France the centralization of royal power and the concomitant decline of corporate jurisdictions had developed too far to make the restoration of these jurisdictions a feasible alternative. The nobility no longer enjoyed the rights it had possessed at one time, but its acquiescence in royal absolutism had been 'bought' by a retention of financial privileges like tax-exemption, a fact which greatly intensified anti-aristocratic sentiment. Through the royal administrative system of the *intendants* the rights of municipal corporations and the independence of the judiciary had been curtailed in the interest of giving the government a free hand in the field of taxation with the result that the urban *bourgeoisie* was divested of local governmental responsibility and the equitable administration of justice was destroyed. Noblemen thus preserved their pride of place in the absence of commensurate responsibilities, urban merchants aped aristocratic ways while seeking preferential treatment for themselves, and both combined social arrogance with an unmitigated exploitation of the peasants. In lieu of the balancing of group-interests in the feudal assemblies of an earlier day each class was now divided from the others and within itself with the result that 'nothing had been left that could obstruct the central government, but, by the same token, nothing could shore it up'.[1]

Tocqueville's analysis was concerned explicitly with the problem of the political community under the conditions created by the French Revolution. He maintained that in the medieval societies of Western Europe, the inequality of ranks was a universally accepted condition of social life. In that early political structure the individual enjoyed the rights and fulfilled the obligations appropriate to his rank; and although the distribution of such rights and duties was greatly affected by the use of force, it was established contractually and consecrated as such. The Old Regime and the French Revolution destroyed this system by creating among all citizens a condition of abstract equality, but without providing guarantees for the preservation of freedom. Hence, Tocqueville appealed to his contemporaries that a new community, a new reciprocity of rights and obligations, must be established and that this could be done only if men would combine their love of equality and liberty with their love of order and religion. This admonition arose from his concern with the weakness and isolation of the individual in relation to government. Because he saw the trend towards equality as inevitable, Tocqueville was deeply troubled by the possibility that men who are equal would be able to agree on nothing but

[1] Alexis de Tocqueville, *The Old Regime and the Revolution* (Garden City, Doubleday and Co., 1955), p. 137.

the demand that the central government assist each of them personally. As a consequence the government would subject ever new aspects of the society to its central regulation. I cite one version of this argument:

As in periods of equality no man is compelled to lend his assistance to his fellow men, and none has any right to expect much support from them, everyone is at once independent and powerless. These two conditions, which must never be either separately considered or confounded together, inspire the citizen of a democratic country with very contrary propensities. His independence fills him with self-reliance and pride among his equals; his debility makes him feel from time to time the want of some outward assistance, which he cannot expect from any of them, because they are all impotent and unsympathizing. In this predicament he naturally turns his eyes to that imposing power [of the central government] [...] Of that power his wants and especially his desires continually remind him, until he ultimately views it as the sole and necessary support of his own weakness.[1]

Here is Tocqueville's famous paradox of equality and freedom. Men display an extraordinary independence when they rise in opposition to aristocratic privileges. 'But in proportion as equality was [...] established by the aid of freedom, freedom itself was thereby rendered more difficult of attainment.'[2] In grappling with this problem Tocqueville used as his base-point of comparison an earlier society in which men had been compelled to lend assistance to their fellows, because law and custom fixed their common and reciprocal rights and obligations. As this society was destroyed the danger arose that individualism and central power would grow apace. To counteract this threat men must cultivate the 'art of associating together' in proportion as the equality of conditions advances, lest their failure to combine for private ends encourage the government to intrude—at the separate request of each—into every phase of social life.

We can learn much from these insights. Tocqueville was surely right in his view that the established system of inequality in medieval society had been characterized by an accepted reciprocity of rights and obligations, and that this system had been destroyed as the *ancien régime* had centralized the functions of government. The French Revolution and its continuing repercussions levelled old differences in social rank and the resulting equalitarianism posed critical issues for the maintenance of free-

[1] Tocqueville, *Democracy in America* (New York, Vintage Books, 1945), II, p. 311.
[2] Ibid., p. 333.

dom and political stability. Again, he discerned an important mechanism of centralization when he observed that each man would make his separate request for governmental assistance. In contrast to this tendency as he observed it in France, Tocqueville commended the Americans for their pursuit of private ends by voluntary association, which would help to curtail the centralization of governmental power.

It is necessary, of course, to qualify these insights in view of Tocqueville's tendency to read into modern conditions the patterns of medieval political life. At an earlier time, when landed aristocrats protected their liberties or privileges by resisting the encroachments of royal power, the centralization of that power appeared as an unequivocal curtailment of such liberties. To-day, however, that centralization is an important bulwark of all *civil* liberties, though by the same token government can infringe upon these liberties more effectively than before, as Tocqueville emphasized time and again. The collective pursuit of private ends, on the other hand, is not necessarily incompatible with an increase of central government, because to-day voluntary associations frequently demand more rather than less government action in contrast to the medieval estates whose effort to extend their jurisdictions was often synonymous with resistance to administrative interference from the outside. In contrast to Tocqueville, Durkheim clearly perceived this positive aspect of modern government and, correspondingly, the dangers implicit in group-control over the individual.

> It is the State that has rescued the child from patriarchal domination and from family tyranny; it is the State that has freed the citizen from feudal groups and later from communal groups; it is the State that has liberated the craftsman and his master from gild tyranny [...]
>
> [The State] must even permeate all those secondary groups of family, trade and professional association, Church, regional areas and so on . . . which tend [...] to absorb the personality of their members. It must do this, in order to prevent this absorption and free these individuals, and so as to remind these partial societies that they are not alone and that there is a right that stands above their own rights.[1]

Important as these qualifications are, they should not make us overlook the reason why Tocqueville's interpretation of the 'great transformation' was illuminating. By contrasting an earlier condition of political life, the transformation brought about

---

[1] Emile Durkheim, *Professional Ethics and Civic Morals*, pp. 64–5.

by the *ancien régime*, the new condition of equality ushered in by the French Revolution, and the possibility of a new tyranny in the future Tocqueville was concerned with 'speculative truths' as he called them. This simplification of different social structures enabled him to bring out the major contrasts among them, and these are not invalidated by the short-run and more deductive analyses that went astray. As I see it, Tocqueville's work becomes intellectually most useful, if we attempt to develop within his overall framework a set of categories that may enable us to handle the problem of the modern political community, which he discerned, in closer relation to the empirical evidence as we know it to-day.[1]

To do so it will be useful to summarize the preceding discussion. Medieval political life consisted in struggles for power among more or less autonomous jurisdictions, whose members shared immunities and obligations based on an established social hierarchy and on a fealty relation with a secular ruler consecrated by a universal church. By the middle of the eighteenth century this pattern had been replaced by a system of oligarchic rule, in which the king exercised certain nation-wide powers through his appointed officials while other important judicial and administrative powers were pre-empted on a hereditary basis by privi-

---

[1] A further theoretical note is in order here. No one doubts the relevance of the distinction between a feudal order and an equalitarian social structure, which Tocqueville analysed. In any study of social change we require some such long-run distinction so that we can know whence we came and where we may be going, though distinctions of this kind may be tools of very unequal intellectual worth. But while it is the merit of long-run distinctions that they enable us to conceptualize theoretically significant dimensions of social life (within the same civilization over time or between different civilizations), it also follows that these distinctions will become blurred the more closely we examine social change in a particular setting and in the short-run. The following discussion will suggest some concepts that are designed to 'narrow the gap' between the long and the short run and hence reduce to some extent the reliance on deductions which characterized Tocqueville's work. But I doubt that the gap can be closed entirely, because in the short-run we are bound to fall back upon Tocqueville's method of logically deduced possibilities of social change, even if we can go farther than he did in comparing actual changes with these artificial benchmarks. Two rules of thumb should be kept in mind, however. One is that this partly inductive and partly deductive study of social change in the short-run should not lose sight of the long-run distinctions, for without them we are like sailors without compass or stars. The other is that this retention of the long-run distinctions imparts a dialectical quality to the analysis of short-run changes. Since we do not know where these changes may lead in the long-run we must keep the possibility of alternative developments conceptually open and we can do this by utilizing the dichotomous concepts so characteristic of sociological theory. For suggestions along these lines cf. Reinhard Bendix and Bennett Berger, Images of Society and Problems of Concept-Formation in Sociology, in Llewellyn Gross, ed., *Symposium on Sociological Theory*, pp. 92–118. This perspective is greatly indebted, of course, to the work of Max Weber.

leged status-groups and the 'constituted bodies' in which they were represented. In contrast to both patterns modern Western societies are characterized by national political communities, in which the major judicial and executive functions are centralized in the hands of a national government, while all adult citizens participate in political decision-making under conditions of formal equality in the more or less direct election of legislative (and in some cases executive) representatives. Centralization, on the one hand, and formally equal political participation, on the other, have given rise to the duality between government and society discussed above in theoretical terms.

Centralization means that such major functions as the adjudication of legal disputes, the collection of revenue, the control of currency, military recruitment, the organization of the postal system and others have been removed from the political struggle in the sense that they cannot be parcelled out among competing jurisdictions or appropriated on a hereditary basis by privileged status-groups. Under these circumstances politics are no longer a struggle over the distribution of the national sovereignty; instead they have tended to become a struggle over the distribution of the national product and hence over the policies guiding the administration of centralized governmental functions.

One unquestioned corollary of such centralization is the development of a body of officials, whose recruitment and policy execution was separated gradually from the previously existing involvement of officials with kinship loyalties, hereditary privileges and property interests. A second corollary of centralization has been a high degree of consensus at the national level. In the political communities of Western nation-states no one questions seriously that functions like taxation, conscription, law enforcement, the conduct of foreign affairs, and others, belong to the central government, even though the specific implementation of such functions is in dispute. The 'depersonalization' of governmental administration and the national consensus on the essential functions of government have resulted in national political communities characterized by a *continuous* exercise of central authority. This continuity is not affected by the individuals filling governmental positions or the conflicts of interest among organized groups which affect the legislative process.

Accordingly, a national government of the modern type represents a more or less autonomous principle of decision making and administrative implementation. For Durkheim it was the state which alone could guarantee the 'moral existence' of the individual, and in his judgement the state was capable of having this effect because it is 'an organ distinct from the rest of society'.[1] Presumably, people as members of a political community regard the overall jurisdiction of this organ as inviolate, because they believe in the achievement and orderly revision of an overall reciprocity of rights and duties, whatever the particular political vicissitudes of the moment.

In the modern political community consensus (or a workable reciprocity of rights and obligations) is strongest at this national level, although as such it possesses an impersonal quality that does not satisfy the persistent craving for fraternity or fellow-feeling. But this emergence of a national consensus concerning the functions of the national government has been accompanied also by a decline of social solidarity at all other levels of group formation. Classes, status groups and formal associations arise from the coalescence of social and economic interests, other groups are formed on the basis of ethnic and religious affiliation: in some measure these collectivities are reflected in voting behaviour. Yet none of them involves a consensus comparable to the acceptance by all citizens of the idea that the national government possesses sovereign authority.

This is not a new issue. From the very beginning of the modern political community, say, since the great debates of the eighteenth century, social and political theorists have complained of the loss of social solidarity, for which the vast proliferation of associations did not appear to be a proper palliative. When writers like Tocqueville and Durkheim stressed the importance of 'secondary groups', they did so in the belief that such groups could counteract both the isolation of each man from his fellows *and* the centralization of government. Yet much of this analysis remained at a level where considerations of policy and an element of nostalgia merged with considerations of fact, especially in the ever-recurring, invidious contrasts between traditionalism and modernity. Despite the eminent names associated with it, we should discard this legacy of obfuscation. The 'great transfor-

[1] Emile Durkheim, *Professional Ethics and Civic Morals*, pp. 64, 82.

mation' leading to the modern political community made the decline of social solidarity inevitable, because (if so complex a matter can be stated so simply) no association based on a coalescence of interests or on ethnic and religious affiliation could recapture the intense reciprocity of rights and duties that was peculiar to the 'autonomous jurisdictions' of an estate society. The reason is that in these 'jurisdictions', or 'law communities' (*Rechtsgemeinschaften*) as Max Weber called them, each individual was involved in a 'mutual aid' society, which protected his rights only if he fulfilled his duties. This great cohesion within social ranks was above all a counterpart to the very loose integration of a multiplicity of jurisdictions at the 'national' political level. In this respect the absolutist regimes achieved a greater integration through centralized royal administration and the people's loyalty to the king, although the hereditary privileges appropriated by Church and aristocracy also subjected the ordinary man to the autocratic rule of his local master. Where such hereditary privileges replaced the 'law communities' of an earlier day, the privileged groups achieved considerable social cohesion, but the people were deprived of what legal and customary protection they had enjoyed and hence excluded even from their former, passive participation in the reciprocity of rights and obligations. Modern political communities have achieved a greater centralization of government than either the medieval or the absolutist political systems, and this achievement has been preceded, accompanied or followed by the participation of all adult citizens in political life (on the basis of the formal equality of the franchise). The price of these achievements consists in the diminished solidarity of all 'secondary groups'.

This 'price' is a by-product of the separation between society and government in the modern political community. Whereas solidarity had been based on the individual's participation in a 'law community' or on his membership in a privileged status group possessing certain governmental prerogatives, it must arise now from the social and economic stratification of society aided by the equality of all adult citizens before the law and in the electoral process. On this basis exchange relations and joint actions may develop to the exclusion of 'governmental interference' or in quest of governmental assistance or with the aim to achieve representation in the decision-making bodies of government.[1] Though it certainly has an impact on the national government, individual and collective action on this basis does not account for the governmental performance of administrative tasks, or, in the larger sense, the continuous functioning of the national political community.

In the societies of Western civilization we should accept, therefore, the existence of a genuine hiatus between the forces making for social solidarity independently of government and the forces accounting for the continuous exercise of central authority in the national political community. This existing pattern is the result of a slow and often painful process. As the central functions of the national government became gradually accepted, organized groups within the society demanded representation in this national political community. Accordingly, 'political community' refers not only to the central functions of government and the consensus sustaining them, but to the much more problematic question whether and how the groups arising within the society have achieved a national reciprocity of rights and obligations. For at the beginning of European industrialization in the nineteenth century new social groups were in the process of formation and had yet to learn (in the words of Tocqueville) what they were, what they might be or what ought to be in the emerging national community of their country.

III

During the eighteenth and nineteenth centuries the societies of Western civilization industrialized and became democratic. We should utilize the knowledge gained from this experience as we turn to-day to a study of the 'developing areas' of the non-Western world. This task is difficult because our theories of the

---

[1] Demands for representation are difficult to distinguish from demands for privileged jurisdictions or outright benefits, because representation in decision-making bodies may be used to obtain these privileges or benefits. It is clear at any rate that voluntary associations are not the unequivocal counter-weight to centralized power for which Tocqueville was searching in his study of American society. Instead, voluntary associations frequently demand governmental assistance even where they reject it in principle, and in this respect they act in much the same way as individual manufacturers tended to do a century ago according to Tocqueville's observations. Voluntary associations are a protean phenomenon. They are evidence of consensus within the society, especially where they pursue private ends as an alternative to governmental assistance and regulation. But they may also be evidence of dissensus within the national political community, in so far as they enlist the national government in the service of parochial interests, and hence seek to secure from the government privileges that are denied to other groups.

'great transformation' in the West have been inevitably a part of that transformation as well. In an effort to disentangle these theories of change from the change itself the preceding discussion has separated the theoretical reflections on this transformation from a consideration of changes in the institutional structure. While retaining the contrast between medieval and modern society it has discarded the nostalgia so often associated with that contrast. And it has utilized the distinction between society and the state in view of its analytical utility and the institutional duality which exists in this respect in the 'developing areas' of yesterday and to-day.[1] In this concluding section I attempt to reformulate this contrast in general terms so as to facilitate a comparative study of social structures.

My thesis is that for our understanding of 'society' and 'the state' in the nations of Europe since the French Revolution the third perspective (mentioned above in Part I) is most useful, if it is considered as an analytical framework rather than as the political theory of liberalism. In the utilitarian contrast between the 'natural identity' and the 'artificial identification of interests', in Durkheim's concern with group-integration and state-interference, or, to cite an American example, in W. G. Sumner's distinction between 'crescive' and 'enacted' institutions we have repeated references to two types of human associations. One of these consists in affinities of interest which arise from relations of kinship, the division of labour, exchanges on the market place and the ubiquitous influence of custom. The other consists in relations of super- and sub-ordination which arise from the exercise of instituted authority and compliance with its commands.[2] The distinction refers to a universal attribute of group-life in the sense that, however interrelated, these two types of human association are not reducible to each other. From an analytical viewpoint it is necessary to consider 'society' and 'the

---

[1] The term 'state' is needed to designate the continuing political identity of the nation irrespective of the governments embodying this identity from time to time. Where monarchical institutions have survived they represent this identity separately from the ruling government. Such institutional separation is not possible under democracies. In this discussion the terms 'state' and 'political community' or 'polity' are used interchangeably, since all three refer with different emphasis to the apparatus and the consensus sustaining the continuous political identity of the modern nation.

[2] Like all such distinctions there is a good bit of overlap between the two types. Affinities of interest which arise from the social structure forever engender relations of super- and sub-ordination, while the exercise of instituted authority forever produces, and is affected by, affinities of interest.

state' as interdependent, but autonomous, spheres of thought and action which coexist in one form or another in all complex societies, although the separation of these 'spheres' is perhaps greatest in modern Western societies.

The generality of this distinction suggests that it lends itself to a comparative study of types of interrelation between social structure and the political community. In medieval Europe two such types were 'competing' with each other as Machiavelli pointed out:

> Kingdoms known to history have been governed in two ways: either by a prince and his servants, who, as ministers by his grace and permission, assist in governing the realm; or by a prince and by barons, who hold positions not by favour of the ruler but by antiquity of blood. Such barons have states and subjects of their own who recognize them as their lords, and are naturally attached to them. In those states which are governed by a prince and his servants, the prince possesses more authority, because there is no one in the state regarded as a superior other than himself, and if others are obeyed it is merely as ministers and officials of the prince, and no one regards them with any special affection.[1]

Government as an extension of the royal household and government based on the fealty between landed nobles and their king and leader thus represented two types of social structure as well as two types of instituted authority. Again, in the societies of Western civilization at the beginning of the present era this duality between society and the state is reflected in two far-reaching developments, which were eventually followed by a third. A market economy emerged based on contract or the ability of individuals to enter into legally binding agreements, while gradually the exercise of governmental authority was separated from kinship ties, property interests and inherited privileges. These developments occurred at a time when the determination of governmental policies and their administrative implementation were confined to a privileged few, but in the course of the nineteenth century this restriction was reduced and eventually eliminated through the extension of the franchise. If we consider these developments in retrospect we can summarize their effects on society and the state. The growth of the market economy and the adoption of universal franchise have given rise to interest groups and political parties which mobilize collec-

---

[1] Niccolò Machiavelli, *The Prince and the Discourses* (New York, The Modern Library, 1940), p. 15.

tivities for economic and political action and thereby 'facilitate the interchange between [...] the spontaneous groupings of society' and the exercise of authority.[1] On the other hand, the 'depersonalization' of governmental functions has accompanied a centralization of legislative, judicial and administrative decision-making and implementation which now facilitates the 'reverse interchange' between the state and society. The efficacy of these 'interchanges' will vary not only with social cleavages and party-structures as Lipset has shown, but also with the 'depersonalization' of government and the propensities of rule-abiding behaviour among the people at large. On the whole Western societies are characterized in these respects by a cultural tradition which ensures the containment of group-conflicts within a gradually changing constitutional framework and a high degree of probity in office and popular compliance with rules. But it is well to remember that even in the West the centralization of government and the democratization of political participation have on occasion created a hiatus that has proved more or less intractable. A striking case in point is the Italian experience with its 'negative interchange' between society and the state, as exemplified by the 'anti-government organization' of the Sicilian *Mafia* which among other things 'protects' the society against governmental encroachments. An extreme case like this serves to remind us that all Western societies have had to grapple with a duality that ranges from the juxtaposition of private concerns and public obligation in each citizen to the juxtaposition of solidary groups based on common interest and appointed officials acting in their authorized capacity.

To say that this hiatus is bridged by 'interchange' from both sides only refers to the end-product of a prolonged balancing of group interests and formal institutions. In this respect the great issue of the nineteenth century had to do with the question whether and on what terms the disfranchised masses would be accorded the rights of national citizenship. The resolution of this issue could be eased *or* complicated through the continued confinement of politics to an élite of notables and through the natural as well as legal obstacles standing in the way of effective political organization. The balance between oligarchic resistance

---

[1] See S. M. Lipset, 'Party Systems and the Representation of Social Groups', *Archives européennes de sociologie*, I (1960), p. 51.

and popular political activation, the rise of central power and the later development of citizenship on the part of all adults posed the problem of how a new reciprocity of rights and obligations could be established *at the national level.* In several European countries this problem of a national political community came to the fore at a time when the 'new' social classes of employers and workers began to make their bid for political participation and to cope as well with the problem of their reciprocal rights and obligations. Ideological controversy was at its height as these and other groups became capable of organized action and as long as they were denied their bid for equal participation in the political process. But as one after another social group has been admitted to such participation, they have in each case used their newly acquired power to pressure the national government into enacting and implementing a guaranteed minimum of social and cultural amenities. In this way a new reciprocity of rights and obligation among conflicting groups could be established by the 'welfare state' at the national level and where this has occurred ideological controversy has declined.

Clearly, this statement does not apply to the 'developing areas' of the world to-day. Instead, we are witnessing ever new attempts to mobilize the 'voiceless masses' through democratic ideas and institutions and at the same time provide these masses with the amenities of the 'welfare state'. This means that all the cleavages of the social structure are given political articulation simultaneously, while governments attempt to plan economic development and provide the minimum essentials of a welfare state. If it be argued that such governments possess only an uncertain authority and relatively little experience, it will be answered that they must make the attempt nevertheless because only on this basis will the mobilized masses positively identify themselves with the new nation. As a consequence of these conditions, ideological controversy is waged with unparalleled intensity, while political leaders attempt to establish a functioning governmental machinery and protect it against the continuous assault of politics and corruption.

In their increasing preoccupation with the 'developing areas' of Asia and Africa since World War II Western scholars have had to grapple with the applicability of concepts which had been formulated in the context of Western experience. Since a simple application of these concepts is found wanting the further we move away from that experience, it is not surprising that some scholars decide to discard them altogether in an attempt to comprise in one conceptual scheme all political phenomena, Western and non-Western. The spirit of this enterprise is best conveyed in the following quotation:

> [...] the search for new concepts [...] reflects an underlying drift towards a new and coherent way of thinking about and studying politics that is implied in such slogans as the 'behavioral approach'. This urge towards a new conceptual unity is suggested when we compare the new terms with the old. Thus, instead of the concept of the 'state', limited as it is by legal and institutional meanings, we prefer 'political system'; instead of 'powers', which again is a legal concept in connotation, we are beginning to prefer 'functions'; instead of 'offices' (legal again), we prefer 'roles'; instead of 'institutions', which again directs us toward formal norms, 'structures'; instead of 'public opinion' and 'citizenship training', formal and rational in meaning, we prefer 'political culture' and 'political socialization'. We are not setting aside public law and philosophy as disciplines, but simply telling them to move over to make room for a growth in political theory that has been long overdue.[1]

In this approach politics is to be considered a universal phenomenon and as a result the distinction is discarded between societies which are 'states' and those which are not, and that just at a time when leading groups in the 'developing areas' are directly concerned with the organization of states and the development of governmental machinery.

The preceding discussion has suggested that this is not a new problem even in the Western experience. The rise of absolutism promoted the centralization of governmental power. But no one reading the record of mercantilist regimes can avoid the conclusion that the efficacy of that central power was often as doubtful as is the efficacy of highly centralized governments in the 'developing areas' of to-day. Again, the destruction of many intermediate centres of authority and the consequent emancipation of the individual through the institution of a national citizenship inevitably accentuated all existing cleavages within the society by mobilizing the people for the electoral struggle over the distribution of the national product. Thus, centralization of power and national citizenship gave a new meaning to the duality

---

[1] Gabriel Almond, 'A Functional Approach to Comparative Politics', in Gabriel Almond and James S. Coleman, eds., *The Politics of the Developing Areas* (Princeton, Princeton University Press, 1960), p. 4.

between society and the state, as Tocqueville observed long ago, and as we have occasion to witness in the 'new nations' of the non-Western world to-day. It may be true, of course, that some of these 'developing areas' are confronted by such an accentuation of cleavages within their social structure and such a lack of effective government, that anarchy reigns, or a political community can be established only by a 'tutelary democracy' or a dictatorship as safeguards against anarchy. Meagre resources in the face of staggering tasks, the relative absence of a legal and governmental tradition, and the precipitous political mobilization of all the people greatly increase the hazards even aside from the additional aggravation of the Cold War. The efforts to cope with these difficulties certainly command our earnest attention and no one can be sure of their outcome. In view of that uncertainty we should try to preserve the insights we have gained from the Western experience into the social foundations of government *and* the political foundations of society. If a balance is achieved between these perspectives we may be able to utilize our knowledge for an understanding of contemporary social change.